DOWN THE DRAIN

JULIA FOX

SIMON & SCHUSTER

New York   London   Toronto   Sydney   New Delhi

Simon & Schuster
1230 Avenue of the Americas
New York, NY 10020

Copyright © 2023 by Julia Fox

All rights reserved, including the right to reproduce this book
or portions thereof in any form whatsoever. For information, address
Simon & Schuster Subsidiary Rights Department,
1230 Avenue of the Americas, New York, NY 10020.

First Simon & Schuster hardcover edition October 2023

SIMON & SCHUSTER and colophon are
registered trademarks of Simon & Schuster, Inc.

For information about special discounts for bulk purchases,
please contact Simon & Schuster Special Sales
at 1-866-506-1949 or business@simonandschuster.com.

The Simon & Schuster Speakers Bureau can bring authors to your live event.
For more information or to book an event, contact the Simon & Schuster Speakers Bureau
at 1-866-248-3049 or visit our website at www.simonspeakers.com.

Interior design by Ruth Lee-Mui

Manufactured in the United States of America

1   3   5   7   9   10   8   6   4   2

Library of Congress Cataloging-in-Publication Data has been applied for.

ISBN 978-1-6680-1150-8
ISBN 978-1-6680-1152-2 (ebook)

Identities have been changed to protect
the innocent and the guilty.

To my dad, thank you for pushing me to write,

even when I struggled to find the words.

Thanks for the mistakes you made which I turned into art.

No matter where life's journey takes me,

for better or for worse,

all roads lead back to you.

But please, whatever you do,

DO NOT READ THIS BOOK.

In loving memory of

Harmony Abrams

and

Gianna Valdes

and

Katharine Pettijohn

This is for the dreamers and the delinquents

Contents

THE AMERICAN DREAM

The year is 1996 and I just landed in the grand metropolis of New York City. The moment we step off the plane and my little feet hit the pavement, I drop my suitcase and cross myself. *"Grazie a Dio,"* I whisper under my breath. On the plane ride, I had asked my dad, "If the plane gets in an accident, will we all die?" To which he casually replied, "Duh." The remainder of the flight was spent in silent prayer, my gaze affixed to the ominous, boundless ocean beneath us. Despite my basic knowledge of the English language, I feel more comfortable speaking my native tongue. I was born in Italy and have spent the last few years in Saronno, a small town in the province of Varese, where the city eerily feels like the remnants of what was once a charming little town. But I see past the shitty graffiti coating the pastel pink–colored walls. To me, it's home.

I'm no stranger to this sprawling city. I've already been here more times than I can count. I was two months old the first time we made the transatlantic trek to visit my dad's family. I even lived here for a while, before disaster struck. But today feels like the very first time. It's like I'm seeing this place through brand-new eyes. And after the mess that went down last time, this is a fresh start, a chance to wipe the slate clean and try again.

It's early September and the humidity hangs heavy in the air, clinging to my skin like a sweet sticky veil. As soon as I step outside, I'm hit by a wave of commotion that overwhelms each of my senses. Everyone talks so loud, and they're not polite at all. Whether they are greeting each other or telling each other to "Get the fuck out of the way," they make sure to cause a scene. I wave at the strange people passing by, and they stare back at me with confusion and alarm. "Do I know you?!" one woman demands. My dad yanks me away and tells me to stop doing that. This is going to be a tough habit to break. I can't imagine walking past someone without acknowledging them, not to mention it's rude. But I don't say this out loud, I keep my observations to myself. I just nod, trying my best to absorb any little bit of information to make this transition easier. For him.

My dad summons a yellow taxi cab with a wave of his hand, as if he were a magician. He tosses my little red suitcase, stuffed with my most precious possessions, into the trunk, and I climb onto the tan leather seats that are cracked and reek of cigarette smoke. My dad tells him the address and the driver, sporting a turban and aviator sunglasses, lets out a thick cloud of smoke. "Fifty bucks."

"Fifty bucks?!" My dad shakes his head.

As we sit in silence crossing the boroughs on our way to Manhattan, I immediately notice how all the billboards advertising movies depict guns and violence. And strangely, there's no naked women. In Italy, it's perfectly normal to glance up at a billboard and have a big pair of bronzed oily tits successfully sell you sunscreen at eight a.m. on a January morning.

Everything is so colossal here. The towering buildings cast shadows that stretch as far as my wide eyes can see, while the people, who look nothing alike, bustle around as if part of some grand dance. I'm a provincial girl from a small town where everything seems miniature in comparison. I feel miniature too, but not in an insignificant way. I feel small in a way that feels exciting, like *I* have yet to be discovered.

My dad aggressively thumbs his beeper, mumbling under his breath, while I roll down the window and stick my head all the way out. I take a deep inhale as the warm jagged air smacks me in the face, instantly recognizing the unique blend of roasted peanuts, molten concrete, and car exhaust that triggers my memory. I know this smell. Before I can immerse myself in the familiar scent, I'm interrupted by my dad pulling me back in by the back of my collar. I don't like how he's always yanking me around.

The ride feels forever long as the car crawls through the gridlocked rush-hour streets. I squirm in the backseat, fidgeting with my bracelet, the gold nameplate that reads "Giulia," that was placed on my wrist at birth. The countless lanes and vast sea of cars overwhelm me. Too many ways to go, I think. The thought of getting lost in this concrete maze sends shivers down my spine. I gulp down the thought and ignore the fact that I'm starting to feel insignificant and inconsequential. Even a nuisance perhaps.

We finally pull up to a towering building, its rusty gray bricks adorned in scaffolding and an emerald-green awning with big faded bronze letters on it. The glass doors swing open and a jolly man with a mustache emerges, eager to assist my dad with the suitcases.

"Javier, this is my daughter, Julia. She's gonna be staying here for a while!"

Javier sticks his hand out and says, "Hola, Hoolia." I giggle. I've never heard my name pronounced like that before.

"Before I forget, this is your address now, if you ever get lost." My dad points to the green street signs on the corner. Before I can read them, he's already disappeared inside the building. I can tell my dad isn't used to having kids around because I'm constantly jogging behind him to keep up.

Once inside, he calls the elevator, and after a few seconds of waiting, he gets impatient and leads me up the service stairs. I trail behind him, down the long windy corridor all the way to Apartment 2F. Without unlocking the door first, he swings it open and shouts, "We're home!"

I'm shocked and ask him, "You don't lock the door?"

He shrugs and replies, "We got nothing of value here."

What about me? I think to myself.

In Italy, Grandpa locked and bolted every orifice of our little apartment at sundown, and we certainly didn't have anything of "value" in that apartment either.

I don't fully trust him but I'm left with no other option. I accept his answer and immediately shift my attention to my brand-new home.

The room is covered in sheets of plastic, shielding the furniture from paint splatter, and the smell of paint is overpowering, but the sunlight streaming in from the windows floods the room with warmth.

My dad takes me on a grand tour of the place, beaming with pride. It's not very big, but it feels massive to me. I've never lived anywhere that had a hallway before. Once we get to the end of the corridor, he announces, "I saved the best for last . . . your very own bedroom!" He pushes the door open and there, perched atop of a ladder, is a man in a beret nonchalantly painting clouds on the ceiling!

My eyes widen and a flush spreads across my cheeks. This is too good to be true. I've never seen anything more exquisite in my life! But mostly, I'm overjoyed to finally have a room of my own like the kids on TV.

I never had the luxury of solitude at my grandpa's. In fact, I was never alone. We were quite literally on top of each other, crammed into the same small one-bedroom apartment my mom grew up in. My brother and I shared the living room with Grandpa, and if our mom was home, my brother would sleep on the pullout couch in her room with her. She was rarely home before bedtime though. When the clock struck midnight and she still hadn't returned, I'd frantically dial her cell number on the old rotary phone until she picked up, just to hear her voice and make sure she was alive. The passing headlights outside only added to my restlessness, as I watched each car pass by, desperately hoping to see hers.

She worked as a nurse and was studying to become a psychologist, with no money, two little kids, and a certifiably insane baby daddy a thousand miles away, so I can't blame her for her late nights.

The nights spent at home with Grandpa were always a blast. He would make us zabaglione with eggs and sugar and put on Lucio Battisti's music. I'd make him record me dancing on his old camcorder as I choreographed my own dance routines. He adored old Western movies, and I'd always have to wait until he was snoring and then I'd change the channel to sneakily watch the trashy late-night game shows. As cramped as it was living with Grandpa, at least it was safe.

The last time I was in New York, we were homeless. How it happened is hazy, but I vividly remember bouncing around between the homes of various family members and friends. The fighting, the chaos, and the tears are seared into my memory. The worst place we stayed was a dingy squat house in Chinatown where over twenty people slept on mats all over the floor. A fight broke out while I was asleep, and when I woke up in the morning, there was a thick puddle of what looked to be blood on the floor by the entrance. Without a word, my dad swiftly scooped me up and we rode away on his bicycle, never to return. And we never spoke of it again.

After that, we began sleeping at my dad's job sites. One of them was a beautiful townhouse on the Upper West Side with arched doorways and a fireplace. It was Christmastime, and while the family who owned the place was away on vacation, they hired my dad to do a partial renovation. Little did they know my dad moved us all in on the first day of the job. Things were running smoothly at first, and my parents even cuddled on the couch by the fire in the evenings as the snow piled up outside. I didn't care that it wasn't technically our house. It was so fun playing pretend, and I was just grateful we were all finally under the same roof.

But soon Mom's mood turned, as it always did. I guess living someone else's life and shuttling all our belongings from place to place wasn't what she considered to be her American dream. With no other option, we moved onto the twenty-foot sailboat docked at the 79th Street

Marina that my dad had bought for a thousand bucks when he was eighteen years old. Unfortunately, it was the middle of winter and there was no heating or proper plumbing on the boat, and the arguing between my parents was getting progressively worse by the day.

The tension was thick and suffocating, making it impossible to escape. Explosive outbursts that spawned violent rages were a frequent occurrence, with objects hurled at my dad, shattering and ricocheting dangerously close to us. My brother was too young to comprehend the reason behind these outbursts, but I knew that our dad had taken our passports and had hidden them from her. She tore apart every inch of the boat, searching for them until she collapsed in tears, sobbing uncontrollably. In a fit of rage, she violently swatted a cup of water off the table that my brother had offered her, in a naive attempt to make her feel better. Water splashed everywhere, dousing my brother and me. I rushed over to comfort her, but she swatted me away like a mosquito.

"Just give me mine then! Keep theirs!" she pleaded through the tears.

She had reached her breaking point. She didn't want to do this anymore. She had higher expectations for her life. The daughter of a hairdresser and a mechanic, she was the first in her family to go to college. She'd done everything right, and yet she was poor, homeless with two little kids in a foreign city. She unleashed her frustrations by hurling insults at him. She called him a loser, a failure, a broke bum. But he wouldn't budge. He wanted to have his family geographically close to him. It probably didn't help that the last time he visited us in Italy, we barely looked up from our game when he walked through the door. Or that my brother would call any tall man with glasses "Papa." At four years old, I darted back and forth between my parents, coaxing my mom not to cry and pleading with my dad to give me the passports. Finally, he told me where they were, and I promptly told my mom. I felt it was my duty to make her stop crying, as she was starting to scare my brother, who had begun sobbing uncontrollably too.

I blinked and we were suddenly back at Grandpa's house.

Grandpa says he is both our mom and our dad, but he's so much more than that. We rely on his small pension to make ends meet, and although we aren't rich, the refrigerator is stocked with delicious food, and he spoils us with ice cream, candy, and soda. When we run out of candy, I eat spoonfuls of powdered chocolate Nesquik. And when that runs out, I turn to the cough syrup in the medicine cabinet. I am a regular at the emergency room and all the doctors know me by name.

I enjoy going to the hospital. I especially love getting shots, often asking the doctors for more. The nurses joke among themselves that they've never seen anything like it before. I relish the brief sting of the needle as it penetrates my skin, and the satisfaction of watching the liquid go in and the blood squirt out. The bright sterile corridors emit a distinct smell of cleanliness that I find oddly comforting. I love wandering around and snooping on the other patients. But mostly, I love the warm, calming sensation of knowing that I'm going to be taken care of.

Grandpa often comments on my parents' lazy parenting skills, and it's hard to argue with him. I can count on one hand the number of times that my mom took us to the movies or to a playground. The last time, she sat on a bench with her friends, chatting and smoking a cigarette as I rode around her in circles on my tricycle. I patiently waited until she had smoked it down to the filter and innocently asked if I could step on the butt. She paused and to my surprise, she handed me the still-lit cigarette. Instead of throwing it on the ground, I put it in my mouth and pedaled away as fast as I could on my little pink bike. When I turned around, she was curled over, laughing uncontrollably, while her friends looked on in horror.

We didn't have a lot of money, so if I wanted something, I knew the only way to get it was by taking it. Once my mom caught me red-handed. After a trip to the supermarket, I climbed into the backseat and began discreetly pulling all my new acquisitions out of my pants. Among them was a jumbo pack of Bazooka bubble gum. Just as I was about to pop another piece of the yummy pink bubble gum into my mouth, she spun around and caught me in the act. I braced for impact but to my surprise, she asked me for a piece of gum, turned on the radio, and drove home.

My mom never had us baptized, which is a sin in itself in a place like Italy. I was furious that she didn't care if we went to hell or not. When the local nuns and priests would stop by for their monthly visits, Grandpa would swear up and down that we had been baptized. I remember them nodding suspiciously while examining the room in search of any photograph of my christening. In Italy, those kinds of pictures are everywhere in the house: the refrigerator, the mantelpiece, the coffee table. They even hang them on the rearview mirrors of their cars. They keep registries of these events, and watching my grandpa lie for me only made me feel worse. After a while, any time the bell rang, Grandpa would tell us to be quiet so we could pretend not to be home.

Grandpa insists on keeping the windows wide open, no matter the weather. He says it's a precautionary measure in case we get bombed; this way the air pressure won't shatter the glass. He has PTSD from the war and is haunted by the loss of his two brothers during battle. I asked him once if he ever killed anyone. He remained silent, but the look of despair on his face gave him away.

The cold marble floors send shivers through my little feet as I bounce restlessly from room to room. To save on gas and electricity, we keep the heat off. During the scorching summer months, we have one small fan that we only turn on when it becomes unbearable. Despite the discomfort, we never complain. He's resourceful, rinsing and reusing paper towels that he hangs to dry on the clothesline on our cluttered balcony. He drinks bottle after bottle of sparkling Lambrusco wine and curses God for taking his wife away too soon. Yet he never once lays a hand on us. He is the only source of unconditional love I know. He is *home*.

I'm excited to be in New York with my dad, but a part of me aches for my grandpa. He rarely ventured out after my grandma died, and we were his whole world. Instead of enjoying his golden years in peace, he was left to raise two wild kids all by himself. He'd whip up dinner for us and pick us up from school. We'd hop on the back of his *motorino* and ride to the garden, where we'd pluck grapes off the vines and pop them straight into our mouths. One summer, we even planted a pine tree, watching it sprout and grow taller year after year. He'd proudly frame my sketches and hang them on the wall, always making sure to point them out to the few guests we had over. *"Hai visto l'artista?"* he'd say with a beaming smile spread across his face.

At night, we'd go around in a circle and recite our prayers aloud before he'd sing us the same verse of the only lullaby he knew, until we were fast asleep.

"When is Mamma and Christopher coming?" I ask my dad in broken English.

Without looking up from his beeper, he replies, "Soon, sweetie."

I'm not convinced by this answer, but before I can further pry into the matter, he grabs my hand and leads me next door. "I want you to meet someone. They just moved in too."

My dad knocks on the door. I hear loud voices blaring from the TV, but there's no answer. He tries again, and suddenly a woman's piercing shriek echoes through the walls. It's not a normal scream but something straight out of a horror film. I glance up at my dad, unsure if maybe we should leave, but he seems completely unperturbed.

We hear thumping and bumping until the door cracks open, and a little boy with shaggy dirty-blond hair steps into the doorway, wearing baggy UFO pants and with a strange blue growth on his nose. I try not to stare at it. Suddenly, a giant, oversize golden retriever appears from behind him, pushing to get past. He struggles to keep the dog inside until, finally, a woman with big bleached-blond hair appears and wrestles the dog back inside.

"Oh, hellooooo! You must be Julia! Your dad was telling us about you! I'm Sharon. So nice to meet youuuuuu! Josh, say hi to Julia!"

Her voice is grating and boisterous, and she speaks with a heavy New York drawl, but she's warm and kind of weird so I'm instantly intrigued by her. "Hey," Josh says with a mischievous look and a smirk that feels way beyond his years.

He is only four years old, and normally I wouldn't befriend anyone younger than me, but as I scan the room, taking in all the black leather and marble accents, I notice he has every video game console available on the market.

Sharon spends most of her time in her room, either chatting on the phone or watching her favorite shows in bed. I overheard my dad say that she's a "JAP"—a Jewish American princess. Whatever that means. Although she has a law degree, she doesn't practice law. Instead, she floats in and out of the building, making drugstore runs and taking the dog out for short walks. She always brings back something to eat, usually pizza or Happy Meals from McDonald's. The only time she doesn't go out is if she gets a chemical peel, and then she looks like a monster for a whole week.

Sharon and Josh split their time between Long Island and the city. When they're in town, I'm usually at their place. And when they're on Long Island, I'm usually at their place. I sneak out of my bedroom window and climb onto the scaffolding that surrounds the building. From there I hop onto their balcony and press my sweaty little palms against the glass until I get the window open. Once inside I play video games, watch MTV, and indulge in the delicious cans of Chef Boyardee they leave behind. It's way better than the Hamburger Helper my dad has at our apartment

My favorite part is sneaking into Sharon's closet and modeling all her clothes in the mirror. She has loads of beautiful fur coats, miniskirts, tube tops, and sexy leather jackets. I put them on, pretending to be her, and talk to myself in the mirror.

Going through her drawers, I stumble upon two ID cards with two very different birthdays, neither of which matches the age she told me she was, twenty-five. My mind is blown when I find a ton of Polaroids of her when she was younger, backstage at various rock concerts dressed like a groupie.

When Josh and I aren't playing video games, we are usually up to no good. Sometimes it's innocent, like freeing our neighbors' cats by slicing their window screen open, or dropping pennies off the rooftop until someone calls the cops on us. Other times we behave like juvenile delinquents. As the complaints from the neighbors start to roll in, one lady in particular seems to take issue with our antics.

Naturally, we decide to scale the barbed-wire fence into her backyard and break into her apartment. We don't take anything, but only because there's nothing good to take. We do it for the thrill.

Josh is the perfect surrogate little brother to me, filling the void that the absence of my actual brother, Chris, has left me with. I couldn't ask for a better temporary placeholder. We spend so much time together that we even start fighting like siblings. He hits me in the face with a baseball bat for no reason, just like a real brother.

Sometimes Sharon locks her windows, and in that case I'm stuck at home, alone and bored. My dad often locks me in my room for the entire day while he's at work. If I have to use the bathroom, I go in the cat's litter box.

We have one TV at home, and my dad reserves it for watching movies, but I figured out how to access basic cable by connecting some wires I found in the hallway. Now, when I'm home alone, I watch *Jerry Springer* and *Maury* for hours on end. I find all the seedy characters on the shows fascinating. They have a mind-numbing element that's irresistible. I feel a sense of calm as I zone out to the chaos.

My dad would never let me watch "daytime television." He says, "It rots your brain." If he only knew that all I did during my time in Italy was sit in front of my grandpa's old television set with headphones on and a bowl of sugar, using a lighter to make caramel clusters to suck on, he would be furious.

I fear my brain has already rotted.

"Read a book," he says.

I've noticed that books are a significant part of his life. He keeps rows and rows of them on every bookshelf, in every closet, and even under his bed. His dad was a writer, and I think he secretly wishes he could be one too. He calls himself an "intellectual construction worker." In Italy, I never read books. My mom only read comic books. She even named me after the main character in the one she was reading while pregnant with me. Prior to my arrival the doctors had told her they had spotted a penis on the sonogram and she even had a name picked out for me, Alessandro. But surprise surprise, I came out with a vagina. I can't help but feel like maybe I was already a disappointment. Everything was blue for the first year of my life. My dad treats books like an escape. He gets lost in the pages of the books he reads, and it seems like he always has to be reading a few books at once. One isn't enough to quiet the noise in his head. He takes me to the bookstore often and lets me choose books from the adult section to take home. Soon enough, I'm doing the same thing. I even steal a night-light from Barnes & Noble, so he won't catch me reading at night with the light on anymore.

Lately I've been stealing anything I can get my hands on. I go to the stores in the neighborhood and they never suspect me. I'm smooth. I never get caught. I steal candy from the dollar store, I steal makeup from the drugstore, I steal clothes out of the laundry room of my building. And sometimes when my dad's wallet is sitting out, I take a small amount of money and stash it in the secret compartment of my music box. It's not much, just twenty dollars here and there. Sometimes fifty. Sometimes five. But it sure adds up quickly. However, I only know how to count to ninety-nine. So I stack piles of ninety-nine dollars until I have so many stacks that I need to find a new place to hide them.

I know stealing is wrong but the security that it gives me is priceless. My parents' constant arguing over money has left an indelible mark on my psyche. I vow that I will never be like them. When I grow up, I'm going to be rich.

My dad works a lot and when he comes home, he's always tired and in a bad mood. The silver lining is that for the first time in my entire life I finally have some independence and I'm starting to form a new identity. I feel like a little lady, the woman of the house. I go to the dollar store and grab a roll of toilet paper when we run out. I get us some cereal and milk since my dad rarely goes food shopping. I'm quickly learning how to care for myself. One morning, my dad comes in to get me dressed for school to find I've already done it. When he bends over to tie my shoe-lace, I yank my foot away from him. "I do it myself."

Sometimes when he gets home from work, if he's not too tired, I'll hop on his handlebars and we'll ride to Central Park, where we catch fireflies in mason jars and make wishes as we release them back into the night. In those moments I feel like I have the best dad in the world. On other nights, we go to the video store downstairs and rent a movie on VHS. Sometimes he lets me watch the movie with him, but if it's for grown-ups, he tells me to go to bed. Even though I'm supposed to be sleeping, I sneak out of bed and watch the movie crouched down from the corner of the hallway anyway.

On the weekends, when my dad isn't working, we go to the diner and order our favorite meal: a cream cheese omelet with home fries and buttered toast with strawberry jam. Later, he sits me down at the dining room table and teaches me how to read and write in English. I have a hard time pronouncing "th," despite my efforts to press my tongue against my teeth and blow; it sounds like "d" and this makes him frustrated. He loses his patience so easily, and I'm starting to get antsy and bored. I wish I could watch *Jerry Springer.*

At night, I lie in bed and cry. I muffle the noise with my stuffed animals because I don't want him to wake up. He's especially grumpy. I'm trying my hardest to be a big girl, but I really miss my mom and my brother. And I especially miss the comfort of my grandpa.

My dad often drops me off at my grandma Margaret's apartment. He says she's a wannabe WASP, whatever that means. She lives in a studio apartment at an elderly person's home ten blocks away. She has the silkiest pearly white hair and the same big blue eyes of which I was the sole inheritor. She lets me give her facials and do her makeup, even though I have no idea what I'm doing. She loves classical music, costume jewelry, her many plants, her senior cats, and the arts. She makes sure I learn the correct way to speak and that I always mind my manners. "May I" not "can I" and "yes" not "yeah."

She has tons of art supplies and encourages me to be creative. We spend hours in Central Park watercoloring, and when we get home she hangs my art on the wall, just like Grandpa. She takes me to the Metropolitan Museum, the Natural History museum, the Whitney, the MoMA. As we stroll, she points out the beauty all around us. She brings me to the opera, the theater, and the ballet. And although we never have good seats, she always remembers to bring two sets of binoculars for us. I never pay attention to the stage because I'm having so much fun spying on the audience members. I love people-watching. I wonder who these people are, what their lives are like, and if they're actually enjoying themselves. A lot of them seem to be sleeping. Grandma doesn't mind that I'm not paying attention. She has a permanent smile glued to her face the entire time.

My aunt Beth is usually always with us, trailing behind with multiple tote bags. They joke that she's Grandma's shadow. "We're attached at the hip," Beth says with a laugh. And since my grandma is in a wheelchair from having had polio as a young girl, this arrangement is very convenient for her. For Beth? I'm not so sure, but she doesn't seem to mind it.

During arguments with my dad, I hear my mom say mean things about my grandma and Beth, about how they are mentally ill and that's why he is too. I wonder if that means I'm going to get sick too. One day Beth casually tells Grandma a story that her therapist told her. Grandma looks up from her paper, her mood quickly shifts, and her eyes narrow toward Beth. "Call her up and fire her."

I stop what I'm doing and zero in on the situation, which is growing increasingly uncomfortable.

"Oh, I don't want to fire her, Mom. She's been helping me a lot. I've been able to connect with her."

Beth's pleas fail to move my grandma, who grows stiff in her seat. "No. She should not be spending the time that you pay for to talk about herself. Call her now and fire her."

Defeated, my aunt Beth sighs and asks her, "Well, what do you want me to say?"

Annoyed, my grandma replies, "Tell her that she's not the right fit for your particular needs."

My aunt nods. Her hand trembles as she reaches for the receiver. She reluctantly punches in her therapist's number. All eyes are on Beth. Even the cat's ears are perked watching this exchange. It rings a few times before she gets the answering machine. I let out a sigh of relief. She struggles to force the words off her tongue.

"It . . . it was so nice meeting with you, but my mom and I just don't think you're the right fit for me. It's nothing personal. You were great. Thanks so much for your time."

She hangs up the receiver and looks as if she's about to cry.

"Don't worry, sweetheart," Grandma says, her tone suddenly warm and nurturing, "we are going to find you someone so much better."

I'm too young to fully comprehend what I just witnessed, but it changes my perception of their relationship permanently.

My dad says to prepare myself because I'm going to start school soon. My palms immediately start profusely sweating as I dread the thought. I have a condition called hyperhidrosis, which makes my hands always clammy. He takes me shoe shopping at Modell's and insists on buying me the ugliest pair of brown Mary Janes. I stomp my feet and tell him I want the shiny blue ones. He says they're too expensive, and I convince him to get me a pair of red high-tops instead.

"Fine since they're only five bucks."

We're both happy and that night he takes me to my very first grown-up movie in a theater. We see *The Fifth Element* and I am absolutely blown away. Milla Jovovich's hair and clothing make such an impression on my malleable little brain. She looks so cool and I want to be just like her when I grow up. On our way home, I rapid-fire questions at my dad about the movie.

"Well, if you behave, maybe I'll put you in a movie!"

My jaw drops. This man really is my hero!

As it turns out, my dad's good friend Nathan is producing a small indie movie in Queens and asked my dad for a small investment. My dad agreed to give him the money on the condition that they find a role for me. That's showbiz, baby!

A few weeks later, I'm on the set of *Fire Dancer*, a movie about a refugee who escapes the war in Afghanistan only to commit suicide later on.

I appear in one flashback, buried among the rubble of a war-torn village. It's grueling labor and I don't even have any lines. It's all so repetitive and underwhelming. Not at all like the *Fifth Element* movie. This turns out to be one of many bad investments on my dad's part because as soon as the movie wrapped, I guess there was some argument over finances that led to Nathan being found guilty of murdering the director of *Fire Dancer*. His severed body parts were discovered in a suitcase on a random street in Queens. As you can imagine, this put a big delay in the completion of the movie, being that both the producer and the director were permanently out of commission. A few years later, we would receive an invitation in the mail to attend the premier of *Fire Dancer* at the Tribeca Film Festival. We said fuck it and went to see it. They cut out my part.

The night before my first day of school, I meticulously pack my backpack. I think of everything: a sharpener, an eraser, a set of colored pencils in a jar so big that it doesn't fit in my backpack. Right before bed, I get on my knees and implore God to please watch over me, as I so often do when I'm scared. I miss my mom and my grandpa more than ever.

In the morning, I get dressed before my dad wakes up. I find the only pair of matching socks and I tuck in my shirt like all the kids do in Italy. I brush my hair and neatly tuck it behind my ears. He comes in, seemingly impressed and a little relieved to find me ready. I just want today to be perfect. No hiccups.

I grip the big jar of colored pencils on my lap with my sweaty hands as my dad bikes me to school. I savor every moment before we finally arrive at the big black doors. I hop off his handlebars and feel the tears bubbling up as I plead with him not to go yet, begging him to come inside with me.

He looks me in the eyes. "Enjoy it now, 'cause it's all downhill from here, kid." Before I can reply, he's already biked away.

Defeated and confused, I drag my feet inside the building and finally find my classroom. But not before I trip and drop the entire jar of colored pencils all over the floor as soon as I step foot through the doorway. One particular girl laughs a little too hard at my mishap and I instantly want to make her pay. I pick up my pencils as fast as I can and scurry to a seat in the back, where I'm promptly informed that we are to only use pens in this class, because the teacher wants to "see our mistakes." I feel the tears boiling up again. I retreat into my corner and check out. I begin doodling when the same girl who laughed at me turns around and whispers, "I'm Mia. What's your name?" Annoyed, I reply, "Julia," and go back to doodling. I still don't trust her.

Later, at lunchtime, I feel her gaze on me. It's like the more I push her away, the more she wants to befriend me. I'm starving but once I unzip my lunch box, it reeks. Someone yells, "Ew, what's that smell?!" and I immediately shut it. My dad must have made his version of a tuna fish sandwich. This is the same man who scrapes mold off old food and still eats it. This is the same man who dumpster-dives and eats food out of the trash can. I'm so embarrassed, fighting back tears, when Mia, who I've decided cannot read social cues, finally stops buzzing around and says, "Wanna see something cool?"

I follow her out of the cafeteria and down an empty hallway. She stops in front of a vending machine and says, "Okay, be the lookout." She slips her long lanky arm inside and up the spout, successfully managing to knock a Twix bar down. She rips it open with her teeth and hands me one. "Now it's your turn!" I accept the challenge and in one swift motion I manage to grab a pack of Skittles.

From that moment on, we become inseparable. We sit together in every class, and when we aren't together, we're on the phone with each other.

Mia's mom, Marissa, is a single mom who teaches at the school and supervises the after-school program we both attend, so naturally I get to know her too. Marissa is beautiful. She's tall and naturally tan, with thick black hair and a deep gaze. Before she had Mia, she used to be a dancer for a famous musician back in Italy, where she's from. It makes me feel happy and less alone to know someone else from Italy.

When my dad picks me up from after-school in the evenings, we go get hot chocolate with extra whipped cream at the diner nearby. Me, Mia, my dad, and Marissa. We go so often that it becomes tradition. It also becomes the part of my day I look forward to the most.

Mia says that I should get a computer so we can talk on AOL. When my dad comes home from work I bombard him, begging him to get one for me. As expected, he tells me, "I don't have the money for it." I decide it's time to part ways with my stolen security fund. I run and get my music box from under my mattress and proudly present him with the dozens of piles of ninety-nine dollars I have accumulated. He counts it and is stunned to find out that it's enough for TWO computers.

He shoots me a look, shakes his head, and mutters under his breath, "I don't even wanna know."

I start jumping up and down, tugging on his sleeve. "Please, Daddy, pretty please with a cherry on top!"

"All right, I'll go get the damn computer."

I hug my dad and call Mia to tell her the news. Marissa answers the phone and asks to speak to my dad. He grabs the portable phone and shoos me away. I listen at the door, curious as to what they could possibly be talking about. I hear him say, "I love you too."

I'm confused but I think nothing of it when an hour later he comes back with a brand-spankin'-new computer from P. C. Richard & Son. Later that night, when we finally figure out how to connect to AOL, we create my very first email address. "Poshspice" is taken so I settle on "gingerkitty123."

Over the next two years Mia and I exist as sisters. We take my dad's boat out and sail the Hudson River, where I bravely dive into the murky

water. Marissa gasps but my dad reassures her that it's good for my im-
mune system. We go ice-skating at Chelsea Piers in the winter and to
the beach at Coney Island in the summer, where we stand on our parents'
toes to meet the height requirement to get on the rides. At school we are
dubbed "The Sleepover Sisters," since we go home together every night.
One of our favorite movies is *The Parent Trap* because we relate so much
to Lindsay Lohan's characters.

It's not uncommon for my dad to come over to Marissa's. Sometimes
he spends the night too. And some nights they go out alone together,
leaving us at home with the babysitter. Our fighting gets so bad that one
babysitter quits midshift, leaving us unattended for the rest of the night.
Another one cries to our parents about how she is traumatized by our
bad behavior. The truth is, we are spending way too much time together
and we probably need a break from each other. But now that our parents
are friends, we never get a night off.

One night while our parents are out, we put on *Romy and Michele's
High School Reunion,* and after watching it three times in a row, we decide we are going to be just like them when we grow up.

"I'm the Mary! You're the Rhoda!" I shout at her.

"No. I'm the Mary!" she shouts back.

When Marissa gets home, she's alone, without my dad. She lies beside us on the pullout couch and begins brushing our hair into braids.
She seems pensive when, all of a sudden, she asks me, "How would you
feel if you had a little brother?" I pause for a moment and tell her I already have a little brother and don't particularly want another one. She
nods. I know this is a strange question but I brush it off. I often imagine
that Marissa is my mom. She's warm and nurturing, but she also has a
fiery wild side. She wears red lipstick, dances naked in the mirror, and
loves going out at night. I'm not shocked when I find her nude Polaroids
going through some old boxes in her loft.

She buys us costumes and plays dress-up with us. She teaches me
how to apply nail polish and lipstick and even supervises me as I shave
my legs, armed with a Band-Aid for when I inevitably cut myself. She

teaches me proper hygiene and how to correctly brush and part my hair with the tip of a comb. She lets us watch TV and doesn't yell at us when we eat cookies after we brush our teeth. Before bed, she kisses us both on the forehead and tells us both how much she loves us.

She does all the things my mother would never do, but she's still not *my* mom. For better or for worse, that spot is taken.

One evening, I walk in on my dad sitting on the edge of his bed with Marissa standing before him. I freeze in the doorway as I watch him pull her close to him by her waist. She leans down, whispers something in his ear, and then they kiss on the mouth.

I gasp and run out of the room. I know it isn't right. I'm confused as to what I'm feeling, it's a new sensation I've never felt before: the bitter sting of betrayal. I lock myself in the bathroom and think hard about how I'm going to handle this. Now everything makes sense. During our habitual sleepovers, Marissa would wait until she thought we were fast asleep and slither out of bed, disappearing into the darkness. I wondered where she was going but I never thought to ask. Now I'm sure she was going to sleep in my dad's room. How could I have been so dumb to think it was innocent?! I feel so stupid.

I push the icky feelings back down, but the image of them kissing is seared in my brain, and I wish I never saw it. I wish I could press rewind on my life and erase that part, but unfortunately I can't unsee it.

I finally explode the next day and decide to confront him. "I saw you kiss Marissa!" I blurt out, standing in the hallway too angry to get close to him.

He starts scrambling to make up excuses. He stutters and cowers as he does his best to gaslight me into believing I didn't see what I know I saw. He says it was just a peck, a love tap, nothing to worry about. "I love Mommy," he reassures me.

I'm not convinced but I make the conscious decision to accept his explanation, since I don't really have a choice anyway. We continue living this way until one day, on one of my mom's biannual visits to New York, she discovers a pair of ripped pantyhose under my dad's bed.

That particular morning, I decided to play hooky and I miraculously convinced my parents that I was sick enough to stay home from school. Big mistake. Armed with the evidence, my mom confronted my dad, who tried to convince her that the pantyhose in fact belonged to her. My mom, without hesitation, snapped back, "I would never wear this cheap brand with all these holes in it!" She was fuming. Her face was beet red and her jaw was doing the twitchy thing it does when she's going to start hitting.

She backed my dad into a corner as she yanked every glass picture frame off the wall, one by one, and smashed it over his head. Then she turned to the kitchen cabinets and began pulling out wineglasses and glass dishes, hurling them in his direction. We were swimming in a sea of glass and I started to get worried for my dad. I ran across the shards and stood between them, imploring her to stop. He took this opportunity to flee the apartment, probably to go to Marissa's house. My mom retreated into the bedroom where she began sobbing.

I trailed behind her, trying to comfort her, but she was inconsolable. Through the steady stream of tears, she asked me if I knew. I felt so ashamed. I kept my gaze low and nodded. I told her about what I saw and she assured me that it was okay and that it wasn't my fault, but I know a little part of her hated me for it. I'd betrayed her in the worst way.

The next few days, I pick shards of glass out of my feet as she quietly tosses every picture of Mia and me in the trash. She also throws away toys, books, stuffed animals, and anything else that might remind her of Mia and Marissa. She withdraws me from school and enrolls me in a new one nearby and then she goes back to Italy.

I sneak one last phone call to Mia.

"My mom says I'm not allowed to see you anymore," I whisper into the receiver so no one can hear me. Mia is mostly mute, almost as if someone is listening in on her end. I want her to say something, anything, but she doesn't. I feel disappointed that she doesn't attempt to make me feel better. Before I hang up, I tell her that one day when we get older, we are going to find each other and live in our own apartment like Romy and Michele. She giggles. I'm hopeful. She hangs up. I hang up.

•   •   •

A couple of months later, my brother moves to America to live with us, and strangely, I'm not as happy as I thought I'd be. After two years of having the luxury of my very own room, decorating it, and making it mine, I don't want to downgrade. I just want to go back to living my fantasy life.

My brother and Josh the neighbor become best friends. Now they play together without me and I'm pissed. My payback is that I dress them up like girls and make them be my backup dancers when I put on performances in the living room.

As much as I pick on my brother, I do like having him around. At least I'm not home alone anymore, and Chris is an excellent listener. He's smart and inquisitive and genuinely loves hearing the stories I stay up all night writing. I can tell he genuinely enjoys hearing my words come to life. As I read, he asks thoughtful questions and makes insightful comments. Sometimes if it's sad, I can hear him softly stifling his tears. He says that I have what it takes to be a real writer someday.

If I want anything, my dad makes me write poems in exchange. A new stuffed animal? "That will cost you fifty poems," he says. "And they better be good, no haikus!" I recite my work to my brother to make sure it meets the standards set by our dad. The poems my dad likes the most, he submits to poetry journals and when they get published, he triumphantly bursts into our room waving the book in my face. "See how talented you are?" he says. He doesn't do this with my brother.

My new school is so much bigger than the last. My last school had an average of ten kids per class, but this one has almost thirty. I like that I can just fade into the crowd and lose myself daydreaming. I spend most of my time in solitude, sucking my thumb, chomping away at my nails, humming made-up melodies, and twirling my hair, tucked away in a remote corner drawing pictures of Mia and happier times. I compulsively write her birthday and her zodiac sign "Leo" all over my books so I won't forget it. "*Julia + Mia 4ever*"

I write long detailed letters to her about my days and how lost I feel without her, knowing I'll never be able to send them. I don't pay attention in class. I don't ask the teachers questions nor do I engage with any other students. They call me "weirdo" and "freakazoid." They make fun of my accent and the way I talk. I don't have many clothes since my dad never takes me shopping and they make fun of me for wearing the same thing every day. One girl points at my shoes and yells, "Ha ha! She has on the bootleg Payless sneakers!" I start to wonder if maybe they're right. Maybe I am a freak. I don't really care though. I prefer living in my fantasy world, detached from reality. I have no interest in making friends again after what happened to me last time. I'm too angry.

My odd behavior draws the attention of my teachers, who alert the school therapist, who then alerts a social worker that I'm displaying troubling signs. At first, I'm thrilled about being plucked out of class every day for an hour or two. The lady with the wild white curly hair asks me about myself. I tell her all about Italy and my grandpa and how I wish I could go home. I suck on cherry cough drops while she takes notes on a yellow pad. "Do your parents get angry at each other?" I fidget in my seat. "My dad says my mom has mad cow disease." After a few visits with the social workers, I realize these meetings aren't normal. They seem to be asking me increasingly complicated questions that I don't want to answer so I better get my shit together and start acting normal.

My dad is notified of my behavior and enrolls me in Transcendental Meditation classes. I don't know what this means but I overheard him telling the instructor, "Her teachers said to put her on ADHD medication! I said, 'Fuck that, I'm not giving drugs to a nine-year-old! Her brain isn't even done developing!'"

I wonder what I need medication for. Maybe I am sick. I can't even remember the last time my dad took me for a checkup.

I'm the youngest person in the Transcendental Meditation classes. We meet once a week in the evenings and talk and meditate. My favorite part is that I get to listen to these strange people talk about grown-up things. Their hopes and fears, their insecurities and shortcomings. This is even better than people-watching at the opera with Grandma. As different as we are, we all have one thing in common: We just want to feel better.

At home, my dad carves ten minutes out of my day to sit in silence and train my brain to stay still. In the beginning it's hard. I twitch and fidget. I fixate and lose track of my mantra. But soon I begin to get it and my thoughts start to slow down, my feelings become manageable, and I start feeling present in my own life.

At school my scribbles start to dissipate, I gradually move my seat to the front of the class, and I start raising my hand and asking questions. For the first time, I'm genuinely interested in learning. I engage with the world around me. I get picked on less too. My classmates start warming up to me, and eventually, I forget Mia's birthday and her zodiac sign altogether. I even make a new best friend. Her name is Danielle. I call her Danny.

Danny's parents are divorced and her mom, Tanya, is in Alcoholics Anonymous, which sounds sort of like my meditation classes—people just sitting around and talking—though it doesn't seem to be working for her the same way. Tanya is beautiful but she's so damaged. She smells like cloves and Chanel No. 5. She's paranoid and anxious and it rubs off on everyone around her. She's originally from Texas, born into a deeply religious family. From what she tells us her mother was a mean mean woman who hit her all the time for no reason. She managed to escape as a teenager, cut off all contact with her family, hopped on a bus to New York City, and has been on her own ever since. When Danny and I complain about going to school, she tells us how lucky we are because she didn't have the same opportunities.

Danny hates when her mom drinks. Tanya relapses a lot and Danny always knows. She has a sixth sense and can tell if her mom has had even one drop of champagne. My mom hates Danny's mom for some reason. She detests things like Alcoholics Anonymous. But I think she's traumatized by what my dad did to her. Maybe she thinks he will do it again with Tanya.

My mom hates anyone I bring around her, and I'm always relieved when she goes back to Italy. I feel like I can finally exhale and slip back into my role of the woman of the house. When she's here, she acts like she's in charge of everything. She doesn't realize that she is no longer a part of our day-to-day lives. My friends are thrilled when she leaves too since they enjoy the lack of supervision that comes with sleepovers at my house. When my mom is in town, I don't like having my friends over because I never know what she's going to do. She might pick a fight with me out of nowhere and demand that my friends leave immediately or hurl insults at my dad loud enough for them to hear. Not to mention, my dad acts differently with me too. He's cold to me for no reason. He acts stricter and he takes the stress from her presence out on me.

I do love when my mom has her friends over though, because I know she will be charming and on her best behavior and she'll cook all my favorite dishes. But as soon as they leave, the fighting commences. When she's away, I do miss her food. When things were better, I would sit in the kitchen watching her cook for hours, mesmerized, subconsciously memorizing every single recipe. These days, I can't get out of the house fast enough. It just feels like she doesn't like me. And to be completely honest, I'm not so sure I like her very much either.

But if there's one thing I'm absolutely certain of, it's that she hates my dad. She even hates his things. And he has a lot of things. He finds most of his stuff on the street or it's unloaded onto him by the residents of the homes he renovates. Most of it is junk. Kitschy trinkets, empty photo albums, boxes of sour wine, old books. He has mountains of things that he doesn't use but continues to collect. The things are stacked on top of each other, oozing out of every crevice of the apartment. When he's out of the house, my mom goes through his mountain of artifacts and tosses them in the trash. This devastates him and only further propels his compulsion to hoard useless junk that he somehow finds great value in. He claims she threw out the only copy of his dad's book. He brings it up all the time like a broken record. I beg them to get a divorce.

As soon as she leaves, I start to hear him on the phone at night. Our rooms are adjacent and the walls are thin. I press my ear to the wall and hear him consoling Marissa and assuring her that they will be together soon. When I confront him, he tells me he's talking to my mom but I know the time difference, and my mom wouldn't be up at four a.m. talking to him. He just can't be honest. My hero is turning out to be nothing more than just another flawed human being. I think to myself how it's not fair that he still gets to see Marissa and Mia and I don't, when I didn't do anything wrong. Why am I being punished for his actions? I feel so much rage toward him for ruining my life. I lose all respect for him. I'm nine years old and I've mentally and emotionally checked out from this family. When I'm home I spend my time locked in the bathroom with the hair dryer on so I don't have to hear the dreadful noise. Unfortunately, I know I have a long way to go before I can physically check out, so for the next few years I'll just have to be in survival mode.

Over time my dad begins to unravel. He becomes increasingly volatile. I think raising two kids alone and maintaining an affair is too much for him, and I never know who I'm coming home to. Sometimes he's funny and caring and easygoing and sometimes he breaks a chair over my head for something as bizarre as not wanting to read the Bible because he decided he's religious overnight. He goes through periods where he gets obsessive about something in particular. It could be a song or a new business venture. He gets manic, wide-eyed, and aggressive. He attacks my brother too, who calls him by his first name now. Beatings with the belt are normal.

I want to love him but I often find myself wishing he could just be an asshole all the time. This way I wouldn't have all these inner battles with myself. I learn to navigate my way through shattered expectations and constant disappointments by putting an impenetrable wall up between us. Every time I let my guard down, I'm quickly reminded why my defenses were up in the first place. It's nearly impossible for me to flourish in an inconsistent hostile environment, especially when my own growth is so intertwined with his. I'm forced to face the unsettling reality that the people who are supposed to protect us are sometimes the same people we need protection from.

I slowly begin to scrub away at my femininity, which has proved to be unsustainable in this environment. "Man up! Don't be a pussy!" my dad shouts at me as I cry. I have to be tougher. I have to be more independent. I have to be resilient. I have to be more like him.

I hide my developing body under baggy T-shirts and pants, and I never wear pink. Pink is for pussies. Danny, on the other hand, wears little skirts and has perfect bubbly handwriting. She takes her time and dots her i's with hearts. Her papers look like a gel-pen purple paradise. Mine are illegible.

But she has another side to her that she doesn't show. She's gotten so used to pretending to be perfect for her mom, it's effortless for her. It's as if she has a built-in switch she can turn on and off. And when she's off, she's so much fun. We roller-skate around the neighborhood. We love exploring and discovering the world around us. And sometimes we get lost in the shadows, the places that are hidden right under our noses, like this secluded forest section of Central Park called the Ramble.

One day we decide to go exploring a little bit farther than usual.

"Stay close, girls!" Tanya says to us before taking a big drag of her stinky clove cigarette.

"Okay!" we say in unison as we run off into the bushes.

We find a footpath on the other side of a hill shaded by trees and decide to follow it. It stops in a remote, desolate area. The vibe shifts as we start to notice how much trash is all around us.

"It doesn't seem like anyone comes to clean back here," I say to Danny.

"Ummm, maybe there's a reason for that?" she says. Before I can answer she's pointing to a long blond wig strewn over a branch of a tree. "What the heck is that?!"

I can tell she's scared, but I'm not ready to leave yet. I'm intrigued, and I'm just getting started. "It's just a wig, it's not human hair." But then: "Oh my God! Is that a whip?!"

I point to the coiled-up black leather whip on the ground. We pause and look at each other.

"Okay this is getting super-freaky," she says.

My eyes light up. "Come on, let's keep exploring!"

I pick up a stick and start sifting through the relics of wild nights past: used condoms, cigarette butts, syringes, vials, empty baggies, broken pipes.

"Look, Danny! Look at all these ropes!" I use my stick to lift the matted brown rope so we can get a better look. "Oh my God! Is that blood?!"

I drop the rope. Danny screams. I scream. We book it out of there so fast. We run and run until we finally find Tanya, who looks furious, aggressively puffing on her long stinky clove. "I was one second away from calling the police! Where the hell were you two?!"

"Condom kingdom," Danny says. Tanya's eyes widen and we laugh all the way home, where we decide to pierce each other's ears. I give myself two piercings on my left ear and one on my right. Danny cries when I try to do hers, so we are only able to pierce one of her earlobes.

Our adventures end on the day of our elementary school graduation.

"I'll see you when I'm back from Italy?" I ask her, hopeful.

She nods. "I'll call you when I'm back from camp."

As I hug her, I clench my eyes shut so as not to start crying. Crying is for pussies.

"I wish we were going to the same middle school," I whisper in her ear. Danny enrolled in Wagner and I opted for the smaller school, East Side Middle. Although the schools are in proximity to each other, they have a long-standing rivalry.

After the graduation ceremony, the boys line up to arm-wrestle me and I beat them all as my dad proudly records my victories on his camcorder.

It's not long before Danny makes a new group of friends. And so do I. We see each other at our after-school dance class, where we avoid each other. We think we're witches too, casting spells on each other from across the room.

My new friends and I hold séances in my bedroom, invoking the spirit of the deceased front man of my favorite band, Nirvana. I tape a picture of Kurt Cobain on my wall and fantasize about dying so I can join him on the other side. "It's better to burn out than to fade away," he wrote in his suicide note. I wonder what he meant by that—not realizing it was a line from a Neil Young song. I dissect every word in his diary and pore over his many biographies. I download his music on LimeWire and weep quietly at the tortured lyrics, finally feeling seen.

We sneak the occasional cigarette here and there, not actually inhaling. We start altering our appearance in subtle ways as we suddenly become self-aware. We ditch our Sketchers for beat-up Converse and start wearing dark lipstick to class. We sit in a circle and paint each other's nails black during recess, singing along to System of a Down.

One scorching-hot September morning during my first week of sixth grade, I'm sitting in my humanities class when a plane strikes the World Trade Center, instantly shattering the peaceful morning air. I find out when a student teacher tiptoes into our classroom and whispers something to my teacher. Instead of keeping this very sensitive information to himself, he abruptly and without warning blurts the news to us, then continues writing on the board, offering no further explanation. We look around the room at each other, puzzled. Maybe he was kidding, I think to myself.

It's only when parents start rushing into the building to pick up their kids that I realize something is really really wrong. I wonder if my dad will come.

Eventually the administrators call all of us into the auditorium, where we sit cross-legged and eager for more news. I hear a boy next to me whisper, "I heard there were two planes." I think, What a strange coincidence that two planes would both have accidents on the same day. The chatter is shushed by the principal, who asks us in a very somber tone, "Does anyone have a relative, a parent or a family member who works at the World Trade Center?"

The room remains silent as a few little arms shoot up from the crowd.

"If you raised your hand, please come to the front of the room."

A few teary-eyed kids stand up, their legs wobbling as they weave through the crowd of eyeballs. They get to the front and are escorted out of the auditorium, leaving a trail of sobs that can be heard long after they're gone.

The principal assures the remaining students not to worry and that our parents will be picking us up shortly. I try calling my dad. No answer. I start to worry. My dad doesn't work at the World Trade Center, but he does work all over the city. My mind starts to drift to a dark place and I begin to wonder if maybe he got a job renovating an apartment downtown and something happened to him. I try calling him again. No signal.

All my friends get picked up. It's now past three p.m. and I'm the last student left. I sit in the cafeteria reading, trying to keep my mind off things. Finally my dad shows up. I'm upset at him for making me worry. He excitedly tells me that once the first plane hit, he grabbed his camera and took his boat out, getting as close as he could to film the wreckage. I wish he would have picked me up so I could have gone with him.

On the way home he mutters something about World War III and I think he's exaggerating. The next day, there's no school. I go to Josh's, where every channel on TV airs the same footage of the buildings collapsing onto themselves over and over again. I just want to ignore it, but I can't.

Sharon drops a copy of the *New York Post* on the table with a photo of the attack and the words "ACT OF WAR" written in large black letters. I guess my dad wasn't exaggerating. This makes my palms sweaty. I wish we could just go back to before.

9/11 ushers me into adulthood before puberty and completely takes over my life. A thick black cloud coats the city. The artifacts are strewn everywhere: a burned page from a book, a woman's shoe, a photograph, a pair of broken sunglasses. The faces on the missing posters stare blankly back at me. There are so many all stacked on top of one another, each telling a devastating story.

At night, I lie in bed and wonder if every plane I hear flying overhead is actually a bomb. I grip my pillow over my ears and brace for impact.

2

BIG GIRL

I'm playing Pokémon cards with Chris and Josh next door when suddenly, I feel a strange sensation in my panties. As I sit cross-legged on a folded newspaper, I glance down to find little red droplets seeping through my pants and onto the paper. When I realize it's blood, panic sets in. I contemplate for a few moments what to do next. A part of me wants to blurt it out, but the other part doesn't want them to know that I'm different from them. I awkwardly stand up, gripping the newspaper against my butt before running home backward. Chris and Josh watch me with a puzzled look on their faces and continue playing, unbothered.

I don't feel comfortable telling my dad so I phone my mom. Her voice betrays her feelings when I tell her the news. She assures me she's not upset, but her tone sounds sad. "I just wasn't expecting this," she says. I can't shake the feeling that I've done something wrong. Once my parents are back home, my dad locks her in the bathroom with me, forcing her to teach me how to properly insert a tampon in my vagina.

My dad's voice echoes through the door as my mom desperately tries to pry it open. "Be a good mother!" he demands as I clutch the plastic applicator in my sweaty palms. She pauses, trying to mask her visible discomfort, and casually suggests, "You should use pads."

I nod obediently, eager for this strange, forced encounter to end. I appreciate my dad's attempt at forcing intimacy between us, but it's clear to me that she has no interest in performing any maternal acts.

"Okay, she taught me how to do it!" I shout through the door.

My dad lets go of the doorknob and I scurry out of the bathroom with my head down, cheeks burning with humiliation.

A profound sadness washes over me as I watch my friends bond with their moms, sharing everything from secret crushes to their dreams for the future. When I told my mom I wanted to learn guitar so I could be a rock star, she scoffed and plainly informed me, "Music is a hobby, it's not a real profession." Maybe she wants to protect me, but it feels like she's projecting her own limitations onto me. As I think to myself that my mom just doesn't realize what I'm capable of, I can't shake the feeling that I'm not good enough.

My new friend Ella says that her mom is her best friend. After school, I timidly tell my mom that she's my best friend. She rolls her eyes and brushes me off. "You sound so American." I know this is meant as an insult. "Mothers and daughters can't be 'friends.'" I can't help but feel like I'm missing out on something fundamental in life.

Ella is the youngest of three sisters. Ella, Kat, and Kayla all live with their mom, Silvia, who divorced their dad after he cheated on her. He ended up marrying his mistress and it's a really sore subject. On special occasions, like their anniversary, she'll hold up photos of his new wife and we all have to tell Silvia how ugly she is in unison. All three sisters have beautiful thick auburn hair and big green eyes. I have really bad acne, but their skin is soft and smooth and blemish-free. They're tall, thin, and naturally tan. All the things that I'm not, but for some reason they love having me over. Lucky for me, Kayla has some behavioral issues and gets into fights a lot, so she spends a lot of time with rich family friends in New Jersey. This means there's usually a bed for me. I start spending every single night at Ella's house, and before I know it, I'm practically the fourth sister.

Silvia gets drunk a lot. One day we even come home from school to find her having sex with her drug dealer in the living room in the middle of the afternoon. We rush past them to Ella's room, shielding our eyes. Ella remains unbothered by the scene, as she's used to her mom's behavior. When they're done, the dealer knocks on Ella's door and hands us a jar of shitty pot for the bother. I've never smoked pot before, but Ella is a pro. She says that when she's done doing her homework, she'll roll one up for us. Ella cares a lot about school. She sits at the front of the class. She raises her hand. She gets good scores on tests. She's everything I wish I could be. I stop coming home, which eventually leads me to stop meditating, and now I can't ever sit still. I lose focus. I get reprimanded. I get kicked out of class. Sometimes I wonder why Ella's even friends with me when she could be friends with the popular girls.

Sublime plays from the computer as Ella downloads songs from LimeWire for us to listen to. I'm transfixed as I watch her effortlessly roll a joint and light it up, carefully placing it to her perfectly puckered lips. She takes a few pulls with ease and passes it to me. My heart pounds through my Playboy tank top. I'm trying my best to play it cool.

I take a small puff and quickly blow the stinky smoke out.

"You have to inhale or else you won't feel it," she says impatiently, her blue eyes now bloodshot. I'm afraid to disappoint her, so I take the tiniest inhale and immediately start coughing uncontrollably. Tears stream down my face until we're both laughing hysterically.

I love being high. I feel warm and fuzzy and everything is so funny. My thoughts are more linear and I can finally hear myself think. Ella teaches me how to roll joints with a filter, "like the French," she says. Sometimes we kiss like the French too. She insists it's just practice for the real deal, but I can sense that she just likes it. We play games like spin the bottle and seven minutes in heaven, and then we pretend like it didn't happen.

Her sister Kat is seventeen and has a live-in boyfriend named José. Whenever I have to find a lighter in her room, I always take the opportunity to snoop through her things. I'm intrigued by this strange, cool girl. Her walls are fittingly painted black and covered in punk rock posters. Amid the mayhem on her floor, she has straws in the shape of a penis, vibrating crotch toys, pink fuzzy handcuffs, plastic tiaras, and mysterious substances coating every surface. Ella informs me that she's a dominatrix and that she beats guys up for money and I'm blown away by how fun that sounds.

Kat always barges into Ella's room to check herself out in the full-length mirror before work. As she studies her reflection, I sit by her feet, adorned in patent-leather platform Mary Janes. Her long legs seem to stretch on for miles in her black fishnet stockings. She catches my ogling gaze through the glass and asks with a sly grin, "Do I look badass?" I frantically bob my head back and forth, startled by her voice, when Ella snaps at her, "Can you get the fuck out of my room?"

Ella is very interested in politics. Her passion is infectious as I too begin learning more of the injustices committed by our government. On a crisp April morning, we skip school and hop on a bus headed to Washington, D.C., to participate in a sit-in protesting the war in Iraq. The night before, we spent hours crafting cardboard signs to bring to the march. I wave around my Bedazzled "No Blood for Oil" sign while Ella fearlessly leads the chants of "Bring back our troops!" at the top of her lungs. The day is emotional, as we are almost arrested for lying down in the street, but the experience only brings us closer.

We decide to get our belly buttons pierced on Saint Mark's, taking turns on the phone outside pretending to be each other's moms, tricking the piercer into doing it. It becomes our little secret as we proudly show off our matching belly rings to our envious classmates in school. I get hooked on the rush of the needle puncturing my skin, and pretty soon we are regulars at the piercing station. I even get my tongue and my lip pierced before the end of seventh grade, all while my dad remains clueless.

When Silvia is out of town, the apartment transforms into a haven for rainbow-haired freaks and leather-clad weirdos. Kat's friends come over and blast Rage Against the Machine and break shit, but nobody cares except for Ella, who tries her best to hold it together. Skateboards are strewn all over the floor, and the scent of bong hits and cheap beer fill the air as I timidly sit on the couch, observing the mayhem.

One of Kat's friends, Mikey, is a regular. He's covered in tattoos and has a scruffy boyish charm, even though he looks way older than us. He buys us a big bottle of Jack Daniel's and warns us not to drink it too fast. I've never drank hard alcohol before, except for the occasional sip of grappa my grandpa made me gargle whenever I had a toothache.

He sits next to me on the black leather couch and reaches his arm underneath, feeling around until he triumphantly pulls out Silvia's hidden tray with her secret stash of pot. "Bingo!" He glances at me and presses his tattooed finger over his lip piercing. "Shhhh."

I nod. "Your secret's safe with me."

He winks at me and starts rolling a joint when I realize I don't know much about him other than he crashes here sometimes.

"Where do you live?" I ask him casually.

"Ah, currently? I've been staying at the St. Mark's Hotel downtown. I'm doing tattoos over there so it's fine for now." He pauses and takes a good look at me. "How old are you, anyway?" he asks.

"Eleven."

"Holy fuck! You're eleven?! You've gotta be kidding me."

I blush and giggle. "What? Why?!"

After shaking his head in disbelief, Mikey says, "You look at least sixteen or seventeen."

I'm shocked. I've never been acknowledged by a grown man in this way. I guess all my baggy clothes couldn't mask what was happening underneath.

"How old are you?" I ask him.

He gets serious for a moment. "Man, I'm fucking twenty-six. Shit really creeps up on you. One day you're a kid and the next day . . ."

He sounds a lot like my dad dropping me off that first day of school and telling me it's all downhill from here. I don't understand why these men are lamenting about getting older. It's not like they're given expiration dates, the same way women are.

I listen to Mikey as he lights up the joint, takes a puff, and passes it to me, but not before hesitating. "Should you even be smoking this? Can I get in trouble for this?"

I nudge him and grab the joint out of his hands, taking a hit, inhaling like a pro. I chase it with a swig of Jack Daniel's. "I'm an old soul, I guess."

He looks in my eyes. "Yeah, I guess you are."

It's getting late and most of the guests have gone home or are too fucked up to move. I get up to shut off the light. I can feel his eyes moving across my body, following my every move. The room is dark except for the glow from the TV screen illuminating our faces. He throws a blanket over our legs and I feel his hand creeping closer to my leg. We both get quiet and pretend to watch the infomercial playing on the TV, but the tension is thick and an unmistakable tingling sensation runs through my body.

He suddenly turns to me and says, "I know it might be wrong but I don't give a fuck. I've wanted to kiss you all night."

My heart rate accelerates. I've never done this before, not like this. This isn't like kissing Ella. This feels grown up.

"Well, then do it," I dare him.

He pauses for a moment before his lips are on mine and I'm tasting his tongue in my mouth. He tastes of smoke and spearmint.

I allow myself to fall backward, pulling him down on top of me, and we continue making out. I'm a virgin. I'm not ready to have sex. Plus, I didn't shave down there. He gets up to use the bathroom, and I take the opportunity to slide into Ella's bedroom, where I hide on the top bunk. I'm only eleven but I know what blue balls are. I lie in bed motionless, my whole body covered by the comforter. I hear the toilet flush. I anticipate he's going to come out and see me gone. After a few minutes I see his silhouette appear in the doorway. I hold my breath so as not to make a sound. He stands there for a moment staring into the pitch-black room before going to sleep on the couch. When I wake up the next day, I'm both relieved and a little disappointed that he's gone.

After this exhilarating encounter, I start shedding the baggy clothes and embrace my figure. I'm hooked to the power I can have over someone by simply just existing.

I have a B-cup size, but the hot-pink padded bra I stole from Victoria's Secret makes them look like double D's. I have a small waist, which I inherited from my mother, and my hips keep getting wider, just like hers. I also have the biggest butt, which boys at school always comment on. One boy in the eighth grade slaps it whenever he sees me in the hallway. Apparently this is a compliment because it makes a lot of girls in my grade jealous, and I admit, I love the attention.

Out of the blue, Silvia announces that she received a job opportunity in California and wants to move the whole family to Catalina Island. This sudden declaration crushes me like a ton of bricks as I gulp down the knot forming in my throat.

"Why don't you just come with us?!" she suggests. "You're practically family!"

I'm not sure if she's drunk or actually being serious but I don't care, I'm ecstatic. I rush home and look up this mythical place called Catalina Island and instantly fall in love with what I see. Sun, sand, skin, freedom! I even find a school on the beach and from the photos online, it looks like paradise.

I immediately inform my dad about my plans and to my surprise, he says I can go. He even talks to Ella's mom on the phone to discuss the logistics. I spend the next few days fantasizing about my future life in California with my sisters, but my excitement is cut short when my mom calls. I forgot about her.

I tell my mom my plans to move and she wastes no time crushing my dreams with a firm "assolutamente NO."

I feel the rage boiling beneath the surface as I plead with her. "How can you have a say in my life when you don't even live here?!"

Tears flood the receiver as I desperately try reasoning with her. I tell her about the weather, the crime rate, and the family of sisters I would have, but she isn't persuaded. Later, when confronted, my dad throws his arms up, saying there's nothing he can do.

"Why can't you ever be a man and stand up to her?!" I shout at him. "You both ruined my fucking life!!!"

I slam the bathroom door, turn the hair dryer on to drown out the noise, and check out all over again.

The next day I go to Ella's house and help them pack up their things. They're mostly preoccupied as they sift through years' worth of clothes from Rainbow and Delia's. They make a pile on the floor of stuff for me to take home. It's mostly junk, but since my dad never takes me shopping, I'm grateful. They're too busy to notice the steady stream of tears spilling down my face. They don't realize how much they mean to me. It's different for them since they have each other, but I don't have anyone.

On the day of the move, I cling to them tightly, not wanting to let go.

"Don't worry, sweetheart, you can come visit us whenever you want!" Silvia reassures me for the tenth time. I nod, but deep down, I know I'll probably never see them again.

In the weeks following their move to Catalina, Ella reaches out to me a few times, but I don't hear from Silvia at all. I guess my so-called family moved on pretty quickly without me. Ella probably has a ton of girls vying to be her new best friend. She doesn't need me, I think to myself. It's time for me to move on.

In Ella's absence, I befriend her other best friend, Trisha. Trisha is beautiful but you can't really tell at first. Her beauty sneaks up on you until one day, you think she's the most beautiful girl to ever live.

Trisha doesn't come to school that often even though she lives across the street. I used to be jealous of her because on the rare occasion when she did show up, Ella would spend the whole day with her and ignore me. I'd watch them laughing, as if they had an inside joke that only they were in on. I didn't get it. Trisha wears the same stained track pants to school every day and smells of stale milk and cigarette smoke. Not to mention all the rumors I've heard of blow jobs with older guys in the park.

One day during our knitting elective after school, she sits next to me and asks to borrow one of my knitting needles. After a little small talk, I blurt out: "I need to know about the blow jobs, is it true?"

She stops knitting and looks up at me. "Oh my God! Are people really still talking about that?!" She continues in her matter-of-fact tone, "It was the summer after fifth grade, and it was only *one* time with *one* guy, and he was my boyfriend that day."

"That day?!" I ask through my laughter.

"Well, I really wanted to try it but I didn't want to get called a slut, so I made him my boyfriend and dumped him right after." Her tone grows more somber. "And then he started spreading rumors about me."

I nod. Makes sense. "How old was he?" I ask.

"Seventeen."

She shrugs. I shrug.

After school, we go to the park and she shows me exactly where the infamous blow job happened, right in the bushes, near the entrance of the playground. "It was nighttime so there weren't any kids around," she reassures me.

After walking her home, we hang out on her stoop for a while until I make the mistake of asking to use her bathroom. She hesitates a moment before responding, "Okay, but it's really messy, don't judge me."

I quickly assure her that it's okay. "My dad's a hoarder," I say with a knowing smirk.

As we walk up the stairs in her building, I immediately recognize the pungent odor growing stronger with each step. It's a distinct smell, unmistakably hers. She unlocks the door and slowly cracks it open. As she peeks inside, a menacing thick cloud of smoke pours out into the hallway. The lights are off and the blinds are drawn but the light from the television casts a flickering glow over the chaos. Once inside, I realize that they live in a small studio apartment with two beds and a couch crammed tightly together in one room. My eyes dart around the endless piles of magazines, dirty clothes, and pill bottles scattered all over the floor. Cups and cans overflowing with cigarette butts litter every surface. The place looks like it hasn't been cleaned once in the past decade.

I'm startled when my eyes land on an old lady lying motionless on a bed, her limp body hooked up to a ventilator. Before I can process the scene, I hear a raspy voice emerge from the shadows. I turn my head to see Trisha's mom's frizzy hair poking up from behind the TV.

"Who the fuck is this? I told you not to bring any of your garbage friends here!"

Something snaps and I see a new side of Trish.

"Oh, shut the fuck up, you drunken old cunt! She needs to use the fucking bathroom!!!"

Suddenly, objects start flying through the air, and I watch in horror as a large mug strikes Ronny, Trish's mom, square in the forehead. Blood starts gushing down her face like water, temporarily blinding her as it streams into her eyes. Without hesitation, I feel Trish grab my arm, and we sprint out of there as fast as we can.

In the midst of the chaos, I'm filled with an overwhelming sense of guilt for having judged Trish. I feel a strong urge to take care of her, but I don't want her to know I feel bad for her. I hate when people pity me, and I don't want her to feel the same way.

Trish and I run all the way back to my place. The phone rings. It's Javier, the doorman. "Hoolia, the police is here."

"Fuck! Your mom must have called the cops on us!"

"What do we do?" she whispers. I have an idea.

"Send them up, please," I tell Javier. I hang up the receiver and lead her out into the hallway. "Trust me," I say.

She nods.

We wait for the cops to call the elevator and then we take the stairs down to the garage and exit the building through the back entrance.

Once we turn the corner, we run like the ground is lava. I lead us toward the best place there is to hide: the Ramble. We climb up on a bench and jump over a stone wall. We're safe. We link arms and walk across the park under the soft glow of scattered lampposts. The park is eerie when it's this empty, at this time of night, but I'm not even scared because nothing is as terrifying as Trisha's mom.

"I hope my dad can stay sober long enough so I can move in with him already."

I nod and ask, "Is she always like that?"

"She falls asleep with a cup in her hand and wakes up with a cup in her hand."

"Well, you can always stay with me," I say.

We hear rustling in the bushes. We freeze. She looks me in the eye and whispers, "If we make it out of here alive," and starts running through the trees laughing. I chase her all the way to the west side, where we decide it's time for a disguise.

We walk aimlessly until we find a twenty-four-hour CVS. With only two clerks working in the entire store, they don't even notice us strolling around covered in dirt. We head straight for the hair section and each shove a box of permanent red hair dye down our pants.

We make our way to the 79th Street Marina, where my dad keeps his crappy sailboat. But as we approach the big metal gate, we realize it's locked and there's no one around to open it. I have no choice but to scale the fence. I jam my Converse sneakers in the little holes, tightly gripping the wire, hoping my hands don't start sweating on me.

I finally manage to get over the fence and unlock the gate. It's been a while since I've been here and I can't remember which dock my dad's boat is on. We tiptoe up and down the docks, careful not to disturb the residents, until we finally find his boat tucked away behind the larger, more expensive ones. I can tell by Trisha's face she's a bit disappointed. I guess she was hoping we'd sail off to sea in luxury.

We climb aboard, careful not to get any splinters, when we realize all the doors are bolted shut.

"It's okay, we can use the hose!" I start mixing the slimy, smelly concoction and slather it onto her long ashy-blond locks, which almost immediately turn a dark auburn color. "Now they won't recognize us."

After what feels like thirty minutes, I start rinsing the dye out of her hair with the hose. The water is icy cold and the dock is illuminated only by the reflection of the New Jersey skyline. "I can't fucking see anything!" I complain.

Once we rinse off our hair, I realize our clothes, fingers, feet, and faces are stained a deep shade of red, and the dock now looks like the scene of a grisly murder.

"We cannot go to school like this!" Trisha exclaims.

I try scrubbing our clothes on the dock with the hose, but it's not working so I suggest we go get soap and lotion. I can tell she doesn't like this idea.

"Don't worry," I say reassuringly, "we're in disguise now."

It's past midnight and the streets are dark and deserted. We link arms as we walk back up the hill toward the CVS. Suddenly, Trish squeezes my arm and nods toward a lone police car parked at the intersection. I feel a chill run down my spine when I see the two cops inside.

"It's fine, they're just parked," I try to reassure her. "Stop looking!"

We pick up the pace and start crossing the street when suddenly the red and blue lights start flashing, illuminating the entire block. Shit. We both keep our eyes ahead as we scurry away, praying they won't stop us. But then we hear the dreaded "whoop-whoop." Trish grabs my hand and squeezes my fingers so tightly that I can feel her pulse pounding through her palms.

"Young ladies, stop walking."

"Fuck," Trish says.

"Let me do the talking," I whisper.

They pull up in front of us and roll down the window.

"Mr. Officer, we can explain. Her mom—"

He cuts me off. "I don't wanna hear it. Get in the fucking car!"

"But it's not safe for her to go—"

Before I can finish my sentence, they both exit their vehicle and forcibly grab us by the back of the head, shoving us into the car by our hair. I bang my forehead against the door on my way in.

"Fucking pigs!" I scream as Trish cries in the back seat. I try to console her, realizing this is all my fault. I start crying too. "I'm sorry. I'm so sorry, Trish. I'm so sorry."

Trisha gets dropped off first. When we pull up, her mom is already outside waiting for her in a stained oversize men's T-shirt and flip-flops. She has a big Band-Aid on her forehead and a cigarette and cup in one hand, house phone in the other.

As the officer opens the car door, Trisha and I squeeze each other in the backseat, holding on for dear life.

"Don't worry, I'm gonna come save you!" I yell as the officers pry us apart and drag her back into her mother's custody. Her mom grabs her by the arm and rushes her inside, turning around once more to yell at me, "Stay away from my daughter!!"

A few minutes later, we pull up to my house. My dad is shocked to see me being escorted by police officers, mostly because he didn't know I was missing.

"What the hell did you do to your hair?" he asks.

I just roll my eyes and lock myself in the bathroom.

Trisha and I become inseparable. She even introduces me to her dad, Johnny. He goes to the same A.A. meeting at the church on 79th Street every single night. And every single night, we stroll into the meeting, starving, and wait for him to finish his commitment. I love going to the meetings. Forget the opera with Grandma or meditation classes, this is by far the best people-watching. My first time there, a woman stands up in front of the whole auditorium and describes in detail the devastating consequences of her alcoholism. She claims she drank a gallon of Georgi vodka a day, without a chaser. One morning she woke up on her bathroom floor, after a blackout, in a pool of blood. There was so much blood everywhere that she didn't even know where it was coming from.

After a couple of months of meetings, nothing shocks me anymore. But I do learn that it's never too late to change your life. The woman who woke up on the bathroom floor was almost fifty before she got sober. This gives me hope for some reason.

After the meetings, Johnny takes us to the 3 Star Diner with his A.A. buddies and orders us grilled cheese sandwiches. Trish whines about wanting a burger. He pauses, thinks about what he's going to say, and firmly yet kindly tells her, "When you're making the money, you can order whatever you want, how about that?"

Johnny is a true New Yorker, an Italian American from the Bronx. He grew up on the streets. His dad used to beat him and his mom was bipolar. I admire Johnny for turning his life around. And Trisha just adores him. She wants to be a daddy's girl so bad.

When I'm not with Trish, I go to the stores in the neighborhood to steal cute clothes for her. A tank top with a bedazzled Playboy bunny, a Von Dutch hat, bell-bottom jeans with suede ties on the front.

I teach her how to steal so she can be self-sufficient and take better care of herself. The goal is to blend in with the private school girls. If people assume we're rich, they won't suspect us of stealing. I understand the power of appearance, and I see how rich people are regarded.

We don't like the private school girls; we want to *be* them. They just seem so *clean*. Their hair is thick and shiny and sits perfectly in a messy bun. They would never cut their own hair like I have to. They get facials with their moms on Sundays. They get manicures weekly. They stay home from school when they have a pimple. Life just seems easy for them.

After school we wait outside for them and taunt them. They laugh at us and call us "white trash" in their $1,500 Moncler puffers while we freeze our asses off in our Baby Phat jackets, two sizes too small.

"Let's go shopping!" I tell her excitedly as I grab her hand and drag her to 86th and Lexington, my commercial utopia. She's the only person who doesn't mind my sweaty hands. Whenever they're clammy, she insists on squeezing them. I think it's weird, but it shows just how much she loves me.

She lets go of my hand as we enter my favorite of all the stores, Orva, a mid-tier department store with a little bit of everything. It's nothing special, but it's the nicest store I've ever been to. We browse the racks, sifting through Triple Five Soul hoodies and Ed Hardy T-shirts, one eye on the employees and the other on the cameras. I used to be invisible, in and out, grabbing only one small thing at a time. But now I do what the rich girls do. I create chaos. I bring a mountain of clothes to the fitting room even though I know their limit is five items per person. They hand me a number tag, and I put the rest of my items on a nearby rack. I try on a pair of jeans and come out to ask for Trisha's opinion.

"Hmm, I'm not sure . . . maybe you need another size," she says. The sales associate rushes to get me the same item in two different sizes, and I grab my other items off the rack and throw the hangers in another room. In the end, I have way more than five items in my fitting room, and they've lost count. We rip out the plastic alarm sensors, leaving small little holes in the fabric, and stroll out of the store waving to the employees.

Just act normal.

I'm addicted to the rush, the indescribable sensation that pours itself over my entire body. My heart beats faster, my step feels lighter, my stomach flutters. I leave the store with a pair of True Religions under my Juicy Couture sweatpants and two Ed Hardy T's. Score! I love my new pants but nothing beats the thrill of walking past the metal detectors and getting away with it.

Trish starts coming to school more, just to hang out with me. We spend every moment we can together. Even her mom warms up to me. When we're not at school, we ride the train for hours, sometimes falling asleep and ending up all the way at the last stop. Last time this happened, Trish got her purse stolen right off her arm, but we went to LeSportsac the next day to steal her a new one.

We take the train downtown, often riding in between cars for a brief rush. We hang out at Union Square and the Cube at Astor Place. We go to Saint Mark's and flirt with the old tattoo artist guy who gives us each a free tattoo. I get a cartoon cat dangling from a rose, in the same spot where my mom has a tattoo, and Trisha gets a tramp stamp. We get our nipples pierced. We are twelve years old but my dad says we are worse than the girls in the movie *Thirteen*. He laughs and thinks it's funny.

My dad comes into my room one day with a very serious look on his face. "Look, girls, I gotta tell you this for your own good . . . Do not smoke that PCP angel dust. It makes hair grow on your brain. Weed, heroin, cocaine . . . all that shit is fine. But stay away from that angel dust!"

Once he's gone, Trisha and I burst out laughing.

We finally get caught shoplifting during a "shopping trip" at Bloomingdale's.

A husky security guard leads us to a small windowless room and orders us to take off our shoes. I hesitate, knowing I've stuffed my sneakers with tons of gold-plated jewelry. The guard asks how old we are and when we tell her, she informs us she's going to have to call our parents as well as the police. After an hour of trying to talk our way out of it, they take our photo and ban us permanently from the store.

Inside the cop car, neither of us seems fazed by the outcome.

"Can you turn your siren on?" I ask excitedly.

"No," the officer quips.

"Fine, how about the radio?"

One winter day, I get home from school and see the light blinking on the answering machine. I press play and hear Trisha's voice, shaky and hysterical, screaming into the receiver. I can barely make out what she's saying through the tears.

"Julia, she's taking me! She's taking me to Oklahoma! I don't wanna go!"

I hear her mom screaming incoherently in the background.

"Mom, shut the fuck up! I don't wanna say goodbye!"

I'm completely caught off guard. I frantically pick up the receiver and try to call her back, but there's no answer. It's too late, they're already gone. Just like that, it's over. Trisha hadn't come to school that day, but I didn't think much of it.

I hate myself for not saving her.

The following days, I feel like a zombie. I can't eat or sleep. I go to school and come straight home to wait by the phone. I play her distressing message over and over again. I ask Jeeves how long it takes to drive to Oklahoma. I listen to Coldplay in bed with the hair dryer on to muffle my sobs.

"Why does everyone always leave me?" I yell into the pillow. "It's not fair!!!"

The call finally comes two weeks later. I'm thrilled when the phone rings and I see an Oklahoma area code. I lift up the receiver and blurt out, "What took you so long?!"

"We just got a phone finally!" Trish says.

"Tell me everything! I've been so worried about you."

"It's actually not so bad. It's hot here all the time and our trailer is pretty big."

"Have you made any friends?" I ask her.

"Yeah, I hung out with the neighbors, and don't tell anyone but I smoked crystal meth!"

"Whoa, that sounds so cool!" I say with just a touch of jealousy in my voice.

"It was, but I don't think I'm gonna do it again."

I work up the courage to ask her the dreaded question: "Are you ever coming back?"

"My mom lost that apartment. She says she needs some time to get on her feet but who the fuck knows."

Trisha seems rather unbothered by my predicament. I decide then and there that I need to move on too. If she can make other friends, so can I.

And this is where Rose comes in. Rose is in some of my classes and she's so different from Trisha. She's different from everybody. I'm convinced she's an angel. She's soft-spoken. She's shy. She's pure. And she's rich. Penthouse on Fifth Avenue rich. I love sneaking into her house after her mom has gone to bed. We sit cross-legged, facing each other on her floor, and pass each other love poems. I write her name on my sneakers; she writes mine on hers. Sometimes we massage each other with oils. Sometimes we dribble hot wax over each other's bodies. Sometimes we take baths together, where I can't help but stare at her enormous double-D breasts, covered in thick purple stretch marks.

The boys in our school don't really like her like that, but I think she's the most beautiful girl in the world. She has the most succulent lips, and when I make her laugh, tears stream down her delightfully freckled cheeks until she pees her pants. Her skin is as fair and soft as snow. Especially her arms; they're my favorite. She always smells of drugstore-bought vanilla body mist, which I find intoxicating. I even know exactly how many minutes it takes to walk to her house from mine. Seven.

"You're my soulmate," I tell her.

"No, you're MY soulmate," she says.

Our friendship is so intense that all her friends refer to us as lesbians. Rose is friends with the popular girls, who all claim that Rose is *their* best friend. And that might be true, but she reassures me that I'm hers.

The popular girls welcome me in their clique when they discover I always have a stale pack of cigarettes from Italy in my backpack. I don't even really smoke them, I just like feeling like a grown-up.

I know Dominique from elementary school. She lives in Brooklyn. We would often have sleepovers at each other's houses and she even told me I was her best friend once. However, she wasn't mine. We fought a lot because she was jealous of my friendship with Danny. The fights mostly consisted of her bullying me and getting everyone else to ostracize me. One day I fought back and she started crying, and she never messed with me again.

Abeline was voted the prettiest girl in school. She's Dominican and lives in the Bronx. She loves to sing and dance and all the guys like her, even Tommy, my crush.

Tara is Jewish and lives on the Upper East Side. She gets her hair chemically straightened and never wears the same outfit twice. She lives with her mom, an accomplished attorney who had her very late in life, and they have a fluffy little white dog that barks a lot.

We call ourselves the Stoned Monroes and we almost immediately start bringing out the worst in each other. We bully the girls in the younger grades if they're prettier than us. We set mice loose in the school. We terrorize teachers to the point of tears. We graffiti "Stoned Monroes" all over the halls. We unscrew the doors off their hinges. We get suspended for fighting.

My grades are suffering and my home life is a nightmare. My mom is now pregnant and I overhear my parents discussing the baby's due date, with my mom reassuring my dad that he's the father. I'm just surprised that they still have sex, as they seem to despise each other.

My mom wants to give birth in New York and take maternity leave, which means she'll be around all the time. I'm not used to having her so close, and it's safe to say that it's just not working out. She invades my space, she encroaches on my freedom, she steps on my independence, she trespasses in my room, and she throws out anything she doesn't like. We have explosive fights where I scream, "I hate you!!" to which she coldly replies "I hate you more." There's no attempt to hide our mutual animosity. I even sleep with my bags packed, ready to leave if things get too violent.

The cops have already come a few times. One time when she was six months pregnant, she whipped me with computer wires in front of two officers who did nothing. I heard my dad in the background, saying, "You can't do that in America, sweetheart." As if she doesn't know that. As if they both don't beat us all the time. As if he ever calls her sweetheart.

I flee. Seeking refuge, I sneak into Rose's welcoming home whenever possible. When that's not an option, I make do with whatever shelter I can find, from unlocked cars to twenty-four-hour delis, rooftops, and park benches. Anywhere is better than being at home.

When my mom goes into labor, I rush to the hospital to be by her side. As she's breathing through contractions, a nurse offers the option of an epidural. But before my mom can answer, my dad chimes in with his own opinion: "No, she wants to have a natural birth." The nurse shoots a look of pure disdain in my dad's direction. "I wasn't asking you, sir. When you're in labor, I'll ask you." Her telling him to politely fuck off is so gratifying. My mom tells him to shut the fuck up too.

Finally, my baby brother is born, and I hold him in my arms, overwhelmed with love. But the moment is shattered when my dad slaps me in the face for not wearing gloves.

On my way home, instead of feeling overjoyed, I feel bitter. He ruined that moment for me. I get my revenge by slithering like a snake into his room at night and stealing cash out of his wallet. The more damage he does, the more money I take.

At school the next day, a girl in my class tells me very loudly that her aunt was the nurse at the hospital who delivered my little brother and she said my dad was a huge asshole. I'm embarrassed.

The only class I excel in is creative writing. Or at least I used to excel in it before I fell in with the wrong crowd. One afternoon, my teacher, Ms. Williams, pulls me aside after class and expresses her concern. "You used to be one of my more promising students," she says. "But now I'm not so sure, and I'm afraid . . ."

I know she's right and I don't try to argue with her. She already affectionately refers to me as the "queen of excuses."

"I hate to see wasted talent," she warns me, her lips downturned, her eyes flooding me with sadness. "Have you given any thought as to what you want to be when you grow up? Will you go to college? Because I'm warning you that on the path you're headed, no reputable high schools or universities will accept you."

I nod. "I know. I'm just trying to get through the day. I can't think that far ahead right now."

She pauses for a moment. "Write about it," she says before waving me off.

I resent the fact that I care what Ms. Williams thinks about me. Normally, I couldn't care less what anyone thinks. Yet the thought of letting her down fills me with anxiety. I wonder if this is how normal people feel about disappointing their parents.

After school, I retreat to the solitude of my bathroom and let the ink flow onto the page, revealing the pain and emotions I had buried deep inside. Each stroke of my pen feels like a release, like a weight being lifted off my shoulders. I write about the suffocating feeling of insignificance and the constant battle to find my place in this world. I write about how lonely I am and how everyone always leaves me, leading me to put on a facade of toughness and aggression. I write about the urge to compare myself to others and the resulting feelings of inadequacy. I fantasize about what life could have been like had I been born into a normal, loving family and all the ways in which I would be different.

The next day, I nervously hand my paper to Ms. Williams at the beginning of class. Later in the day, she approaches me in private and asks for my permission to read it for the class as an anonymous submission. "No one will know you wrote it," she reassures me. "I was moved by your writing, Julia."

She insists that my work could serve as inspiration for my classmates. All the while, I wonder whether she's going to ask me if I'm okay. I'm nervous to have something so personal be shared with what feels like the world. But I concede and give her my consent.

The next day, Ms. Williams reads my writing aloud to the class. My hands start to sweat as I hear her reciting my pain. My trauma feels dreadfully familiar, even when it's in her voice. Some of my classmates snicker and purposely make noises, and every time they do, I feel stupid and insignificant. "Corny," someone remarks, and even though they don't know who wrote it, I do. And that's enough for me to feel humiliated. Ms. Williams doesn't ask me if I'm okay.

From that moment on, I vow to keep everything inside and never share my vulnerability with anyone ever again.

• • •

One day, Tara has a free crib and invites a few of us over. "Just the girls," she says. But when we arrive, a bunch of boys from all the other classes show up with us. Tara tries to act cool about it, but I can sense she's anxious. Her mom can be quite strict. We listen to Fabolous and Eminem and smoke Newports on her balcony as we pass around cans of Sparks and Smirnoff Ice. One of the boys, James, rolls a joint and passes it around. "Smoke some weed, chill out," he tells Tara, who has a secret crush on James, knowing that Dominique has a thing for him too.

Tara hesitates. We begin chanting, "Smoke it, smoke it, smoke it." She takes a pull and we all cheer.

Dominique goes to sit on James's lap. Tara's gaze is fixed on them. She's frozen. Rose and I notice she's acting funny and guide her into her mom's room, where she begins trembling and whimpering, "I hate myself! Can you please ask everyone to leave? I need everyone to get out of my house now!"

I run back out to the balcony and tell everyone to leave. Between the sighs and groans, Dominique yells, "Why is Tara such a wack bitch?!" loud enough for Tara to hear it. On their way out, they steal whatever they can, Dominique trailing behind them, laughing.

Rose and I comfort Tara as she cries. "I'm so ugly! Nobody likes me. I try so hard to be perfect but I'm not! I'm short and fat and ugly!"

"Who cares what boys think," I tell her with a shrug. "Boys are fucking dumb, in case you haven't noticed."

Wrong thing to say. Tara's cries turn into full-blown wails.

"Tara, you are so beautiful!" Rose says. "Are you kidding me? Look at you! You're hot! So many guys wanna hook up with you!"

"No, they don't!!!!! They wanna hook up with you guys 'cause you both have big boobs and blue eyes!!" Tara springs up and locks herself in her mom's bathroom.

Rose and I look at each other, shaking our heads. "I need a cig," she says.

We go to the balcony and admire the view from the twenty-first floor.

"We are practically in the clouds," Rose says.

"I can see my building from here!" I excitedly say. "Oh wait, maybe that's not my—"

Before I can finish my sentence, Tara rushes toward us with a maniacal grin and swings the doors shut, locking us on the balcony.

"Ummm," Rose says with a confused look on her face. "Did she just lock us on the balcony and run away?"

I start tugging on the door and fidgeting with the handle. "It's definitely locked," I tell her. When Tara's face appears at the adjacent window, I start yelling, "What the fuck, Tara! I'm gonna kick the glass in if you don't open this door!!" She struggles to get the window all the way open but once she does, she swings her leg over it, straddling the frame, her perfectly pedicured foot dangling over twenty stories high. Rose starts crying and frantically pleading with her, "What the fuck are you doing, Tara?! Please, Tara, please, get back inside!"

Tara giggles. "Don't cry, Rosie! I love you! It's better this way. Nobody wants me. Nobody loves me . . ." She swings her body over and scales the side of the building until she's on the ledge of the balcony facing us. "It would just be better if I died." Rose is sobbing now and I have to force myself to cry. It's like I'm here but I'm not. I see her and I hear her but I'm not here.

The sun starts going down, and after what feels like forever, we finally convince her to retreat. Through the glass, she makes us promise we won't be mad at her for what she did to us. "We promise we won't tell a soul and won't hold it against you," we tell her in unison. Once she's convinced, she releases us. Her entire demeanor changes and she's back to normal.

"Are you guys hungry? Do you want some pizza rolls?" she asks us with a warm, inviting smile, as if she didn't just almost force us to watch her kill herself.

"I have to go home," Rose says with a frown. "My mom is gonna be pissed if I come home late again."

"Me too," I say, avoiding eye contact.

"I feel like you guys are mad at me," Tara whines.

"Oh my God, never," I say. "We are totally suicidal too. Don't even worry." I reassure her with a hug and we get the hell out of there.

Tara doesn't come to school the next few days. We call her house over and over and get the machine.

"What if she actually did it?" I ask Rose.

"Should we tell her mom?"

"Do we snitch?"

"No, you're right. We can't."

Tara finally shows up a week later in a brand-new Abercrombie outfit and a fresh tan.

"Where the hell have you been? We were so scared!" Rose tells her.

"Aww you missed me! That's so cute! I was with my dad for a few days and he took me shopping!" she squeals with excitement as I roll my eyes.

Abeline isn't allowed to hang out after school, she always has to go straight home.

Although I pretend to be sad about it, I'm thrilled. I count the minutes every day until the bell rings and school is out so I can get Tommy alone, without Abeline all over him.

They don't even have anything in common. They never have deep conversations.

Before they started dating, he and I spent hours chatting online. Eventually he began to confide in me about his life. He told me how hard his mom works as a single mom and how he never sees her. His dad doesn't pay child support. His brother is hooked on drugs. I feel special carrying his secrets. We still message, though not as much now that he's with Abeline. He even calls me on my house phone, where he always ends our conversations with "I just wish your brain could be in Abeline's body." I'm not sure if this is a compliment or a complaint, but I'll take it.

It's ten p.m. on a cool Saturday night. I'm chatting with Tommy on AIM. I turn to look at my friend Alice, peering over my shoulder at the computer screen. She reads aloud the words on the screen: "My mom is out of town, you guys should come over!" Her eyes widen and a sinister smile spreads across her face. Alice and I just got close recently but I've known her forever. She stole my ring in elementary school and I hated her for it.

She recently did a complete rebrand and lost a bunch of weight using diet pills that give her the jitters. She also started tanning and wearing makeup and cute clothes, so we let her in the crew. I suspect this sudden transformation is due to her own secret crush on Tommy. I tease her about it. "Ew, he's like a brother to me! Gross!" She brushes me off but I don't buy it.

When Rose is grounded, I spend my time with Alice because she is just as devious as I am. Late at night we pass time in the 24/7 Mc-Donald's, blowing spitballs at people until they freak out. After school we stroll into buildings at random, holding clipboards, and knock on people's doors pretending to be fund-raising for our schools. Cash only. Rose would never do this with me. Just like how Rose would never go to Tommy's house and betray Abeline. But Alice would.

"Let's go bitch!" she yells. I jump in the tub and start shaving my legs. She straightens her thick brown curly hair. We spray our entire bodies in body mist and sprint out of her building.

We hop the turnstile and jump on the train, taking it all the way to Inwood. It's past midnight when we finally get there. We wander around looking for his building.

We start yelling "Tommy" aimlessly, when a man comes to the window with a shotgun yelling "Shut the fuck up or I'll bust your asses wide open!" We look up and see him waving the long metal nose at us. We shriek and run for our lives.

After what feels like forever we find his building.

"How do I look?" I ask her.

"Like shit. How do I look?" she asks.

"Like shit," I say, laughing.

Once inside, Tommy leads us through the dark apartment, all the way to his room, where his brother is asleep in another bed.

"What took you guys so long?" Tommy says. "I was about to pass out."

"Umm you should be flattered, 'cause we almost died getting here!" Alice says.

He laughs and I start wondering if I should have come by myself. I feel myself crawling inward, feeling self-conscious. What am I even doing here? This feels wrong.

We drink a few beers and when it's time to go to sleep, he hands us each a pair of boxers and we all squeeze in his tiny twin bed, with him in the middle. I lie there for what feels like an eternity, hands sweating, heart pounding, thoughts racing through my head. He suddenly turns on his side to face me. I wait a few seconds and follow his lead. My body is parallel to his now. I scoot my butt into his lap. A few seconds elapse. I feel something hard crawling up my backside. OH MY GOD! I think to myself. *He has a boner!!!!!* My hormones are on fire as I feel my vagina tingling and I want to slide down on it so bad, but I'm a virgin and Alice is sleeping in the bed with us and his brother is in the same room.

I can't help myself, I have to explore it.

I quietly slide under the blanket until I'm face-to-face with IT. Wow, it's beautiful. I put my hands around it and grip it tightly with my sweaty palms. I move my hands up and down, his body twitching at my every move. I stick my tongue out and taste the tip, as if sampling an ice cream cone. It doesn't taste bad! I put my mouth over it and before I can even start sucking, he ejaculates all over my hair. I shoot up from under the covers and run to the bathroom. I begin scrubbing the gelatinous goop out of my hair, half thrilled, half horrified.

When I get out of the shower, the sun is coming up. I tiptoe back to his bed to find him already asleep and spooning Alice. When we wake up in the afternoon, I pretend as though nothing happened and we never speak of it again.

Miraculously, we all graduate middle school. Mostly because the administration doesn't want us there another year.

The morning of the ceremony, we all get ready at Rose's house. We try on her mom's dresses, which are all too big. I decide to wear a dress I stole from Betsey Johnson on Madison Avenue. I burn the tip of my eyeliner with a lighter and smear the thick black paste in my waterline. I slather bright red lip gloss all over my lips and straighten my jet-black hair with an iron. We take photos on my disposable camera.

At the graduation, people cheer as the principal calls my classmates' names one by one. I'm dreading the moment he calls me. I'm afraid no one will clap for me. But to my surprise, when he calls my name over the microphone, the crowd erupts into madness. I receive a standing ovation from all my classmates. I'm overwhelmed with love and sadness all at the same time. I already learned from my elementary school graduation that I'll probably never see most of these kids again.

After the ceremony, I can tell my mom is annoyed. She makes a comment about how trashy I look and leaves immediately. I can't help but feel like she's shocked that people actually like me. I shrug it off. I won't let her attitude ruin my last day with Rose before I go to Italy for the summer.

That night we get wasted in the park with the neighborhood kids and spend the rest of the night wandering the streets together, talking about the future.

"I'm sad we're not going to the same school," Rose whines. Unsurprisingly, neither of us got accepted into any of the good schools that don't require metal detectors.

"At least we'll both be downtown and our schools aren't that far," I say with a hopeful smirk. She wipes the tears out of her eyes as I wrap my arms around her. "And plus, my house will always be seven minutes from yours."

I walk her home and we spend a few minutes lingering in her doorway.

"One more cig?" she asks. We pass our last Newport 100 back and forth before I kiss her on the forehead and walk home crying.

MOTHERLAND

We arrive in Italy and my mom drives us four hours north to the little house in the mountains that's been in our family for years. It's not the most beautiful home, but it's survived two wars and been the site of some of my fondest childhood memories. My mom would often drop Chris and me with our grandpa in June and pick us up in September.

When we were kids, Grandpa would pour buckets of cold water on the boys who came howling at our window at night. We caught spiders and scaled walls to pick wild strawberries from the neighboring garden. We built airplanes out of firewood and drank water straight from the waterfall.

The town is small. Everyone is related in some way and everyone knows each other's business. Growing up, the locals always made me feel like a celebrity just for living in New York. They'd shout, "Americana!" And stop to take photos with me, spending hours explaining to me how we were related, telling me stories about my mom when she was a little girl.

The moment we arrive, we are greeted by our neighbors and family friends, who all remark about how long it's been and how different I look. I can't tell if it's a compliment or not.

I put my stuff down, change into my cutest outfit, and immediately run down the road to my cousin Chiara's house. She's a year older than me and the funniest person I know. We met in town when we were kids and later found out that, surprise surprise, we were related. Chiara smokes like a chimney, drinks like a sailor, and curses like a truck driver. Her dad hits her a lot too. I stepped in between them once and ended up getting chased around the house with a wooden paddle. He does make the best paninis, though. It's tradition that we always go back to their house for lunch, since she spends every night sleeping in our attic bedroom.

The bartenders in town have no problem with serving us alcohol or selling us cigarettes. Chiara doesn't wear as much makeup as me and she certainly doesn't wear thongs or padded bras like I do.

"You're such a show-off," she says to me as I get dolled up for a night out.

"I'm American now," I snap at her confidently. She rolls her eyes, dismissing me. "Italian women are raised to be modest and blend in."

I stop applying my mascara and make eye contact with her through the mirror. Chiara pauses to absorb my statement and examines herself in the mirror. Over time her eyeliner gets bolder and she starts borrowing my array of slinky tank tops and low-rise jeans.

We skip arm in arm down the mountain and to the bar, where we down shots of vodka back-to-back until we are too shitfaced to walk. I flirt with the hot older guys who ride motorcycles and drive muscle cars. The younger boys in town don't excite me the same way. I get such a rush when I succeed at the art of seduction. Most of them don't care when they discover I'm only fourteen.

Chiara is annoyed by my antics. "I don't see why you need all these guys to like you. It makes you seem desperate and insecure."

"You're just jealous 'cause they like me more than you!"

"Of course they like you more, you have your tits in their face all night!"

I push her, she slaps me, I slap her back, and in a moment we are in the dirt, wrestling. I have her pinned to the ground, sitting on her chest and laughing, when I hear someone say, "Girls, come on, you're too pretty for this!"

I look up and lock eyes with the most beautiful man I've ever seen. I immediately get off of her and readjust my clothing, but he's already gone.

The next day, I'm playing UNO with Chiara and a local kid when the mystery man strolls by again. "Girls," he says with a wink and a nod, but he's only looking at me. I feel my heart pounding in my cheeks. I smile and nod back, my eyes following him all the way to his car, a purple Porsche Cayenne. He slides into his vehicle with such ease, each one of his movements falling into the next effortlessly. I've never seen such a graceful man. He starts his car and heads back in our direction, slowing down as he passes us again. He steals another glance and our eyes lock for a sliver of a second, but in that moment it's like lightning.

A few weeks pass without any more sightings of the mystery man. I begin to lose interest until, one night as we're sitting on a bench on our cobblestone street chatting with a neighbor, I see him drive by. He flashes his headlights, parks the car, and gets out. He holds up a bottle of Anima Nera, which means "Black Soul" in Italian. It's a rich velvety liqueur that tastes of anise and licorice. He says hi to the neighbor, ignores Chiara, and introduces himself to me:

"I'm Giovanni, what's your name?" He has a strong Venetian drawl that I find irresistible. I notice how long his eyelashes are, and his cologne, which is a little sweet, almost feminine.

"Julia," I stutter. "And this is my cousin Chiara."

"Hi, Chiara, nice to meet you," he says, before shifting his attention back to me.

"I hate to break up this little lovefest, but I'd like a drink," Chiara says, completely oblivious to how embarrassing she is. He laughs and hands her the bottle of Anima Nera. She takes a big gulp before passing it to me. I take a swig, and then another and another, before I can't stand straight anymore.

Chiara disappears with the neighbor and it's just Giovanni and me. We sit side by side, tucked away under a small bridge, talking about life. He's doing most of the talking while I try my best to hide how drunk I am. He tells me he's twenty-three and he's been coming to this town his entire life. He can't wait to bring his children here one day. He tells me about his job and how he works for his dad's company in Venice. He says his dad is an asshole and his mom is overbearing, nagging him about getting married and settling down. I nod as the world around me warps and my brain spins in circles beneath my eyelids. I nod as he trails off, doing my very best to keep my composure and seem like a *big girl*.

"I can't believe I didn't meet you sooner," he whispers as he leans in and gently places a kiss on my lips. My eyes are still closed when he abruptly stands up. "I'm gonna get another bottle out of my car."

I stumble behind him, trying my best to walk in a straight line. He digs around in his trunk and pulls out a bottle of red wine. He opens it and takes a sip before passing it to me. I pretend to sip and pass it back. We stand there awkward, giggling, under the moon and millions of stars lighting up the sky above us. "You have beautiful eyelashes," I tell him.

He leans in to kiss me again. This time he picks me up and I straddle him in the middle of the cobblestone road. We fall down on the ground laughing and kissing, tongues wagging. He unhooks my bra and lifts up my shirt, kissing my breasts. I pull his pants down and admire his penis for a moment. He's uncircumcised. It's not the biggest, but it's pretty. I suck it for a few seconds before deciding this is the night I'm going to do *IT.* I pull my pants down and squat over him, sitting on it. This isn't sexy at all and it feels painful and unnatural.

It doesn't go in immediately. He thrusts harder and harder until I feel something snap deep in my gut. My eyes widen and I'm jolted back to reality when I see his perfect penis coated in blood. I stand up as drop-lets of blood stream down my legs and land all over his Polo cable-knit sweater with the American flag on it. He seems shocked for a moment and then immediately annoyed that I've ruined his sweater.

"You didn't tell me you were a virgin," he says.

"You didn't ask," I reply.

"I better get you home," he says, walking me back toward my house in silence. We part ways with an awkward peck on the cheek. I run up the stairs and watch him walk home from my bathroom window. He pulls his sweater off and examines it for a moment before tossing it in his trunk. Once he disappears into his house, I quickly hop in the bathtub and start scrubbing at my skin ferociously when I hear a car pull up. I peek out the window and see the neighbor dragging Chiara's limp body out of his back seat, completely covered in vomit.

I sprint to her aid and lug her dead weight up the three flights of stairs. I draw her a bath and rinse the chunks of vomit out of her hair, all the while wishing she weren't incoherent so I could tell her all about how I just lost my virginity. I wish I could call Rose. I wish I could talk to someone.

I tuck Chiara in bed and run down to the cellar, where I hop on my bike and pedal as fast as I can into the sunrise. I feel the morning dew on my skin as I bike through the clouds, soaring up the mountain. I arrive at a small secluded stone church, drop my bike, fall to my knees, and beg for forgiveness. As tears stream down my cheeks, it starts to rain. I think to myself how no amount of water will ever wash off the filth and shame that I feel.

The next day, before I can even process what happened, word spreads throughout town that I'm a whore. My friend's aunt woke up during the night and heard us outside. She cracked open the window and saw us doing it. She even told Giovanni's mom, who now thinks I'm a whore too.

"I overheard the clerk calling you a lowlife whore at the store today," Chiara tells me.

I shrug. I don't care what anyone thinks about me except Giovanni.

Late at night, he slows down his car in front of my house and beams his headlights, signaling me to come down. We sit in his car and talk; sometimes we make out. But mostly, he just criticizes me for having calloused hands, biting my nails, or not brushing my hair properly. He shakes his head and sighs: "You're just a kid." I hate that he doesn't take me seriously.

On nights he doesn't come, I sit at the windowsill scanning each passing car, hoping it's him. I lie in bed at night clutching my stomach, using my pillow to muffle my screams. When I see him around with other women, women closer to his age, I glare at him shamelessly. The next time he sees me, he tells me to stop making his friends uncomfortable or else he won't come see me anymore. The thought of him abandoning me scares me into submission, and I comply. He takes me to a desolate church and we make love under the stars.

During the day, I take walks alone up the mountain and lie in the dirt. I bargain with God, simultaneously cursing Him and pleading with Him. "Please, God, make Giovanni fall in love with me. I promise I'll be good. I'll quit smoking and I won't steal money from my dad or my grandpa anymore."

My mind is consumed by Giovanni, and he knows how much power he has over me. He controls me with crumbs and I beg him to let me go. He says okay, but he always comes back. We get stuck on this loop for the rest of the summer until, one morning as I sit on my rooftop, I see him packing suitcases into his trunk down the street. I skip downstairs barefoot and run to the end of my small driveway and wait for him, trying my best to act as if I just happened to be there. As he passes my house, he slows down like he always does and we lock eyes. He nods, I nod, as if we have an unspoken agreement. He steps on the gas and I watch as his car turns into a little purple speck far off in the distance.

I so badly want to chase his car or yell at him to stop, but I know I can't.

I'm his dirty little secret and he's made it clear that I need to protect that.

· · · ·

Once I'm back in New York, I can't wait to pick Rose up after school. I eagerly stand outside as kids pour out of the building. After waiting for what feels like forever, I begin to worry that maybe I missed her. Kids hug and link arms and hurry away together until I'm the only one left. I stand awkwardly by myself, biting my nails, until I finally see her emerge with a group of girls. As I suspected, she's already made a bunch of new friends. She spots me and quickly says bye to them as I sprint across the street and embrace her, lifting her up and spinning her in circles. "I love you I love you I love you," I whisper over and over, nestled in her neck. I take a big inhale. She's wearing JLo's fragrance.

I begin telling her all about Italy and Giovanni and late-night motorcycle rides and how easy it is to buy cigarettes. But she seems distracted as she taps away on her Nokia.

"How was your first day?!" I ask her excitedly.

"It was okay." She continues tapping. "How about you?"

"Not good. They confiscated my pipe at the metal detectors this morning and—"

She cuts me off. "Should we go meet everyone at John Jay?"

I shrug and nod, remembering when Rose didn't care about hanging out with anyone but me. Once we arrive at the park, I'm unimpressed. I can't pinpoint what it is but I feel different. It's as if I aged ten years in one summer and all the things I found fun before no longer excite me. Everyone else, on the other hand, seems exactly the same. Childish. They crowd around me as I tell them in detail about my wild escapades in Italy. They gasp when I tell them I had sex behind a church. After a while, everyone scatters and I get bored. When I find Rose and tell her that I want to leave, she looks confused and almost offended. I can tell she wants to stay so I don't ask her to come with me and for the first time ever, I go home early.

The next few days, I find myself daydreaming about Italy. I miss my grandpa and my friends. I miss freely walking into a bar and ordering a drink, and I especially miss Giovanni. I'm suffocating in my house with my mom and the baby. I decide I want to move back to Italy and I approach my mom with the proposition. "If you let me move to Italy, I'll be out of your hair."

She loves the idea and a few weeks later, I'm saying bye to my friends again and I'm on a plane with her back to Italy. She enrolls me in the same Catholic school she attended as a kid. She meets with the head priest and he informs us that he found a family willing to host me for a couple of months. I'm annoyed and wish I could just live alone, or an hour away with my grandpa, who has recently been diagnosed with prostate cancer. My mom says, "He needs to get through his chemo and with the way you behave, you'll send him to his grave early." It's dawning on me that the reality of my situation isn't matching up with what I had fantasized. I didn't sign up to live with a bunch of strangers.

On the drive to my new surrogate family's house, my mom makes sure to reiterate that I better behave. It starts raining as we drive in circles through the depressing little town on the periphery of Como. We finally find the house and pull into the driveway. I scrunch my face up in disgust at the big morbid gray house before us. "I can't live here! This place is scary!"

My mom whips around and shushes me. "It's either this or homelessness!"

I roll my eyes and stare off into the smog as my mom rings the doorbell. She catches a glimpse of her reflection in the glass and begins fixing her hair. The door swings open, and a young girl with a short pixie cut greets us with a tight-lipped smile. She leads us inside, and my eyes dart around the room, taking it all in. The room is cold and spotless. Nothing is out of place. A tall, skinny middle-aged woman with short hair emerges from the kitchen in a tracksuit and slippers and welcomes us in.

"You must be Julia!" she proudly says in broken English. "We happy to meet you."

I reply to her in Italian and her smile instantly turns into a frown.

"Oh, what a shame, I was hoping we could all brush up on our English while you were here!"

She laughs. I shoot my mom a look.

"I'm Rossana, this is my daughter, Letizia, and you'll meet Paolo, my husband, later. He gets home late most nights."

She gives us a tour of their home and shows us where I'll be staying: a small guest room with terra-cotta tiles and a twin bed. On the other side of the room, I spot a desk with a computer on it. Score! I'll wait until everyone is asleep and log on to AIM.

During dinner, my mom does most of the talking as I pick at my food. I try asking Letizia questions and receive one-word answers in return. I start wondering if she hates me. As dessert is served, I start dreading the moment my mom will have to leave. I feel like a little kid again.

After dinner she hands me a little Nokia. "There's fifty euros on here. Don't spend it all at once because I'm not giving you more."

I walk her out to her car, where we hug and she reminds me again to behave. I watch her headlights fade into the distance. Once she's gone and the coast is clear, I light up a cigarette, but I only take a few pulls before I'm called back inside.

"I think I'm gonna go unpack," I tell Rossana.

"I'll help you!" she insists.

I feel her judgy eyes scanning my belongings as I pull them out of my suitcase. I fold my clothes and place them in the closet, and she immediately takes them out and refolds them.

"So why did you want to leave New York?!" she says in disbelief.

I don't tell her about the fighting or Giovanni or my grandpa being sick. "I just like Italy more. Best country in the world," I say with a forced smile.

"Brava!" She pats me on the back.

Once she finally leaves, I dart to the computer and press the power button only to be met with a password. Fuck! I take out my phone and call Rose, but every time I hit her voicemail, money gets deducted from my phone card.

I want to text Giovanni, but I promised myself I would never reach out to him again. I even deleted his contact from my phone. However,

I have his number memorized. The mere thought of hearing his voice invigorates my soul and sends a wave of adrenaline throughout my body. I type out my message a few times before finally mustering the courage to push the send button.

"Hi G. It's Julia. I live in Italy now. If you're ever in Como, we should meet up."

I read my message over and over until it starts to sound foolish. I'm embarrassed. I lie in bed staring at the lights from the passing cars dancing on the ceiling. My thoughts echo in my brain, only amplified by the silence enveloping me. Hours of stillness pass as I begin to wonder, What the fuck did I get myself into?

It's still pitch-black outside when Rossana marches into my room. She calls me into the kitchen, where Letizia is already seated, drinking a cappuccino and eating a croissant.

"*Buongiorno,*" I say with the friendliest smile I can come up with.

"*Ciao,*" she says without lifting her gaze.

After breakfast, Rossana rushes us to get dressed and drives us to a desolate train station in the dark. Once she's gone, I light a cigarette on the platform and watch the sunrise in the freezing cold. I'm thinking how much this sucks when Letizia gets in my face.

"My mom knows you smoke. She found a cigarette butt on the lawn. She said you can't do that anymore."

I take a big inhale and blow it at her. I laugh. She doesn't. She coughs, and once the train arrives, she makes sure to sit in the farthest seat from me.

We're already off to a great start. And to make matters worse, Giovanni never answered me. Letizia gets off at the last stop, and I follow her. I walk a couple of yards behind her, keeping a close eye on her, since I have no idea where I'm going. Once we approach the school, I see swarms of kids scattered at different cafés, sipping on espressos and puffing on cigarettes. We pass a big sign that reads "Internet Café." I peer inside at the smoke rising from a dark staircase leading down to a basement. I pause for a moment and look back at Letizia. I say fuck it, and make a sharp turn and run down into the basement.

Once downstairs, I'm greeted by the familiar sound of Amerie's "One Thing" playing on MTV from a small TV on the wall. The music is loud and the kids are even louder. I run straight for the rows of computers and sign on to AOL. I log in and see Trisha is the only person online. I start frantically typing: "Trish!! You're not gonna believe I moved to Italy . . ." I see her typing. My eyes glance at the clock as I eagerly wait for her reply. The typing stops. I follow it up with: "I miss you." I look at the clock. I'm already late for class. Finally, a message appears: "I know! Rose told me! I moved back to NYC from Oklahoma. I live with my dad in Harlem now. Sad ur not here :(" I feel sick to my stomach. Not only is Trisha back in town, but she's hanging out with Rose and I'm not there! I try to feel happy for them, but a part of me feels like life just went on so easily for them without me.

"You talk to Rose? I've been trying to get in touch with her."

"Ya. I'm seeing her tomorrow. She has a boyfriend. Ace. You can check him out. He's on her top 8 on MySpace."

"Wtf is MySpace?"

My heart pounds as I wait for her reply and I'm notified she logged off. When I take my eyes off the screen, I realize the café is empty and everyone has left for class. I ask the clerk for directions and he points me in the direction of my school. I sprint through the piazza, full of adrenaline and anxiety.

When I walk into class late, Letizia raises an eyebrow at me before whispering something to her seatmate. The professor pauses his lesson and asks me my name.

"I'm Julia Fox."

I hear a few snickers across the room. "Oohh, the American girl!"

I nod and he points me to an empty desk. I take out my books and begin doodling and daydreaming, when the professor calls on me to answer a question.

"Can you please repeat the question?" I ask.

"Who can help out Miss Fox?"

Letizia raises her hand and repeats the question in a snarky tone: "What's the difference between an adverb and an adjective?"

I feel my face burning up. The temperature in the room suddenly feels ten degrees warmer. I should know this answer. I *do* know this answer. I know I know it. Creative writing is my best subject. But I'm too nervous. I blank.

"I . . . I'm afraid I don't know."

I hear gasps around the room harmonizing like a shitty choir.

I was never taught proper grammar. I never learned about anatomy or art history. I never learned about Greece and the Roman Empire. I learned that Christopher Columbus discovered America. I'm overwhelmed by the amount of classes I'm forced to take: Latin, German, geometry, calculus, among many more. And each professor assigns hours of homework per night, making it impossible to breeze by, as I always did in the past. To make matters even worse, we have school on Saturdays.

As soon as school is out, I desperately call my mom and beg her to let me come home. "No, Julia. You wanted to do this and now you have to see it through." She hangs up on me. I call my dad next and he says, "Absolutely fucking not. We paid good money for you to go to this school!" He hangs up on me too. I call them on repeat and send them a slew of text messages until all my phone credits run out.

On the train ride home, Letizia informs me that the two girls who sit behind me in class are keeping track of the color of my thongs in their notebook.

As soon as we get home, Rossana ushers us into the dining room to commence the four hours of studying required for the next day. I shake my head. Doesn't this woman have a life? She places a plate of snacks on the table and tells us, "When you're finished, you can both use the computer for half an hour." I'm relieved, as I finally have something to look forward to. After a few interminable hours at the table, we finish our homework. Rossana looks it over and once she's satisfied, she excuses us from the table.

Letizia skips into my bedroom as I trail behind her. She plops down at the desk and calls out for her mom. After a few minutes, her mom comes shuffling in, instructing us to close our eyes. I try peeking at the keyboard as she enters the password but I can't quite make out what she's typing. Once she leaves, Letizia puts on a computer game and begins playing it in silence.

After a few minutes, I work up the courage to ask her, "Can I please use the computer when you're done?"

Her eyes are fixed on the screen. "Yeah, when I'm done."

I sit on my bed, rereading over my texts with my parents. Rossana knocks on the door and announces, "Okay, girls, thirty minutes is up. I'm shutting off the computer. It's time for bed."

I shoot up from the bed and tell her, "But I still haven't had the chance to use it!"

Rossana shoots a look at Letizia, who fires back, "I lost track of time!"

Rossana shakes her head. "If you can't share, I'm taking away computer privileges!"

Letizia sighs and groans as her mom comes up from behind her and smushes the power button with her long bony finger.

"I didn't even save the game!" Letizia slams her hands down on the desk and runs out of the room. Rossana trails behind scolding her. I fucking hate it here.

The next morning, I impatiently ride the train, ignoring Letizia and staring out the window at the ever-changing landscapes zipping past us. Once we arrive at the station, I'm the first to hop off the train, bolting straight for the Internet café.

I type "MySpace" into the search engine and hit enter. I'm redirected to a website where I'm prompted to make an account and log on. I type my friends' names one by one into the search bar. I finally find Rose's profile and scan her Top 8, and sure enough, there he is: Ace.

I click on his profile and I'm stunned to see he has over 10,000 friends. There's no way he has that many friends, I think to myself. I click on his default photo and browse through his photo album. I'm shocked at what I see: piles of cash, a scale next to a mountain of cocaine on a glass table, and so many guns. As I shield the computer screen from any potential onlookers, I wonder what he's doing with Rose. Is it serious between them? What do they talk about? Is she doing drugs with him? I'm flooded with concern.

I open AIM and message Trish again: "I have no more minutes on my phone. Can you please tell Rose to call me?"

Before she can reply, I have to go to class. I spend the whole day waiting for Rose to call or text. I write poems for her in my notebook, like I used to. I write her detailed letters of what I'll say to her when I finally get the chance to speak to her, so I don't forget anything.

After school, Letizia and I go straight home and do our homework in silence and when it's computer time, I run to the room first and wait for Rossana to enter the password. Letizia sits on the edge of the desk, watching me navigate the Internet.

"What is Myspace?" she says. I can tell she's fascinated by the slew of characters appearing on the screen. "Do you know these people?"

I log on to AIM and by a miracle Rose is online.

"Rosie! Please call me. I texted you from my Italian number. I really need to talk to you!"

Moments later, my phone starts vibrating. It's her. I dive for my phone and run into the bathroom.

"Rosie! I miss you so much. I'm so miserable. I made a huge mistake moving here. I hate it. They make us do so much work and we have to go to school on weekends . . . and high school is five years! Not four like in America. Rosie, are you there?"

"Uh-huh," she says.

"Are you mad at me?" I ask her.

She pauses. "No! I could never be mad at you. I'm just so busy—"

"I cut her off. "I saw you have a boyfriend! He's really cute. How did you meet him?"

"Ace?! He's not my boyfriend. We're just hooking up."

"Don't lie to me!"

"I'm not!"

"Do you like him?"

"I guess. I'm just so over people asking me about him, to be honest."

Ouch.

"Okay, well, I just wanted to check in, you feel so far away."

"I *am* far away."

"That's not what I mean."

"You left, Julia. I don't know what to say. I have to live my life too."

The conversation stalls between awkward moments of silence.

"My mom's calling me, can I call you back?" she asks.

"Yeah, of course. I love you. Call me back!"

She hangs up and I know she won't be calling me back. I calmly get undressed, turn on the hot water, curl up into a ball on the shower floor, and cry. After a few minutes, I'm startled by a knock at the door.

"Don't use up all the hot water!" Rossana yells through the door. "It's almost time for bed!"

I swallow some water and yell, "Okay!"

I slide back down on the floor, put my head on my knees. I fucking hate it here.

The following morning, I'm relieved to learn that lectures are suspended due to "Culture Day," where each classroom transforms to represent a different country. I'm strolling the halls alone aimlessly when I walk by "Spain" and notice a giant bowl of sangria unattended on a desk. I bee-line for the bowl and double-fist cups of sangria back-to-back. Before I know it, I'm crouched over the toilet, puking my brains out. I hear a group of girls enter the bathroom. One of them yells, "Wait, is some-body puking in here?" I open the stall and sheepishly announce, "I guess

I drank too much sangria." The girls erupt into laughter and pat me on the back. The girl with the long ashy-blond hair remarks, "Are you kidding me? I fucking love this girl! Someone go get her some water." The brunette girl runs out of the bathroom to go get it. "I'm Barbara." She sticks out her hand before changing her mind. "You know what, why don't you wash your hands first." Everything she says is followed by belly laughter. The brunette girl comes back with a cup of water and I gulp it down and thank them.

"Where did you come from?" Barbara asks.

"I'm from New York."

"Oooohhh, so you're the girl from New York! We heard about you! In all seriousness, what the fuck are you doing here? Are you crazy?!" I'm bombarded with questions from all directions, when one of them says to me, "We're gonna go to the café. Wanna come with us?" I smile and nod.

They end up taking me to the same basement café I've been going to. My eyes dart to the computers at first and I have to fight the urge to go online. Barbara fires question after question in my direction. They listen, transfixed, as I tell them stories about my life in New York. I show them my nipple ring, and they lose their minds. They're all in the grade above me. Barbara is the funniest of the bunch. Tatiana is the pretty one and Sara is the sweetest. I learn that they are all in serious long-term relationships. Sara's been with her boyfriend since middle school. And Barbara's engaged and even wears a ring on her finger. She's been with him since she was eleven. He's older than her but her family loves him and supports their plans to wed. Tatiana has a thing for fucking the married men in her small town. She's been dating the butcher in secret for the past two years. I'm shocked at this discovery. In America, people go through relationships like toilet paper and childhood is prolonged well into our thirties. I can't believe how experienced these girls are. They wear heels every day to class. They wear layers of bronzer and their highlighted hair is always perfectly coiffed. The only thing we have in common is that we all chain-smoke cigarettes, but they don't do it in a rebellious way. They do it in a chic way. I look so much younger than them in my Nirvana T-shirts and ripped skinny jeans.

When it's time to go, they all make sure to get my phone number. We kiss on the cheek and make plans to meet at the café the next morning. I skip to the train and for the first time in a while, I feel a glimmer of hope.

I visit my grandpa on the weekends so I don't have to spend my free time with my host family. I love the comfort of the little apartment in Saronno, where we sit around and watch TV all day. He still has his wine and cigarettes, only this time I do too.

I take care of things around the house. I help him bathe, administer his chemo shots, and prepare his meals.

I wait until he goes to sleep and go through the cabinets, excavating all the artifacts we left behind when we moved. I go through my mom's drawers and try on her old clothes in the mirror. I find the spare set of keys to her empty apartment in Como. I unplug the landline to hook up to the Internet on my laptop and chat all night with my friends in New York. When Grandpa catches me on the computer he yells, "You're going to bankrupt me!!!" I roll my eyes. How expensive can it really be?

One night, I log on and Trish messages me immediately. "Rose got sent away to rehab!!! Her sister said 2 guys came in the middle of the night and kidnapped her and that their mom paid them to do it!! No one has heard from her since!"

I log on to Myspace to scour Rose's page for clues but her page is gone.

"What happened to her MySpace?" I ask Trish.

"Her mom found it and saw what was on there and freaked out and made her delete it."

I have no links to Rose anymore. I'm forced to let her go.

Over the next few months, my appearance begins to soften. I go from punk to prep. I start wearing less makeup and dye my hair back to brown. My clothes have fewer tears and more brand names. I trade in my ripped-up Converses for a pair of Prada sneakers I find at an outlet.

I throw away my band T-shirts and start wearing turtlenecks. I beg my mom for a Gucci belt so I can match my new friends. She says no so I ask my grandpa, who grudgingly gives me the money. I look forward to going to school, where I hug my friends in the halls and everyone wants to meet the cool girl from New York.

Letizia notices my growing social status and begins warming up to me. She even lets me copy her homework at night. Every morning her mom drops us off at the station, where we freeze our asses off watching the sun rise. I light up a cigarette and now Letizia asks me for one. "You better not tell your mommy!" I tease her. She rolls her eyes.

She tells me she has a crush on a boy who rides the train with us. He's hard to miss with his six-inch electric-blue mohawk and pounds of metal in his ears. She waits for him every morning at his stop and makes me change seats in the hope that he will sit in the glaring empty spot next to her.

One morning, he finally does. I feel Letizia's palpitating heart as I sit across from them with a smirk on my face. She doesn't have the balls to say hi. I'll show her how it's done, I think to myself.

"Hi, I'm Julia."

He looks startled as he glances up from his comic book. "Hi."

His hollow blue eyes shift back down to his book. Letizia looks amused.

"What's your name?" I ask him.

"Alessandro," he says, bordering on annoyed.

"This is my friend Letizia."

Her cheeks turn bright red. He glances at her and nods. She manages to awkwardly wave back.

"I'm staying with her since my family is back in New York."

Alessandro perks up. "You're from New York?"

We spend the rest of the ride talking about music. I mention Leftöver Crack, a popular punk band from New York, and he loses it. They're his favorite. Letizia glares at me. We both wave as he gets off the train.

"So what did you think?" I ask her.

She violently whips her backpack over her shoulder and hurries off the train. I'm panting as I try to keep up and also smoke my cigarette.

"Are you really mad at me for that?!" I yell after her.

She ignores me and keeps walking.

On Saturday nights, while Letizia stays home playing computer games, I go to the discoteca with my friends. I put on a pair of skintight Miss Sixty jeans and sharp black stilettos. I straighten my long brown hair and pile on loads of shimmery eye shadow. I ride on the back of Tatiana's off-brand Vespa without a helmet, so as not to mess up my makeup.

When we arrive, we don't get carded. Instead, we are handed a wad of drink tickets and ushered inside. We make our way through the club and head straight for the bar. Barbara orders a "Cuba libre." It's just a fancy way of saying rum and Coke, but I like the sound of it so I get the same. We dance to Gigi D'Agostino. Italian techno pulses throughout the dance floor when I spot Alessandro's electric-blue mohawk swaying in the crowd.

I ditch my friends and head straight in his direction. He's so tall in his platform boots. I climb up on a stool and tap him on the shoulder. He turns to face me, squinting under the flashing lights. "American girl!"

He seems totally different from the train. He scoops me up off the stool and I wrap my legs around his body. I can smell the liquor on his breath as we dance, intertwined. He pauses and we lock eyes for a moment before he dives straight into my mouth, swallowing my tongue and licking me all over. We fall over onto the couches as I straddle him, making out, crazed, drowning in each other's sweaty saliva. I think about Letizia. She would hate me for this. I tell myself to think rationally. She never would have stood a chance with him. And she's a huge bitch.

I hear Barbara's loud cackle. "Is that Julia?! Oh my God! Who the fuck is this guy?!"

I hop off the couch and readjust my boobs into my bra. I glance over at him. His lips are swollen and his spikes have wilted. Barbara grabs me by the wrist and drags me away before I can get his number. I guess I'll just have to wait until I see him on the train.

• • •

A few days later, I wake up to my cell phone vibrating relentlessly on the nightstand. I reach over. It's my mom.

"What's going on?" I say, half asleep.

"They don't want you there anymore. What did you do?" She sounds pissed.

"What? Nothing! Why?" I'm wide awake now.

"They didn't say. Just act normal. Don't say anything to them about it. Okay?"

"Okay, I won't."

"Just go to Grandpa's house until I get there in a few weeks. Okay?"

"Okay."

She hangs up. I lie motionless, heart pounding, thoughts flying through my head. What the fuck did I do? Did Letizia find out about me and Alessandro at the club? Why do I fuck everything up? Why does nobody want me?

I can't go back to sleep, so I get out of bed and start packing.

That morning, the drive to the station is quieter than usual. I stare out the window so as not to risk making eye contact with either of them. At the station, I walk to the other side of the platform and smoke by myself. When the train arrives, I make sure to sit in a different car. I feel humiliated, abandoned, ashamed, guilty.

At school, word gets out that I've been given the boot and the rumors start swirling. It was the smoking, the piercings, the clothes, the attitude. Basically, I'm just a bad influence. The teachers laugh and call me "orphan." I laugh too, so they think it's a joke.

I tell my mom I'm at my grandpa's, but I actually move into her place, which is close enough to the school where I don't need to take the train anymore. I start walking to school and I don't see Alessandro again. But I don't care, I've already moved on.

His name is Marco and he's a few grades above me. I'm so in love with the idea of having a boyfriend that I completely overlook the fact that I'm not physically attracted to him. I heard a rumor that his mother is part of the royal family in Belgium. The girls all agree that he's marriage material. He waits for me every day after school and carries my backpack like a perfect gentleman. I feel safe behind him on his Vespa as he drops me off from school. I hate kissing him, though. His lips are small and his tongue feels firm and prickly in my mouth. Not at all soft and succulent like Giovanni's kisses. I suck it up, literally and figuratively. It's the price I must pay in exchange for finally having a boyfriend and being like the other Italian girls.

Marco surprises me with YSL Cinéma perfume because I told him it was my favorite. He buys me gold earrings and concert tickets to see the Stereophonics perform live in Milan. He does everything right. But somehow I just can't bring myself to love him back. When the ick and the guilt become too much to bear, I break up with him. He then waits for me outside class with tears in his eyes and begs me to take him back. I feel bad for him and convince myself to overlook the daunting fact that I just don't like him and give it another try.

This cycle continues until one morning, I see his sister barge into my classroom out of the corner of my eye, face red, voice shaky, tremors of anger pulsing through her body. I blink and she's right in front of me screaming her head off, belligerent.

"You piece-of-trash whore! Stay the fuck away from my brother!!! You're nothing but trash! Everybody thinks so!"

She wags her finger in my face as she spews her venom. I'm too stunned to speak. I feel the burn of my classmates' stares on the back of my head. The room is silent but I hear the whispers, the gasps, and the snickers. No one says a word. Once she's satisfied with my humiliation, she disappears into the hallway.

I spend the rest of the day obsessing over all the things I should have said. I feel stupid for just standing there like a fool and allowing her to trample all over me like that.

· · ·

One morning, the head priest in charge of our school comes into our classroom with a grim look on his face.

"Go home, pack your bags, we're going to Rome. The pope has died."

I hear gasps as my classmates hug and cry on each other's shoulders. I'm just glad for the half day and can't wait to get home and watch my favorite reality dating program, *Uomini e Donne*. As I flip through the channels, I'm met with the music video for "One of Us" on every single channel. Images of the pope are broadcast on loop. Footage of the smoke signals from the Vatican take over my television set. I can't escape it.

The next morning, we meet at the train station and after two long train rides finally arrive in Rome where we are met by thousands of mourners. We join the crowd waiting to get a glimpse of the dead pope's body.

A helicopter flies overhead and someone screams that it's George Bush. The line into the cathedral is miles long and barely moving. My feet hurt and I'm starting to get cranky. I smoke my last cigarette. I ask my friend Leonardo for one but he says he's running low. This sets me off into a rage. I flip him off and call him an asshole.

After sixteen long torturous hours, we make it inside the Vatican. The line is even slower inside. Everyone must kneel before the pope's casket and say a quick prayer. It's finally our turn and I guess being in the presence of a dead body makes me have a change of heart because when I spot Leonardo, I say sorry for yelling at him. We hug for a millisecond, when I feel a strong grip on my shoulder. The head priest rips us apart, swings me around, and slaps me in the face in front of everyone, including the dead pope. I'm stunned.

"This behavior is unacceptable in the Vatican, you animal!"

I'm frozen. Leonardo is speechless.

"Why didn't you get slapped?" I ask him.

He shrugs and scurries away from me.

The rest of the trip, I'm fuming. Did I seriously just wait sixteen hours to get slapped in the face in front of the dead pope? I didn't even get to have a moment with him!

·   ·   ·

At the end of the school year, all the students crowd around the bulletin board in the lobby, anxiously checking the lists. One list means you passed. The other means you will have to repeat the year. I push through the crowd of crying, shaking kids and spot my name on the naughty list. I failed. I call my mom and tell her the news, imploring her to let me come home for the summer. We compromise. I have to stay in Italy but I can switch schools if I want to. I enroll in the other Catholic school across the street. This one is run by nuns.

"They will be nicer," my mom assures me.

"Great, so they won't hit me?"

Most of my friends go away on vacation with their families, but I'm left in the city all summer long. I get lonely spending so much time by myself and my mom's apartment is an echo chamber for my nagging thoughts. Sometimes I go to my grandpa's house, but he's so out of it all the time.

I ride my stolen bike around the lake, hoping to bump into someone I know. One evening, I'm biking through the piazza making my rounds when I hear someone yelling, "Foxy!"

I whip around and see Veronica, a girl from my old school. She was a grade above me in a different department.

"You smoke?" she asks, waving a neatly rolled joint in my face.

"Weed?" I ask.

"Hashish. Afghan."

I park my bike, and we walk to a secluded area, where we pass the joint back and forth. I get so blazed I can't even formulate a sentence. Veronica finds it hysterical when I can't remember where I parked my bike. Once I get home, I see a text from her inviting me to her house for dinner the next day. I'm thrilled to finally have someone to smoke and chill with.

The next day, I go to the address she sent me and realize it's a hotel. And not just any hotel. This one is in the heart of the city, right on the lake, with gold finishes and velvet drapes. I take the elevator up to the penthouse and I'm greeted by a beautiful heavyset Russian woman speaking near-perfect English.

"Nice to meet you, Julia! I'm Svetlana," she says with a warm hug. She almost immediately starts telling me all about her modeling days in New York in the eighties, when Veronica emerges from behind her. Her eyes are red as if she has just been crying.

"Mom, stop talking her ear off! She's here for me!"

She takes my hand and drags me into her bedroom, where she starts rolling a joint. Her room does not match the decor in the rest of the house. She has stickers on every surface. Her walls are covered in posters. It's as if her entire room is a shrine to Jim Morrison. She asks me if I like the Doors. "How can I say no?" I ask her, looking around her room. She laughs.

She leads me onto the marble balcony, where we crouch so her mom won't see us and hit the joint until we are ready to munch. At the dinner table, I'm too stoned to speak. I'm busy observing the family dynamic. Her dad, an Italian furniture mogul, is forty years older than her mom. He's steady and stable, wise and calm. He listens to Veronica and speaks to her in a soft, nurturing tone. Her brother is a pretty-boy prick, and the disdain he has for his sister is obvious. He shoots down everything she says and barely acknowledges me at all.

Any time the conversation veers in a direction Svetlana doesn't like, she hijacks it and redirects it. "In my country, me and my twelve brothers and sisters all ate with our hands from the same plate! You kids have it so good!"

We eat the rest of our meal in silence.

After dinner, her mom hugs me and makes sure to tell Veronica, "Why can't you be more polite, like Julia?" Veronica drags us away and back into her room, making sure to lock the door behind her. She then goes into her private personal bathroom and closes the door. I hear her hacking and gagging and I know she's throwing up. When she comes out, I go in and do the same.

Veronica and I spend the rest of the summer glued to each other's side. She doesn't care about parties or nightclubs. She's content with smoking weed and stuffing our faces, then throwing up. For this reason, we spend most of our time at my mom's house, where we can navigate undetected. Veronica doesn't have a boyfriend like my other friends do. She hates boys. She loves art and teaches me about fashion. We go to all the fancy stores, where her mom has accounts open.

"I want you to have this," she says, holding up a pink Marc Jacobs cardigan with crystal embellishments. "He's my favorite designer."

I look at the price tag. It's seven hundred euros. "Are you sure?" I ask her.

"My mom won't know."

I don't even like pink but I happily accept it.

Once I start at my new school, I don't care about making friends because I know Veronica will be waiting for me once the bell rings. She's all I need. I barely ever think about my old life in New York. I can see myself living in Italy forever. This is what I told my mom to convince her to let me come back home for ten days during Christmas break.

When I get to New York and step inside our apartment, I'm shocked at how small it is. It feels even more cramped than when I left it over a year ago. I have no place to put my things and it looks like I'll be sleeping on the couch.

My baby brother, now walking, bounces around, while my other brother, who is a whole foot taller than when I last saw him, plays video games in what used to be our bedroom. My dad still floats in and out of the front door all day, while my mom cooks and yells at him from the kitchen. I realize pretty quickly that I'm already getting in their way. It's obvious that there's no room for me here.

I pick up the house phone and dial the only number I still remember by heart. "Julia?!" Trisha squeals as she picks up on the first ring. She instructs me to meet her a block away at a dealer's apartment.

Once I arrive, Trish charges at me, jumping on top of me in excitement. She looks so much older now. Her hair is longer, blonder, and she has a fresh French manicure on her long nails. I glance down at her shoes and notice she's still wearing Converse.

"I died when I saw your number on my phone! It's a Christmas miracle. Wow, you look so pretty. I can't believe how light your hair is!" The words pour out of her mouth. Before I can say anything, she leads me inside the dim studio apartment that smells of stale bongwater and beer. Through the smoke, I notice a few seedy characters sitting in the shadows. Trish introduces me to Kyle, an overweight white boy playing video games from his bed in the center of the room. "It's his apartment," she says. He barely acknowledges me when I say hello. I scan the room and notice another heavyset guy in his mid-twenties weighing large nugs of weed on a little kitchen scale. He goes by Dougie Digital. I recognize another girl I know from middle school, Jaqueline. She looks so frail now. She used to be so loud in middle school but now she won't even speak unless she's spoken to. She gives me a limp hug and sits back down on the couch, watching Kyle play video games, anxiously ripping out strands of her hair.

"Is Rose out of rehab?" I whisper to Trish through the music.

"Yeah, but she won't talk to anyone anymore. She has new friends."

The bathroom door swings open and a tall figure appears in the doorway. As he makes his way toward us and the light hits his face, I recognize him. It's Ace. Rose's ex-boyfriend. He walks to the center of the room, commanding everyone's attention with his stance. He notices me and doesn't say hi. Instead, he reaches out and drops a white pill in my hand. I study it for a moment, holding it up to the light. "Is that a naked lady?" I ask.

"They're the best ones!" Trish says. "Take it!"

I pop the pill into my mouth and contemplate spitting it out when their backs are turned, but Ace will not stop staring at me. He looks different in person than in his overedited Myspace photos. His skin is milky in contrast to his jet-black hair. His high cheekbones and sharp features are made more defined by the clenching of his jaw. He asserts dominance over us like an art form. I can feel everyone's eagerness to please him. He makes a joke and immediately turns to see if I laugh. I do. His dark beady eyes dart around the room as he catches every subtle movement. His eyes are everywhere and I feel them peering into my soul, trying to figure me out.

"You really Italian?" he asks.

I nod. "Yeah, I live there."

He licks his lips as he talks. "You speak Italian?"

"*Si*," I say with a giggle.

He nods in approval. "Your family's in the Mob?"

I shake my head no, when I'm suddenly hit with a warm wave of euphoria crawling up my spine, enveloping my entire body. My brain feels like it's being tickled by a feather as I close my eyes and fall back on the bed. I crawl under the comforter, wiggling my toes and feeling the soft sensation on my fingertips. Then I feel someone touching me. I open my eyes and Ace is in bed with me. As he inches closer and closer, my heart begins pounding and I feel like I'm on fire.

I struggle to get my knit sweater off under the covers and he helps me remove it. He begins tracing his fingers up and down my arms and back, sending goose bumps across my entire body. He runs his hands through my hair. He wraps his hand around my neck and pulls me in to him. He licks his lips before kissing me hard and passionately. We forget there's an audience and have sex like we are the last two people on earth and the human race depends on it. I climb on top of him, still under the covers, and ride him until I feel the fireworks in my vagina and I cum all over him. It's my first penetrative orgasm and I'm overwhelmed by the euphoric bomb that just exploded between us.

I turn over and stare into his eyes, which have been enveloped by his pupils, like two black shiny marbles.

"I love you," he whispers.

I pause as an anxious feeling washes over me.

"I love you too," I tell him.

I pull the comforters off me and run into the bathroom naked. I turn on the light and look in the mirror. I'm horrified at my reflection. My once blue eyes have been swallowed by my pupils, and I can see every vein and pore in my skin. I hear a knock on the door and immediately shut off the light. I crack the door open and Ace politely asks, "May I join you?"

"Yes, but we have to keep the light off," I tell him.

He agrees and sits down on the toilet. He pulls me down onto his lap and whispers in my ear, "I swear, when you walked in the room, I said to myself, 'I'm gonna marry that girl.'"

I find comfort in knowing he can't see me blushing. "You don't even know me!"

"Trish said you're mad thorough *and* you speak Italian. You have a beautiful smile. I like your peacoat."

I laugh as he trails off after listing all the menial things he likes about me.

"I don't believe you. It's just the drugs talking."

He pauses and his tone changes. He's determined. "You saying you don't believe me?" He dashes out of the bathroom and comes back a second later with his cell phone. "Mom, you're not gonna believe this. I met my wife! She's from Italy and she's smart and stylish and sexy. Say hi to my mom."

He holds the Razr flip phone in my face as I hesitantly place it to my ear.

"Hi, I'm Julia. Sorry for calling so late. It's nice to meet—"

Before I can finish my sentence, he grabs the phone back and shuts it. He grabs me again and smothers me in kisses.

"Is Ace your real name?" I ask. He's caught off guard. He nods, and his eyes dart away quickly.

I feel the ecstasy wearing off and I start fidgeting anxiously. "Can I have another pill?" I ask him.

"Baby girl, slow down."

I feel myself turning inward, crawling back inside the depths of my mind. He notices the shift in my energy and says, "All right, get dressed. I got some work to do anyway. You're coming with me." He swings open the door and yells, "Dougie, get the car, we're going downtown."

I start gathering my clothes, which are scattered all over the apartment. No one seems startled by our manic romance spiral. Trish looks at him with puppy-dog eyes and asks, "Can I come?"

"There's no room in the car," Ace snaps. I look at Trish longingly but even she knows that what he says goes.

We get into a silver Honda Civic, Dougie in the driver's seat, Ace directing in the passenger seat. We drive down the FDR, windows down, music blasting, my gaze transfixed on the neon trails of lights. I sit quietly in the back seat listening to Ace rap along to all the lyrics of every song that comes on the radio. Occasionally he pauses the music to answer the phone and berate whoever is on the other line. When he hangs up, he looks at Dougie and they laugh until they have tears in their eyes.

We pull over on 42nd Street. Ace turns around and instructs me to move over and not talk to the man heading toward us. He gets inside, they make a quick exchange, and in an instant we're back on the road. Ace unwraps a folded-up tissue and jiggles the white pills in his hands. He waves one in front of me, teasing me with it.

I manage to snatch it out of his hand, and he turns to Dougie and says, "She's so feisty and Italian. I love her. She's perfect."

I feel the wave of ecstasy washing over me again and I want nothing more than to crawl up in the front seat and nosedive into Ace's lap. I massage his neck and head and stick my tongue in his ear. I whisper, "Come sit back here with me." He makes Dougie pull over and hops in the back seat with me. I lick his neck and kiss him all over as he unhooks my bra with one hand. I pull his throbbing penis out of his pants and climb on top of him. I ride him hard and fast and soft and slow. He pulls my hair and whispers, "I love you" in my ear. We pull over on a dark street and Dougie gets out of the steamy car to let us finish.

Dewy and disheveled, we begin walking down 8th Street.

"I gotta make another sale," Ace says.

He grabs my hand and leads me down the street toward a group of kids drinking forties on a stoop. I immediately notice their clothes, because they're barely wearing any. The girl with the bleached-blond hair has on glasses and a crop top and a pair of pink patent-leather platform boots. The tall skinny girl with the black hair has on a neon-green mini-skirt and white Pleasers.

I squeeze Ace's hand tighter. They both spring up and kiss him on the cheek. The girl with the black hair reaches into her bra and hands him a wad of crumpled dollar bills, while the blond girl with glasses stares me up and down.

"Is this your new girlfriend?" the brunette asks.

"This is my fiancée, Julia. She's from Italy.'"

I smile and tug on his hand.

"I'm Liana," the blond girl says without a smile.

When we walk away, I ask him, "How do you know them?"

"They're just some whores. Right?" He shoots a look at Dougie, who nods in agreement. I start feeling insecure when we walk by a tattoo shop.

"Let's get tattoos!" I say enthusiastically. I can tell by Ace's expression that he's uncertain. "If you love me as much as you say you do, then it shouldn't be a problem."

He looks me in my eyes and says, "Okay, if we do this, you can't ever leave me."

"Okay, done."

"And you have to move back to America."

Shit. My mind jumps to my life in Italy and Veronica and my grandpa. I push the thoughts out of my head and say, "Okay, I will."

As I sit in the chair getting his name tattooed on my wrist, Ace seems restless, maniacally tapping away on his silver Razr. The tattoo artist asks me, "How long have you two been together?" Before I can answer, Ace interjects, "It doesn't matter how long we've been together, just do your job." The rest of the session is awkward and quiet and not at all romantic.

It's past midnight when we get back to Kyle's apartment. I rush inside and proudly show off my new tattoo. Trish seems concerned but forces a smile anyway.

"Meet me in the bathroom," she whispers and walks away. I follow her to the bathroom. I can feel Ace's eyes on me as I move across the room. Trish locks the door and lets the water run. She whispers, "Are you sure about this, Julia?"

I'm annoyed that she's not happy for me, but mostly I'm just pissed that she's fucking up my high.

"Yeah, it's fine, don't even worry, I'll be back in the summer and it's gonna be fine."

"What about Rose? She's gonna find out."

I feel the anxiety constricting my chest. "Well, they're not together anymore. It's been over a year and didn't you say she won't even talk to you? I think it's fine."

Am I convincing her or myself?

Trish nods. "Okay, I just don't want you to regret this. You don't know Ace. He's crazy."

We're startled by banging on the door. Trish's eyes widen as she quickly flushes the toilet. I crack the door and Ace pushes it open.

"What are you telling her about me?" he says aggressively.

"Oh my God, Ace, don't be crazy! I was taking a piss!"

"And I was showing her my tattoo!"

He doesn't seem convinced. He grabs my arm and leads me out of the bathroom. "Okay, party's over, guys, everyone's gotta go!" he yells.

I say bye to Trish, who looks disappointed. Ace makes Kyle get up out of his own bed and sleep on the couch. We get in the bed and as I pretend to fall asleep, I hear him frantically tapping away on his phone until I drift off to sleep.

The next day when I open my eyes, I'm startled and for a moment don't remember where I am. The room is dark and cold and quiet. Kyle snores next to us and Ace's body is wrapped around mine, restricting me from going anywhere. My head pounds and my body feels like it's been hit by a car. My bladder feels like it's about to explode but I'm paralyzed by the fear of waking Ace up and having to face him. He feels like a stranger. I don't know him and he now has my name written in large Gothic letters down his entire forearm. What did I get myself into?

I slither out of bed naked, trying to locate my clothes among the plastic bags and empty cartons of food. Ace rolls over. I freeze.

"You weren't thinking of leaving, were you?" His voice is low and raspy.

"No, I just don't wanna be naked in front of your friend."

"Come here," he commands, holding his arms out.

I'm relieved that he still seems to like me, even though I'm not so sure.

Over the next ten days, my brain absorbs a shit ton of drugs as well as everything there is to know about him. He shows me his sketchbook and I'm floored by his talent. I'm also impressed by his ability to code and take apart computers. He's a wizard at graphic design too.

"I'm a nerdy gangster," he says, and I laugh.

He tells me about his connections to the Mob and that he has an open case for an attempted manslaughter charge. "I stabbed this mother-fucker in the eye in broad daylight on 96th Street." He says this with a proud smirk, as if he's showing off.

I'm caught off guard but also weirdly turned on. "What did he do?"

His posture stiffens. "What are you? The feds? Don't worry about it, he deserved it."

I nod, a thousand questions flooding my mind.

"They're gonna drop it to an assault charge. They're not gonna get me, don't worry." He reassures me with a kiss.

"Should you be smoking weed?" I ask.

"'Should you be smoking weed?'" he mimics me in an exaggerated Valley Girl accent. "I'm a gangster. I do whatever the fuck I want!"

His stories are always changing. First he tells me he's Italian, then he's Albanian. I suspect that he isn't telling me the truth but I don't want to get off this manic ride. I can tell he doesn't like when I ask too many questions. His body shifts uncomfortably when I ask him about his dad.

"He's an Irish guy. He has the lightest blue eyes. I don't really know him like that. He got locked up a few times and my mom didn't take me to see him. When he got out he married some chick and had a couple of kids." He shrugs.

"Do you ever see them?" I ask.

"Nah."

On my last night in New York, he takes me to a party in Tribeca.

"I gotta make a few sales," he says. When we enter the room, everyone pauses to look at us. The crowd parts with each step he takes. I feel the jealous eyeballs and hear the loud whispers.

"*That's* his new girlfriend? I don't get it."

He holds my hand while kids line up to greet him as if he's some kind of king.

"This is my fiancée, Julia," he says proudly. "She's from Italy."

I recognize some kids I know from the park and let go of his hand to say hi to them. I'm talking to them for a few seconds when Ace swoops in from behind me and drags me away by the arm.

"What the fuck? What's going on?" I ask him.

He clenches his jaw and squeezes my arm tighter. "I got a bad vibe. Get in the car." He physically places me in the back of the Honda, where Dougie has been waiting for us, and we speed away.

When we get back to Kyle's place, he ignores me as he paces manically and does bumps of coke off his hand. I finally stand up and announce, "I think I'm gonna go home. I haven't spent any time with my family—"

He cuts me off. "No, you're not." His tone is sharp, and his eyes are hollow.

"What do you mean?"

"You're not going home. You wanna go fuck that dirty skater kid."

I look at Kyle or Dougie to back me up—surely they can see he's being irrational—but they just shrug and stare blankly at me, almost amused.

"What kid? You mean my friend from middle school? I was just saying hi to him!"

Ace waves his hand in my face, dismissing me.

I sit back down and cross my arms. "No. I'm not leaving now."

Ace's face lights up. He starts laughing and looks over at Kyle and Dougie. "I love her, she's perfect!"

I crack a smile. He holds out his fist. I lean in to get a good look at the shimmery white pile of cocaine on it and inhale it. I instantly forget about what just happened and feel myself ascending from the inside. A lightning bolt strikes my spine and shoots down into my panties, causing an over-whelming tingling sensation in my vagina. I jump on top of him, sucking on his neck and licking his face. I straddle and grind on him as he carries me into the bathroom. I rip my top off and drop to my knees. I unzip his pants and devour his flaccid penis with my mouth. He struggles to get it erect. He squeezes his eyes shut and clenches his butt cheeks. His toes curl as he thrusts his penis into my mouth with every ounce of strength in his body. My mouth is numb as I slurp on the salty sweat juice. I feel the buzz start to wear off and I'm jolted back into reality, his shriveled penis still in my mouth. I stand up and wipe my face with my hand. "I need another bump." He digs through his pants on the floor and pulls out a handful of glistening glass vials. He unscrews one and dumps it all out on the toilet seat. He rolls up a twenty-dollar bill, hands it to me, and I dive straight in, nose first. He sniffs whatever is left and bends me over the toilet seat. I feel a wave of warmth run through me as his penis hardens inside me. We have sex all night, pausing only to sniff lines off the toilet seat.

The sun peeks in the window and I whisper to him, "I have to go. I still have to pack."

He squeezes me tight. "If you love me, you won't go."

"I'm coming back this summer. It's only six months."

"You better."

I retrieve my clothing with dread in my eyes.

The streets are empty as he walks me to my parents' house. We hold hands, walking in silence, occasionally glancing at each other and giggling. He pulls a bag of pills out of his pants and hands me one. "Xanax, so you can sleep on the flight."

I squeeze him tightly, heart racing, profusely sweating and disheveled. We kiss for a long time, not wanting to let go, then I stumble into my building.

I cry the whole plane ride back to Italy, partly because I'm sad to leave and partly because I'm coming down off a shit ton of pure-grade-A fish-scale cocaine. I decide not to take the Xanax, since it's all I have to remind me of Ace.

The moment I land, I immediately go find Veronica and show off my new tattoo. She listens in amazement as I tell her about my time in New York. After a while, she asks, "Does this mean you're moving back there?"

I pause. "I don't know, maybe?"

She looks shattered.

"You can come with me, don't worry. I'll never leave you."

We hug and she pulls out a fat joint loaded with Afghan hashish.

I spend more time at my grandpa's house since my mom's apartment doesn't have Internet access. I stay up all night waiting for Ace to sign online. We haven't spoken since I left and I can't help but feel a sense of impending doom. I grind my teeth and bite my fingernails until they're bloody nubs. When I ask Trish, she tells me she hasn't heard from him, either.

"I think he's pissed, Jules."

"Why?!" I tap away frantically at the keyboard while my grandpa snores ten feet away from me.

"He thinks you have a boyfriend in Italy."

"What?!"

I glance down at the tattoo on my wrist and scrape the crust off in hopes that it will just magically pop off, but it's still there, glaring back at me. I'm growing desperate, scouring his Myspace, searching for clues. I decide to message Jacqueline and ask her if she's seen Ace.

"You didn't hear it from me but he was chilling at this girl's house."

My heart stops. "What girl?"

"Her name is Alyssa. Her mom's a stripper or something lol."

I remember the Xanax and run to get it. I pop it in my mouth and chain-smoke cigarettes until I finally see his username appear. The seconds feel like hours as I wait for him to message me first. I finally say fuck it and open the chat box and type, "You forgot about me already?" I hit send. I see him typing in the chat and then he stops. I hold my breath, waiting for him to reply. After a long moment he writes: "you need to get back here."

"Do you still love me?" I ask him.

"Do you still love me?" he asks.

"Yea," I reply.

"Prove it."

"How?"

"Come back," he says before signing off.

Ace has such a hold on me. He's my favorite of all the drugs. I love the way I feel when I'm with him. I get high on his power. I'm the queen to his king and I have to find a way to get back to him.

The next day I call my dad and beg him to let me come home. He screams, "NO!" and hangs up. I won't even bother wasting time and asking my mom. I'm left with no choice but to ask my grandpa.

I slither into my grandpa's room as he's watching TV. I'm sweating from the burning shame. It takes me a few minutes to work up the courage to tell him this lie. I take a deep breath and announce, "I'm pregnant and I need money for an abortion."

The color drains out of his face. "You're joking, right?" I look down and shake my head. "I told you, Julia, you're on a bad path!" I nod in agreement.

Once I have the crisp bills in my hands, I don't feel relieved. I feel awful. I tuck the feelings away and focus on my mission. Problem is, I've never bought a plane ticket before. I suddenly remember there's a travel agency by the train station, so the next morning I march over gripping my passport in my sweaty hands. I wipe my hands on my jeans before I step inside. I don't want them to suspect anything is amiss. As soon as the travel agent sees my American passport, she begins speaking to me in broken English. I go along with it and pretend I can't speak Italian so she won't inquire further about my reason for travel.

She books me a flight for a week from today. I get butterflies when she hands me the plane ticket. This is really happening! I run to Veronica's house to tell her the news. She breaks down in tears. "You're my only friend—my best friend. What am I gonna do without you?"

I wipe the tears from her cheeks and brush the hair out of her face. "I got a return flight. If it sucks, I'll come right back. Okay?"

We spend the next week at my mom's apartment chain-smoking weed and binging-and-purging Nutella. The morning of my flight, Veronica insists on taking the bus with me to the airport.

"Someone is coming to pick you up when you get there, right?" she asks.

"I hope so."

She drags my massive suitcase as I lug my heavy bags across the terminal.

When we arrive at security, we hug and ugly-cry like two long-lost lesbians.

"I'll see you so soon, I promise!" I yell at her.

"I love you!" she yells back. She keeps her eyes on me until I disappear into the crowd.

On the plane, my mind descends into darkness thinking about my grandpa. I'm a piece of shit. I didn't even say bye. I tell myself it's okay, I'll go visit him over the summer. I think about Barbara and Letizia and my other friends from school. They're going to be so pissed that I didn't tell them I was leaving. I think about my teachers at school who will probably call my mom. I think about Veronica. My heart hurts.

HOMECOMING FIEND

When I land at JFK, I get my bag and run outside and inhale the familiar polluted New York air. Smells like home. I've lit a cigarette, my eyes darting through the crowd, when I hear a familiar voice.

"Julia!"

I turn around and see Trish running toward me, her pink Converse sneakers stomping on the concrete. Her hair is now a dark chestnut brown. I'm relieved when I spot Ace behind her. She jumps on top of me and knocks us both over. Ace reaches down, my name glistening on his arm in big bold letters, and scoops me off the ground. I straddle him as he carries me all the way to the car, where even Dougie seems happy to see me.

Once inside, I ask, "Where are we going?"

"I got us a dope spot on the Upper West Side."

Adrenaline rushes through me as we drive past my parents' building. Their windows are open and I can see them moving around inside. I'm so close to them and yet they feel so far away.

We pull up to a massive doorman building on Riverside Drive.

Dougie grabs my bags and Ace leads us to an apartment on the twenty-fourth floor. The apartment is bare except for a printer, a stack of paper, a paper cutter, and a bed. A preppy kid with acne scars wearing a bathrobe, emerges from a door with a fat blunt in his hands.

"His name is Patrick," Ace whispers. "His family owns this apartment and the one next door. He's a private school kid who wants to feel like a gangster."

"I'm having a party here tonight," Patrick says, "but y'all can crash for as long as you need."

"What's the printer for?" I ask naively.

"We're making money!" Ace says.

"This is the only printer in the world that can do it," Patrick says proudly. He drops a fifty-dollar bill in the scanner and copies it exactly.

I pull it out, examining it against the light. "It's not right," I say. "The texture is off. It's too dry. I need an iron and some butter or oil."

Patrick nods, runs to the apartment next door, and returns with butter. Ace watches in amazement as I take over the operation. First I drench the paper in butter, then I iron it dry, and then I put it through the printer.

"The money feels smoother and more realistic this way."

I don't know how I know how to do this. I just do. It's strangely instinctual.

Partygoers begin spilling in, crowding around me as I cut stacks of money in the paper cutter. Ace drifts in and out, keeping a close eye on me. I'm sorting through stacks of faux cash when the blond girl with glasses from 8th Street enters the room.

"Hey, I'm Liana. I think we met."

"Yeah, I remember."

She's traded the crop top and platforms for a pink Care Bear T-shirt and sneakers. It's a stark contrast from what I'm wearing: a Gucci belt and black stilettos. She opens her Hello Kitty lunch box and pulls out a nug of weed.

"Do you have papers?" she asks.

I shake my head no.

"Whoa, what are you doing here?" she says in awe when she sees my money printing station.

"Exactly what it looks like," I say with a laugh.

"Should we see if it works?"

"Okay, let's try the deli."

On the walk, I ask her, "How do you know Ace?"

"He used to date my friend but I just know him from around."

We stroll into the deli and ask the clerk for rolling papers. He places a pack of Rizla papers on the counter. I fumble through my bag and pull out the crumpled fake fifty-dollar bill. He holds it up to the light before placing it back down.

"This is a fake bill," he says.

Liana and I shoot a look at each other.

"Oh, shit, someone just gave it to us. Okay, never mind!"

We're running down the block laughing when I spot a hot dog vendor.

"I have an idea," I tell her.

I order a pretzel and hand him the folded fifty. He glances at it, puts it in his pocket, counts out forty-eight dollars in change, and hands it to me.

When we get back upstairs, Ace rushes in, drink in hand, yelling, "Where the fuck did you go?! I was looking everywhere for you!"

Everyone freezes and stares at us. I lead him to a walk-in closet so we can talk in private. Before I can say a word, he has his hands around my neck, slamming me repeatedly into the wall. The rod comes crashing down and I'm sure everyone can hear us. "You don't fucking leave without telling me!" he whispers through clenched teeth. I nod and fall to my knees, and he walks away, leaving me in the closet on the floor.

Hearing him go to the apartment next door, I run out of the closet and lock myself in the bathroom. I pat down the redness on my neck and wipe away the mascara tears staining my face. I comb through my hair with my fingers and rinse my face off with cold water. I plaster on a smile and walk back out to the quiet room. Everyone has left except Liana. Without a word, she passes me a fat joint and we smoke it in silence.

Ace comes back in and abruptly instructs Liana to leave the room. I keep my eyes fixed on Liana. She looks back at me, and I nod, indicating that I'll be okay.

Ace crouches in front of me. "I'm sorry I lost my cool. I just love you so much and you can't just disappear like that." I avoid his gaze. "Baby, look at me," he pleads. I look into his glassy eyes filling up with tears. He gets on his knees and wraps his arms around me.

"You're not the tough guy you claim to be. You're a fake and a phony. Real men don't hit girls."

My words fly at him like darts, instantly popping his overinflated balloon-size ego. He loosens his grip and hops to his feet, jaw clenched and eyes twitching. His tone changes, and even his accent becomes more pronounced as he grinds his teeth with anger.

"Listen, you little brat, I'm a gangster, whether you like it or not. Maybe I overestimated you. Maybe you're not cut out for this lifestyle."

I cut him off. "Okay, tough guy, whatever. See, you're not even really sorry. Are we done now?"

He inches his face closer to mine, backing me onto the bed. I fall backward, and he climbs on top of me, straddling me and kissing my neck before wrapping his hand around it. He tightens his grip and whispers in my ear, "Do you love me?" I hesitate. He squeezes me harder. I nod and he kisses me violently, sucking on my tongue and biting my lips.

"I love you so much," he whispers. "I finally met my match." He lets out a desperate laugh, tears forming in his eyes. "Julia, please, I beg you, forgive me."

"I want to but you make it so hard. You can't do that to me anymore."

He wipes the tears from my cheeks, lies down on top of me, his head nestled in my hair, and we both cry. The crying turns into kissing, which turns into sweet passionate lustful orgasmic sex.

When we're done, I go into the bathroom and notice there's a phone on the wall. I lift it up and put it to my ear and hear a dial tone. I turn on the shower, hoping Ace will go back to the party. I wait a few minutes and crack the door open and see that he's gone. I lock the door again and call Veronica. She squeals with excitement when she answers the phone on the first ring. "Is this my love Julia?"

My eyes instantly fill up with tears. I swallow them back down and manage to say, "I miss you so much."

"How's it going?" she asks.

"I'm okay. I learned how to print fake money—me and Ace got in a pretty bad fight."

"If he fucking hurts you I'm going to come over there and fucking murder him. Tell him I said that."

I giggle and brush it off. "Has anyone said anything about me yet?"

"Nope! You're in the clear!"

I'm relieved but a little part of me is saddened that no one has noticed I'm missing. I hear a knock on the door and abruptly hang up the phone. I jump out of my clothes and into the shower.

The next day Ace informs me that he has to go beat up some private school kids for Patrick.

"Why?! That's a really bad idea. Don't you have an open case already?!"

"Listen, sweetheart. I'm a gangster. This is what I do." He pulls a fat stack of hundreds out of his pocket and dangles it in my face. "Come on, you're coming."

Ace, Dougie, and me pile into Dougie's Honda. Ace's amped up. The phone rings. It's Patrick. Ace ends the call with: "When are mother-fuckers gonna realize that this shit makes me horny! My dick gets hard thinking about curb-stomping motherfuckers!" He lets out a maniacal laugh and turns around to catch our reactions. He sees me rolling my eyes. "Oh, this bitch doesn't think I'm about that life! Let me show you now, sweetheart." He shifts his attention over to the school as acne-studded teenagers trickle out of the building. "Where's my brass knuck-les?" Dougie reaches into the glove compartment and pulls them out.

Ace puts them on, kisses them, and bolts out of the car in the direction of the school.

I watch closely through the window. There's too much traffic and I can't hear what's going on but I see Ace swing at someone. Agile and swift, he has his target cornered like a predator in the wild. A crowd forms as people chant and cheer. We hear a siren in the distance and Dougie swiftly pulls the car around. I roll the window down and scream for Ace to get in the car, but he doesn't hear me.

His eyes are like two soul-sucking black holes obliterating anything that they come in contact with. I see his iron-crusted fist fly through the air in slow motion, connecting with the kid's temple. The kid stumbles backward before collapsing on the ground. Ace snaps out of his trance, scans the crowd, and sprints back into the passenger seat with the most accomplished grin on his face. He turns to me. "Did you see that?" he proudly asks with the same enthusiasm as a kid asking his mom about a soccer match. I nod as Dougie steps on the gas. Ace flips the vanity mirror down, examining his face. "Not a scratch, baby." He beams.

As we weave in and out of traffic, Ace's phone rings. It's Patrick. Ace puts it on speaker.

"I got 'em good! You seen that?! I was like bopbopbop, knocked him the fuck out!"

"Ace Ace Ace, listen to me. Someone snitched and said I hired the hit. I don't know who. The cops are here and the kid is getting an ambulance."

"So what's this gotta do with me?!" Ace asks defensively.

Patrick stutters. "I'm just letting you know—I would delete my MySpace if I were you. I heard some kids saying your name to the cops."

Ace glances back at me through the mirror. "Am I too famous to be committing crimes now?!" he boasts. Patrick forces a laugh. I look down, shaking my head. Ace hangs up and laughs, waving the stack of hundreds in the air. "Quickest five G's I ever made!" Dougie holds out his fist, giving him a pound.

"Does this mean the cops are looking for you?" I ask.

"Captain Obvious over here!" Ace cracks. Dougie's bellowing laugh echoes through my brain, giving me a headache. The rest of the car ride is silent and I can tell he's stressed out.

We go back to Patrick's apartment. Ace rolls a fat blunt and passes it to me. "I'll be back. Dougie, let me talk to you for a minute." Dougie longingly eyes the blunt in my hands before following Ace out of the apartment.

Ace doesn't return for hours. When he does, he's agitated and panicky. "Get up! Dougie's downstairs. We gotta bounce!"

"What do you mean? What happened? Where did you go?"

"Patrick snitched."

I sigh and shake my head. "I knew this was a bad idea!"

"Don't worry, he got what was coming to him," he coldly replies.

"What do you mean?"

He waves me away. "Just pack your shit and let's get the fuck outta here!"

I frantically gather my belongings, sloppily throwing them in my suitcase.

"Where are we gonna go?" I ask once we're in the car and Dougie has started driving.

"Shhh! Let me think!" Ace shouts at me.

"Fine, I just won't talk anymore," I say as I cross my arms and shift my attention in the opposite direction.

"Dougie, stop the car," he commands.

"I can't pull over here."

"Stop the fucking car!"

"What are you doing?" I yell as Dougie steps on the brakes.

Ace jumps out of the car, opens the back door, and drags me out kicking and screaming. "I fucking did that for you! I beat up that kid for you! To show you I'm man enough for you! This is all your fucking fault!!"

I'm left on the side of the road, jaw agape, stunned at this revelation. He jumps back in the passenger seat and they speed away. Tears spill out of my eyes and numb my lips as I wander aimlessly under the FDR, wondering if this really was all my fault.

I hear Ace's voice calling my name from the silver Honda. For a split second I envision myself running away and getting on my return flight and pretending none of this ever happened. I hear his voice again as they trail behind me.

"Come on! Get in! I'm sorry! We're going to Trisha's!" he yells from the open window. I hesitate for a moment, throw my hands up, and walk back to the car.

We get to Trisha's small converted two-bedroom apartment in Washington Heights that she shares with her dad. "He lets me do whatever I want 'cause he feels guilty for missing the first half of my life," she says with a cool emotional detachment that I envy. Lucky for her, her dad can literally sleep through anything.

As we walk up the narrow staircase, a neighbor's door cracks open and a little boy, no older than four years old, eyes me up and down and whistles, shouting, "Wadup, ma?"

Once inside, I'm met with thundering Italian techno music and a snaggletoothed Chihuahua running in circles. "Shut the fuck up, Gucci!!!" Tricia snaps. I maneuver my suitcase through the obstacle course of soiled wee-wee pads as she guides me to a dirty tagged-up loveseat. "Don't worry, it pulls out. Ace's slept here mad times." I glance at him and he immediately shifts his gaze. "Oh! And I made a drawer for you!" She proudly opens an empty drawer in her beat-up dresser covered in scribbles and stickers.

Before I can thank her, Ace says, "Trish, can I have a word with you?" His tone makes it sound more like a command than a request. He walks out of the room and she trails behind him like a lost child. I sit in silence for a moment, wondering what they could be talking about. I begin unpacking my suitcase and neatly place the contents inside the drawer. I find my return ticket and hold it in my hands. The door swings open. I instinctively crumple the ticket in my palms. I'm relieved to see it's Trish.

"What ya got there?" she asks.

I put my finger to my lips. "Shhhh." She raises the volume on her computer speakers. "It's my return flight. I might use it."

Her smile fades. "No, Julia, you can't leave again!"

"I know, but you didn't tell me he was crazy, Trish!"

"Yes, I did, I tried to warn you! Rose literally got sent away 'cause of him."

I shush her when I hear the floor shaking from approaching footsteps. I shove the ticket under a pile of jeans and shut the drawer. Ace cracks Trisha's bedroom door.

"You guys want anything from the store?" Any time Ace goes to the store, he's gone for hours. I shake my head.

"Can you leave us some blow?" Trish asks. Ace chucks a vial across the room and she catches it midair. She dumps a frosty little mountain of coke onto her desk and crushes it with her lip gloss and a MetroCard. "Shit. Do you have a dollar?"

I shake my head.

"Let me get a tampon," she says. When she leaves the room, I read the graffiti covering her entire couch. I see some tags I recognize. I notice one of her cushions is cleaner than the rest, like it's recently been flipped over. I turn the cushion over and see my name in big red letters with the words "ugly" and "dirty" next to it. My cheeks burn like I've just been slapped in the face. I quickly turn it back over.

Trish stomps back in, holding the pearly blue scented tampon applicator like a trophy. She tosses back the coke and jumps up with a "Whoop!" She swings her head back to get the drip and hands me the applicator. I blow two massive lines into each nostril. I feel the powder seep into my nasal cavities and trickle up my forehead all the way down to the back of my skull.

My mind races as I bop my head to techno beats on repeat. Do they really think I'm ugly? And who is they? And has Ace seen it? Can I trust Trish? What's going to happen when people discover I'm missing? What are my parents going to do to me?

Trisha taps away on the computer, browsing random girls' Myspace pages that all have "Italian Stallion" or "Proud Guidette" in their bios, occasionally commenting, "I want hair like this" and "Do you think she's hot?" She clicks on their images and drags them into a folder on her desktop. I pick at my cuticles, anxiously waiting for Trish to leave the room again so I can erase the slander from existence.

She catches my reflection in the mirror. "What's wrong? You look like a ghost! Do you need a drink?"

A long Newport 100 dangles from her manicured fingers, her blue eyes bloodshot and on high alert. I can't help but think that she's turning into her mom. She spins around on her computer chair to face me. I can sense her panic through her accelerated speech. "Are you, like, not having fun here?"

I want to tell her about what I saw on the couch. "I think I just need a drink."

Once she leaves the room, I grab a thick silver graffiti marker from her desk and sloppily color over the cushion. The room smells like paint fumes when she returns, and she pauses and sniffs around before glancing at her desk. Her eyes move to her desk and then back to the couch as she hands me a plastic Big Gulp cup. I wrap my warm hands around it, watching in silence as the freezer-burned ice cubes disappear into the vodka and orange juice.

When Ace finally returns, I leap into his arms. I feel so insecure and I need him to validate me. I lead him into the bedroom, where he sits me on the edge of the bed and undresses me like a doll. He runs his tongue down my neck and over my chest. He kisses my stomach until his head is in my lap. He spreads my legs and sticks his tongue out before he spreads me apart like a flower, until he is covered in my juices. I gasp. "I've never done that before!" I say in disbelief as he licks his lips and smirks.

"I know these are your favorite, the Double Stuf," he says, handing me a pack of Oreos.

"You remembered?"

"I remember everything you say."

I'm moved to tears by this seemingly insignificant gesture. That night, we fall asleep entwined in Trisha's small twin bed, swimming in a sea of cookie crumbs.

I wake up the next day to find Trish sitting on the couch and Ace at the foot of the bed in his boxers, one fist clenched, the other gripping my return ticket.

"I can explain that," I say as my voice cracks.

"You were planning on leaving?!"

I crawl back into the comforter. "No, it was just cheaper if I bought a return flight. It was a good deal!"

Trish keeps her gaze low as Ace tears my ticket into pieces, tossing the shreds all over the bed before storming out of the room. I bury my head in the pillow and hear Trisha's muffled voice whispering, "I swear, I don't know how he found it!"

I peek out from under the pillow. Fighting back tears, I manage to utter the words, "It's okay." But it's not okay. Nothing is okay, and now there's no way out.

We spend the next three weeks holed up at Trisha's. I miss my flight back to Italy. Ace misses his court appearance.

"It's a trap," he says. "They're gonna take me back to Rikers. That private school pussy's pressing charges. They're lookin' for me."

Trisha's home quickly becomes a revolving door of shady characters. Men in basketball shorts. Men in tailored suits. Some have guns. Some have gel in their hair and tweeze their eyebrows. Some have thick New York accents, and some don't speak English at all. Sometimes Ace leaves with them, disappearing for hours at a time.

"Where does he go?" I ask Trish.

"I think he's just selling coke, babe." She changes the subject. "Should I get a boob job? Look at this girl." She pulls up a large photo of a bronzed brunette. "This is the size I want. A small C-cup."

I pretend to be interested, nodding as she continues scrolling through this stranger's Myspace page. "Trish, you're fifteen. You can't get a boob job."

"I know but I have to start saving now if I want it!"

"I want a Myspace page," I tell her, "a public one." The account I've been using is secret, just to look at what my friends are doing.

"Ace's not gonna like that," she says in a warning tone.

"Okay, but why can he be on Myspace all day and I can't?"

She hesitates for a moment before opening a new tab on the screen. "You can't tell Ace I'm helping you do this." Her long acrylic nails clack away, swiftly moving across the keyboard. "I can show you how to use the codes to make it like mine if you want."

She gets up, allowing me to sit at the computer. I scroll through her list of friends and request all the names I recognize. A message suddenly pops in my inbox from an old middle school friend named Heather.

"Julia!! I saw a missing persons poster on 59th Street with your face on it! Are you ok? Everyone is looking for you!"

My palms instantly start sweating profusely. "Trish!" I yell frantically.

She rushes over. Her eyes widen as she reads over my shoulder. "We have to call Ace," she says.

"No, I have to call Veronica."

Trish scrunches her face. "Who's Veronica?"

I dig my suitcase out from under her bed and start frantically searching for my Italian cell phone.

"It's not here!" I yell.

"What isn't here? Who's Veronica?"

I ignore her and continue sifting through all the miscellaneous sentimental artifacts from my life.

"My cell phone is gone!" I scream. Trish drops down to her knees, helping me look for it, tearing apart her entire room.

"Don't trip, Jules, you can always get a new one. It didn't even work here."

I shoot her an icy glare. "It's not about that! It has my best friend's number on it."

Trisha's energy shifts, and I soften.

"I think Ace stole it." I sigh, defeated.

She nods. "Me too."

Trisha's phone starts ringing. It's Ace. I grab the phone out of her hands.

"They know I'm missing. The cops are looking for me and there's posters with my face all over the city."

"Do they know you're with me?"

"I don't know but it's a matter of time."

"Baby, don't worry about it. I got you. I love you so much. I'm not gonna let anything bad happen to you."

I want to scream that he already has, that I know he stole my phone. But I push it out of my mind and force the words "I love you too."

"My Italian princess. You know what I'm gonna do? I'm gonna go get all the posters and personally hand-deliver them all to you, okay?"

I force a chuckle but I'm not feeling any better.

Ace strolls in hours later with a small stack of posters in his hands. "We drove up and down the whole city!" he declares proudly, waving the posters in my direction.

"I look so ugly!" I say, yanking the posters out of his hands. Not only did they choose the ugliest photos of me in existence, but when I get a closer look, I notice all my identifiable information is wrong. My birth year is not 1992, I am definitely not five-nine, and I certainly weigh more than 110 pounds. I crumple the loose papers and shove them deep in the trash before Ace and Trish can notice how little my parents know about me. It's embarrassing. I suddenly feel justified in running away. I did the right thing. I'm with people who care about me now.

Ace cleans up when Vinny comes over. He puts on dress pants and gels his hair. I tease him about it. "We do business together," he says dismissively. Ace says that Vinny is climbing the ranks in an Italian crime family. "He's gonna be a made man soon," he declares proudly.

"What's this I hear about a missing poster?" Vinny asks as soon as he spots me. "How old are you, anyway?"

"Sixteen."

"Is there a reward?"

I shift uncomfortably. "No."

"Ace, let me have a word with you."

I accept my cue to leave and quietly shut the door behind me. I press my ear against the door and hear Vinny mumbling about "fifty thousand dollars." My eyes widen as a wave of paralyzing fear engulfs my body. I can't let them sell me back to my parents. Ace would never go for that, right? I have to stop them.

I swing the door open. "If you guys think my parents would pay fifty thousand dollars for me, you're out of your fucking minds." I burst out laughing, trying to get them on board with aborting this mission. "They don't even have that kind of money!"

"Babe, we would split it with you!" Ace says.

"No," I say, in shock. "It's not happening."

I slam the door shut, grab the house phone, and rush into the bathroom, locking the door behind me. I quickly turn on the hair dryer to muffle the noise. My heart feels like it's exploding through my chest as I dial *67 and punch in my dad's phone number, my hands shaking with fear. As it rings, I secretly hope he won't answer so I can just leave him a message, but I'm jolted back to reality by the sound of his familiar voice.

"Hello?"

"Hi, Daddy, it's me." My voice trembles.

"Julia? Where the fuck are you? Do you know Interpol is looking for you!"

"Please! I'm okay! Just stop looking for me, okay?"

"Not until you tell me where you are!" I sense him growing more agitated.

"Look, I told you I didn't want to be in Italy anymore! It took you guys three weeks to notice I was even missing! And you chose the ugliest photos of me for the poster! And all the information on it is wrong! You were never gonna find me with that, trust me. Just stop looking for me, I'm doing great. And if anyone calls about a ransom, don't give them the money. I'm fine. Goodbye."

I hang up the phone before he can answer and shut off the hair dryer. I walk into the living room and dig a roach out of the ashtray and light it at the window, watching the outside world go 'round without me.

The next morning, I'm woken up by the buzzer. I stumble out of bed and shuffle out to the living room, where I find Trisha's dad, his big belly spilling over his boxers, peeking out the window through the blinds.

"What's going on?" I ask, covering my mouth as I yawn.

"There's a fuckin' squad car outside, that's what's going on," he shouts at me. "Get back in the fuckin' room!"

I run into Trisha's room and shake Ace until he wakes up. "The cops are here!" He jolts up and begins pacing around, ducking under the windows and listening at the door.

"What are they here for?" Trish asks.

"Could be me," I say.

"Could be me," Ace says.

When the buzzing finally stops, Trisha's dad rushes into the room and slaps Trisha across the face so hard that it sends an echo across the entire room. She holds her face as tears well up in her eyes.

"Don't you fucking start crying now! We're the only white people on the whole fuckin' block, and you and your little friends are makin' it hot for everyone else! That's how you get us all killed, Trisha!"

I run to her aid, wrapping my arms around her as he towers over us.

"And you—" He waves his wobbly fat finger in my face. "You and your boyfriend need to find somewhere else to stay. Party's over. Pack your shit."

"Dad, no!" Trisha shrieks. "You can't do this!"

"It's okay, Trish," Ace says. "We have to leave anyway. They know we're here."

"Where are we gonna go?" I cautiously whisper, afraid to rouse any dormant anger in Ace.

"I got a spot," he replies cryptically.

The spot, as it turns out, is none other than Ace's childhood bedroom in his mother's cramped apartment in the Bronx. She greets us at the door, draped in a pink silk robe with a glass of red wine in one hand and a lit cigarette in the other. The scene is straight out of a film noir.

"Ace! I wasn't expecting company! The house is a mess!"

I peek inside at the spotless apartment.

"This is my fiancée, Julia," Ace says proudly, showing off his shiny new trophy.

"Wow! She's even more beautiful in person!"

I lean in to hug her, clutching her small frame and inhaling the sweet scent of cocoa butter.

"We're gonna be staying here for a bit. It got too hot in the city," Ace declares as he pushes past her, heading straight for his room, which looks like a landfill frozen in time. Overflowing ashtrays and dirty boxers are strewn across the floor as if he left one day in a hurry and never returned.

"I'm not allowed to clean in there," she whispers, throwing her arms up. "What can I do?"

Ace's mom is a warm and timid woman with jet-black hair and olive skin. She's petite and modest, reading romance novels and dancing to Puerto Rican music in her spare time. She's nothing like Ace, and I can tell she walks on eggshells around him. "He's just like his dad," she whispers to me after he snaps at her, and I can't help but feel sorry for her.

One evening as the dust settles from yet another explosive fight with Ace, he storms out into the night, leaving me to clean up the ruins. I carefully gather the porcelain shards of the lamp he chucked at me before he dangled my upper body out an open window. My hair is tangled and my body aches with pain. Mascara-tainted tears are streaming down my red swollen face when I hear a gentle knock at the door.

"I'm ordering Indian food. Do you want anything?" She cracks the door open, stealing a peek at the war-torn bedroom. Her eyes widen at the sight of the debris littered across the floor. I nod silently as she holds out her little hand and leads me to the living room.

"You just get comfortable," she assures me, "I'll set the table."

I watch her shuffle around the kitchen, pausing only to sip from her jumbo wineglass.

"What was Ace's dad like?"

She stops moving and pauses to think for a moment.

"He was *very* handsome," she replies, a hint of nostalgia in her voice. "He had the most electrifying blue eyes. It's where Ace gets his fair skin . . ." I nod as she trails off. "All the girls were head over heels for him!" She throws her arms up in disbelief. "Nobody could believe he wanted to be with me. I was just this tiny shy little girl, and he was this big scary tough guy."

I can sense there's more to the story besides what she is choosing to remember.

"Why didn't it work out?" I ask, watching her smile fade quickly to a frown.

The answer, I realize, is buried under years of pain and regret.

"He had a temper. He would push me around. He would break everything in the house. One day Ace and I came home, and every single thing in the house was broken. The TV was off the wall, the windows were shattered, plates, picture frames, all my clothes cut up and damaged. He broke everything in Ace's room too." Her gaze shifts to the floor. "It really traumatized Ace. He could never just relax after that."

My mind races back to my own childhood, to memories of my parents and the lasting impact they had on me. As I think about Ace's outbursts, a wave of sympathy washes over me. I realize that he's also a victim of his upbringing. He can't help being violent. It's all we know.

"What was he like when he was little?" I ask, determined to figure him out so I can fix him.

She's lost in thought as she transports herself back to another time. "He wasn't like other kids," she begins. "He was always serious, never really interested in playing with the other kids. His cousins would be out having fun, and he'd be glued to my side. He was weird. He only liked talking to grown-ups! And he was always so smart and so talented artistically." She smiles, the good old days shining bright on her face as her mind wanders through the past. "He always liked nice things. The kid had excellent taste. I mean, look at *you*!" She laughs. I crack a smile. "I think he always looked down on me 'cause we weren't as well off as some other people. But I always gave him everything he wanted. Whatever I could, I mean."

Her smile fades when she spots an envelope on the table. She reaches for it and tears it open, squinting to read the fine print. In an instant, her face falls. "'There is a warrant for your arrest,'" she mutters, setting the paper down with a sigh. There's silence as she takes a long gulp of her Malbec. Then she turns to me, forcing a smile. "I'll just leave this here so he sees it when he comes back," she says casually.

Shaking off the heavy moment, she perks up and adds, "I hope you like vanilla ice cream!"

Once she has her back turned, my eyes dart over to the envelope. My heart drops like a rock. The letter is addressed to a foreign name I've never heard before: Simon Velez. The name sends a wave of anger and betrayal through my veins. I can't believe he lied about his name! I can't help but wonder what else he's been keeping from me. I glance down at the tattoo on my wrist, his ridiculous nickname permanently etched into my skin, and begin anxiously picking at it.

I rarely see Trish anymore. Ace says I shouldn't trust her.

"You saw what they wrote about you on the couch?" he says, rejecting her repeated phone calls.

He dismisses my requests to go outside or see people or go to parties.

He spends his days on Myspace and playing World of Warcraft, barely acknowledging my presence. He's been keeping me locked up like a forgotten prisoner, never allowing me to leave the house by myself. We only venture out of the house at night to grab a slice of pizza, always looking over our shoulders. I barely recognize myself anymore. I feel like a shadow of my former self. My clothes no longer fit. My once clear complexion is now speckled with zits.

When I complain, he dismisses my concern with a sinister grin, telling me it's for my own good, that guys won't be attracted to me now and he can have me all for himself. He lies to me often, about everything, and I begin to lose sight of what is real and what is a figment of his imagination. What if I'm just a figment of his imagination?

Sometimes I wake up in the middle of the night and he's nowhere to be found. He disappears often and when he returns, he's always armed with a convoluted, confusing excuse. His phone died and he got locked out, Dougie's car broke down on the highway, he got lost on the way home. I know he's lying but I've learned to pick my battles wisely, and when I do try to speak up for myself, I'm almost always met with rage.

"We're on the run! Get that through your thick skull. You wanna get me locked up?"

After our fights, Ace used to comfort me, pleading with tears in his eyes. He'd get on his knees and beg for forgiveness, promising to never lay a hand on me again. Once I'd forgiven him, we'd have passionate, explosive makeup sex. I was addicted to it. Now he just pushes me aside and goes back to his computer, keeping his eyes glued to the screen.

I no longer feel bound by passionate love, but I've threatened to leave him so many times that he barely acknowledges my hollow warnings. I decide it's time to take some of my power back. I start devising an escape plan. I collect loose change scattered around on the floor and memorize the schedule for the bus to Manhattan.

I glance at the clock. It's 6:04 p.m., only eleven minutes until the last bus leaves for the city. I grab my suitcase from the closet and begin stuffing it with whatever I can find.

"I'm leaving," I announce as he taps away on the keyboard.

As expected, he brushes off my words as empty threats, but I won't be deterred. I zip up my suitcase, feeling the grounding weight of the quarters in my pocket. His gaze is still fixed on the screen when I see the time, 6:08. I rush to the front door and quickly unlock it, shutting it quietly so as not to startle him out of his Internet trance. I charge down the hallway toward the elevators. I'm already out of breath by the time I press the button. The adrenaline courses through my veins as I wait for it to arrive. I glance back at the door, half expecting him to burst through it at any second. After what feels like forever, I make a run for the staircase, dragging my heavy suitcase down the flights of stairs.

I suddenly hear the door creak open and my heart drops. I let go of my suitcase and try to run away, but Ace jumps through the air, down an entire flight of stairs, and lands directly in front of me, blocking my path. He yanks my suitcase up, snapping the metal handle off, and begins to beat me with it. I scream in agony, begging him to stop, but he covers my mouth with his palm and drags me back up the stairs by my neck. Once we're back inside the apartment, I look at the clock. It's 6:15.

A few weeks later, there's a knock at the door. Ace tiptoes to the peephole and rushes back into the bedroom. "It's DTs," he whispers. I jump out of bed and listen in the doorway.

"We know you're in there. We just wanna talk," they shout through the door. "We can do this the easy way or the hard way!"

They slide a card under the door, and once they're gone, I quickly pick it up.

"We should just see what it's about, maybe they're looking for me," I suggest.

Ace seems hesitant. "We can't keep running, and it's not like they can arrest you through the phone," I reason.

He nods reluctantly. I grab the phone and dial the number on the card, masking our number with *67. "Put it on speaker," he instructs me. Time seems to stop as we huddle over the phone.

"Detective Malone speaking."

Ace pauses and I encourage him. "Hey, I think you guys are looking for me. You left a card under my mom's door."

"Ace, Ace, Ace, we've been lookin' for you, kid," Detective Malone

confirms. "You got a girl with you. She's sixteen, and her dad's been bust-
ing our balls. If you send her home, the DA won't press charges. 'Cause
right now, it's looking like kidnapping and statutory rape."

Ace looks at me, fuming. "I didn't kidnap her, she chose to be with me!"

I think about the word "kidnapping," keeping my eyes low to avoid
his gaze.

"Spare me the details, please. Whatever the case may be, she has
to go home," Detective Malone says firmly, sending a glimmer of hope
my way. "And you gotta come down to the station to sort a few things
out."

"What things?" Ace asks.

"We wanna ask you about a fight that occurred outside a school a
few months back. Don't worry, we won't arrest you. We just need your
version of events."

Ace hangs up and immediately calls his lawyer, a public defender.

"Listen," his lawyer advises, "if the cops wanna talk to you, there's no
way around it. I'll go with you in the morning."

Ace hangs up and lets out a deep sigh. The fear emanating from him
is palpable, a far cry from the cocky, arrogant tough guy I first met.

"I don't know if I should do it," he says softly.

"We'll both do it. I'll turn myself in in the morning while you go to
the station," I suggest.

Later that night, we don't argue, we don't fight. Instead, we order
chicken and waffles and watch silly Adam Sandler movies all night,
laughing and pausing only to make love.

At dawn, I help him get dressed in a suit and tie. It's the first time
I've ever seen him dressed up like this. He could almost pass for normal
at a glance. I wrap my arms around his lean frame and whisper in his ear,
"Don't worry, I'll see you later. Okay?"

"You promise?" he asks me with the same naïveté as a child.

I bite my nails on the long bus ride to Manhattan. A part of me is nervous and afraid. The other part feels lighter, like I've just been relieved

of a soul-crushing weight. I stare out the window, the feeling of dread intensifying as we get closer to Manhattan.

The moment I arrive at the precinct, I take a deep breath and casually announce to the lady at the front desk, "Hi, I'm Julia Fox. I ran away from my home. I'm turning myself in."

The lady pops her gum and shoots me a puzzled look. "Umm, okay, wait right here."

I take a seat on the linoleum chair and stare at the clock for what feels like forever until two officers appear before me. One is bald, and the other is overweight.

"Well, well, there she is!" the bald one says. "Come with us, please."

They lead me to a little room with a desk and sit directly across from me.

"We just wanna ask you a few questions," the fat one says, "to make sure you're okay."

"I'm fine," I say.

Their eyes scan the bruises on my arms. "How did you get those?"

"I just bruise easily. I'm not, like, being abused or anything."

"How could you do this to your parents?" the bald one asks.

"I didn't think they would care," I say, shrugging.

"What about your boyfriend, what's his name?"

"Ace," the fat one interjects.

"Oh, right, that troublemaker."

"Can I go home now please?" I ask politely.

"Your dad is on his way to come get you now."

"He is?"

"Should be here any minute."

I slouch in my chair and zone out as they continue firing questions at me. "What kind of activities is Ace involved in? Where were you guys hiding out? Do you know if he owns a pair of brass knuckles?"

My mind drifts to Ace. He must be done at the station by now.

I snap out of it only when I hear my dad's familiar voice coming from the main room.

I shift nervously in my seat as an officer leads my dad into the tiny room. He shudders when our eyes meet. I can tell by his face that he wishes he could slap the shit out of me. I'm relieved there are cops around.

The walk home is silent. He looks at me only to shake his head and mumble under his breath, "You really pulled some shit this time, Julia."

He speed-walks as I trail behind him, struggling to keep up.

Once I'm home, my mom emerges from her bedroom, and she too barely acknowledges me or the bruises covering my entire body.

"You gained so much weight," she points out as I pass her in the hallway.

Feeling rejected, I run for the house phone and lock myself in the bathroom. I dial Ace's number, but it goes straight to voicemail. A helpless feeling washes over me, and I feel powerless. "I'm going for a walk," I yell to no one in particular before sprinting to the bus stop to go back to the Bronx.

It's dark out by the time I arrive. I push the buzzer and I'm let inside. I knock on the door. My heart races as I hope for him to be on the other side. But when the door cracks open, it's not him. It's his mom, greeting me with her usual robe and a glass of wine in hand.

"Julia! What are you doing here? Why didn't you call first?"

I feel like a massive burden. "I'm sorry, I don't know your number by heart and Ace's phone was off. I panicked."

"Well, that's okay! Come inside!" She steps aside, allowing me entry.

"Is Ace here?"

She shifts her eyes to the floor. "They booked him, honey."

"What does this mean?"

"He's waiting to see the judge. We'll have to see in the morning if they let him—"

I interrupt her, my voice shaky. "Can I sleep here?"

She hesitates, and I suddenly feel like a stranger, like I didn't just live here for the past three months.

"Um, yeah, I don't see why not," she finally responds.

I force a smile, a sense of impending doom looming over my head.

As I enter his room and survey the mess, I instinctively begin tidying up, placing each item back in its designated space. I pick up his worn boxers and press them to my face, inhaling the sweet-and-sour scent of his sweat. I can't help but feel like a piece of me is missing, like the sensation of running your tongue over the space where a lost tooth used to be. Inquisitively, I thumb through his sketchbooks, which are covered with graffiti tags, doodles in bubble letters, and the occasional masterpiece.

My gaze wanders toward his computer chair, now unoccupied, and I sink into it, basking in its familiar comfort. I reach over and press the power button, but a password prompt stops me in my tracks. I notice a hint option and click on it, revealing the word "bloodz." I remember him telling me about his stint in the street gang during his high school years. I rack my brain, trying to remember what he said his gang name was.

Suddenly, I remember the words "Bloody Oz" written in red graphic bubble letters on one of his notebooks. I enter the words into the password box, and with a click I'm granted access to his secret hidden universe that he always kept separate from me.

I scan his desktop, aimlessly clicking on various icons until my attention is drawn to a cluster of icons in the corner of the screen. I begin rearranging them only to reveal an inconspicuous untitled folder buried beneath. A wave of curiosity washes over me, and without hesitation, I click on it. What I find leaves me stunned: an entire collection of X-rated photographs. Some look old. Some look recent. As I scroll through the images, I spot Liana in one of them, naked in bed between Ace and another girl, her thick signature glasses peeking up from under a sheet as her friend's bare leg is draped over his body.

As I scroll through the endless photographs, the mouse pad becomes slick with sweat. My heart thumps in my chest so loudly that it drowns out any other noise. Despite the stab in the heart that each picture brings, I can't seem to stop myself from clicking. My eyes fixate on one girl in particular—a petite girl with long chestnut hair, a spray tan, and the biggest boobs I've ever seen. She appears in numerous photos, often accompanied by Trish. Thoughts zip rapidly through my brain. How could they do this to me? Was Trish in on it? Did she cover for him?

The worst part is that I can't even call him and tell him I know about him cheating on me. I have to put these feelings on a shelf and wait until he gets out, secretly hoping that maybe there's an explanation.

In the morning, Ace's mom creeps into the room and gently nudges me out of my restless sleep. She doesn't know that I spent the entire night going through every document, album, and folder on his computer. I slept no more than thirty minutes.

As she ushers me out of his room, I take one last lingering glance at the space I once called home, knowing that I'll never step foot in here again. The evidence I uncovered has tainted what few good memories I have of this place, and I'll never be able to unsee it, as much as a part of me wishes I could.

With a heavy heart, I follow Ace's mom out of the apartment, choosing to leave behind all the humiliating secrets trapped within those walls.

I'm struggling to mask my anger on the bus ride to city hall when it becomes too much to bear, and I blurt out, "Did you know Ace's girlfriend before me?"

She eyes me suspiciously and nods in response. "Yes, why?"

I take a deep breath before continuing. "What did she look like?"

She pauses for a moment. "Not nearly as pretty as you, don't worry."

I can't help but smile at her words. "Did she have huge tits?"

Ace's mom nods with a hint of sympathy in her expression. "Yeah, the poor thing had very bad back pain."

"I think he is still hooking up with her," I admit, my voice barely above a whisper.

She sighs and shakes her head. "Whatever it is, now is not the time to deal with it," she tells me firmly. I nod in agreement and shift my gaze out the window, feeling a range of emotions too complicated to put into words.

We spend the entire day waiting at the courthouse, with Ace's lawyer, the public defender, advising us to stay put. "It looks better if there's people in the chamber," he tells us. As the hours drag on, I feel myself crossing the five stages of grief. I'm in the "denial" stage when Ace is finally called before the judge. I spring to my feet at the sound of his name, watching him intently as he shuffles across the room in shackles, still in the wrinkled shirt and tie from the day before. My anger evaporates when I see how pale and miserable he looks. He turns to face me just long enough to mouth the words: "I love you."

The judge doesn't look as happy to see him as I am. "How many last chances can a person get?" she demands. "We were so good to you. We gave you bail, we offered you the program, and we even let you keep your freedom. All you had to do was stop fighting. You ever hear the expression 'Fool me once, shame on you. Fool me twice, shame on me'? That's it, no more chances. I'm sending you back to Rikers. No bail."

She strikes her gavel with finality. Ace spins around, his shackles clanking as he lifts his hand to his heart. I rush toward the wooden railing separating us and call out to him, "I love you so much. Find a way to call me!"

A security guard shouts, "Ma'am, you can't do that. I'm gonna have to ask you to leave."

I ignore him and lock eyes with Ace.

"Make sure my mom puts money in my commissary!" he shouts as another security guard drags him away.

He disappears into the back room. His mom follows me out into the hallway.

"That was like a scene out of a movie," she says with a sigh. "I need a drink."

"We need to put money in his account," I say urgently.

"Doll, it's gonna take a while for them to process him. I'll keep checking the system. I've been down this road before. You go home and get some rest."

As we ride the 6 train, the air between us is thick with tension. We arrive at 86th Street, and I give her a quick hug before getting off. On my walk home, I pass Kyle's apartment, where Ace and I first met. I sit on the stoop, mentally transporting back to the first night—taking ecstasy and getting tattoos, feeling like we were invincible. It's not so hard to believe that just nine months later we would be here. We were doomed from the start.

The next few days, I find myself confined to the bunk bed that I now have to share with my brother. I lie there, clutching the house phone in one hand and the hair dryer in the other, using it to drown out the noise in the apartment, but mostly to drown out the noise in my own head.

Whenever the phone rings, I close my eyes and pray that it's going to be Ace on the other end. My dad starts to notice my withdrawal and becomes concerned. He barges into my room with a worried look on his face.

"What happened to all your friends? You used to have so many friends."

"Shut up!" I scream at him in agonizing pain. "Get the fuck out!"

Four days later I finally get a call from an unknown number. I answer it and I'm met with an automated recording.

"An inmate at Rikers Island . . . Press pound to accept the call."

I press pound and hear his familiar breathing on the other end.

"Baby, you there?"

"Yeah, I'm here," I manage to say before I break down sobbing.

"Baby, don't cry. I'll get out, don't worry."

I get ahold of myself and listen closely as he instructs me on his visiting days, what I need to bring for him, and how to put money in his account. I grab a pen and scribble down his inmate and case numbers as well as "Boxers no logo. Socks white. Tank tops white. XL sweatpants gray. Sweatshirt gray. No red. No blue."

After a few minutes, the call gets disconnected, but I know what I have to do. That night, I wait until my dad is fast asleep and slither into his room on my stomach, pulling out five twenty-dollar bills from his wallet.

The next day, I take two trains and a bus all the way to Rikers Island.

Once we cross the long bridge onto the island, I'm instantly hit with an awful stench of sewage and mold. The facility looks grim and out of place against the vibrant New York City backdrop.

They shuffle us from base to base like cattle, barking orders and often singling someone out for some good old-fashioned public humiliation. Sometimes that person is me. I get yelled at because I don't have quarters for the locker, I get yelled at because my arms are bare, I get yelled at for standing in the wrong place to wait for the bus.

But that's not the worst part. The waiting is the worst part. Luckily the people-watching here is supreme. After a few hours of being shuttled around, I finally make it to the visiting area, where I'm told to wait in an adjacent room enclosed by bars. Why does it feel like I'm the inmate?

I sit alone, watching people have their visits for an hour, before I'm called. When I'm led onto the floor, I feel a wave of eyeballs roll onto me. I'm escorted to a small plastic table where I'm told to wait some more. I notice the colorful murals covering the walls, probably to make the children feel comfortable, I think to myself. I sit down on the miniature chair and a few minutes later, Ace appears in a gray jumpsuit and plastic slippers.

I stand up and leap into his embrace. I take a big inhale. He smells different.

A guard snaps at us, "No touching!" Ace releases me instantly and we both sit down. I notice that his eyebrows look freshly tweezed and penciled in. My jealousy kicks in and my mind travels to the dark place where the voices are telling me another girl visited him and dropped off supplies first.

He immediately senses a shift in my energy. "What's wrong?"

"Nothing," I say passive-aggressively.

"Two seconds in and you're already being a bitch. Please don't do this right now. You have no idea how much I need—"

I cut him off. "Did you cheat on me?"

His eyes widen. He stutters, "Cheat on you?! Are you crazy? When would I have had the chance?"

"Please! You disappeared all the fucking time!"

People start turning around to see the commotion. "To make money! So you could smoke weed and sit on your ass eating Happy Meals all day!" He's yelling now.

"I didn't wanna do that!!!" I yell back. "You made me do that!"

A guard comes over and informs us that he will end our visit if we continue arguing. I didn't just travel two hours and wait another four hours to get kicked out. I take a deep breath and collect myself, changing the subject. "What have you been doing?"

"Besides dreaming about you? Nothing."

"Did you make friends?"

"There's no friends in jail, sweetheart. I ran into a few guys from the neighborhood but I'm just sticking to myself and staying out of trouble."

"That's good," I say wryly.

"There's no one else, Julia. I only wanna be with you. Since the moment I laid eyes on you, I thought to myself, I'm gonna marry that girl." I chuckle and roll my eyes. "I'm serious! You're my soulmate. You're my match. I want to marry you."

He rips the corner off the visit slip and rolls it up to make a ring. "Julia, will you marry me?" He grabs my hand and slides it on my finger.

"No touching!" the guard yells as he swiftly makes his way toward us. "That's it, buddy, visit's over."

Ace jumps to his feet and begins arguing with the guard. Everyone turns to watch us.

"If you don't cool it, I'm gonna put her down as banned!" The guard grabs him by the arm and then shifts his attention to me. "You stay here!"

Ace and I keep our eyes fixed on each other as he's dragged away. I remain seated at the table, staring at the empty seat in front of me, trying to ignore the gawking eyes. I twirl the paper ring around my finger and smile.

Before boarding the bus to leave Rikers, I deposit forty dollars in Ace's commissary so he can call me. I beg my dad to get me a cell phone. "If you go to school," he bargains with me. Following my grandma's advice, he enrolls me in Saint Vincent's, an all-girls' Catholic school in Midtown, and gets me a silver Razr.

I spend my days glued to my phone, afraid to miss any of Ace's calls for fear of how he might react. His jealous outbursts are more frequent. Any time I mention the photos on his computer and call him out on his lies, he calls me heartless. "How can you do this to me while I'm locked up?!" After a few weeks of attending Saint Vincent's, I decide to drop out, since I spent most of the school day locked in a bathroom stall talking to Ace. I can't balance his emotional load and going to class.

He fluctuates from rage to complete despair and helplessness in a matter of seconds. I can't keep up with his ever-changing moods, and I never know which version of him I'm talking to until it's already too late. I'm on a roller coaster from hell that I just can't seem to get off of. When I hang up on him, he calls me repeatedly. If I shut off my phone, he starts calling my house phone and talks to my dad. I discover they have been having long conversations. Ace even managed to convince my dad that he's actually trying to help me. He's infiltrated every aspect of my life, and the only time I feel at peace is at night, when he's locked in his cell.

He always knows exactly what I'm doing, who I'm talking to, and where I'm going. Sometimes he's even able to tell me what color shirt I'm wearing. He warns me that he's having me followed. I don't know who to trust anymore, and I'm losing my mind. I discover that Trish, who still had my Myspace log-in, was sending Ace photos of my conversations.

This sends me in a spiral, and I contact my cell phone provider to have Ace's number permanently blocked from calling me. But then the letters start arriving, each more graphic and gruesome than the last. One specific letter describes in detail how he wants to murder me and my entire family. First he would tie my father and little brother to a chair and rape my mother in front of them. Then he would chop her body into little pieces before executing the rest of my family before me. For the grand finale, he would kill himself. The letters are usually accompanied by detailed and very realistic sketches of demons and angels and my naked body nailed to a cross.

I decide that I've had enough. I'm going to end things with him. After weeks of him calling the house phone, I finally decide to pick up. I speak at a low octave, calm and cool, so as not to agitate him.

"I really think I just need to focus on myself. I'm not trying to date other people, so don't jump to conclusions. This isn't healthy for either of us. Please, you have to let me go."

"Let you go?" he asks, chuckling. "I'm never letting you go! You belong to me! I have your fucking name on my arm! Everyone knows you're mine!"

"If you don't let me go, I'm gonna kill myself!" I plead with him, tears streaming down my face, desperate. "You make me wanna die, Ace! You ruined my life!"

I place the phone on the counter. I can still hear him yelling unintelligibly. I frantically pace around, opening drawers, until I spot a shiny little box cutter. I hold it in my hands and without a second thought, I slash my wrist with it.

I pick up the receiver and tell him, "I just slit my wrists and I'm gonna die and it's all your fault."

I hang up and lie on the floor, dozing off as droplets of blood ooze onto the white kitchen tiles around me. I'm startled when I hear the buzzer. I stumble up to answer it. "It's the police."

I run to clean the blood off the floor. I slip the razor blade in my back pocket and throw on a long-sleeved shirt to cover the gash. I open the door to four officers, three men and a woman.

"Is there a problem?" I ask casually.

"We received a call about a suicide attempt. Are you the only one here?"

I nod.

"Where are your parents?"

"Work."

Truth is, my mom moved back to Italy with my baby brother. My grandpa's health had gotten worse and she needed to be close to him. My dad is there for a few weeks, helping her with the baby, but I can't tell them that. I'm pretty sure it's illegal to leave a minor unattended.

"Do you mind if we have a look around?"

I nod as they scan the apartment.

"Can you show us your wrists?"

I hesitate as they all crowd around me. I lift up my sleeves, revealing the bloody gash. One of the officers picks up his radio and says, "She's injured. We need an ambulance."

I immediately pull back. "No! Please! You don't understand, I'm really fine! I was just frustrated! I don't actually wanna die."

"We can't make that call," the female officer says. "Most likely they'll just sew you up and let you go home."

I take a deep breath, surrendering to the situation. I don't have any more energy left in me to fight.

I'm taken to the mental emergency room for a full psych evaluation at New York–Presbyterian. The room is more of a stall, no bigger than five feet by five feet, with a hard plastic bed. No pillow and no sheets. This is a holding cell meant to be occupied for less than twenty-four hours. Since my parents aren't coming to get me, I'm forced to stay in the cubicle for over seventy-two hours. No phone. No TV. But strangely, I feel free. I'm no longer in fight-or-flight. I can finally exhale. I feel a sense of peace and tranquility.

I spend my time writing poems and drawing pictures. I read books and make up songs to sing to myself. The nurses ask me if I know when my parents will be coming to get me. "I think soon," I tell them, knowing damn well that nobody is coming. I'm secretly relieved they're far away from this chaos. They're safe from Ace.

Eventually they escort me upstairs to the eleventh-floor to the psych ward. Everything is a different shade of green. Lime green, pale green, hunter green. The fluorescent lights make the whole place look sterile and depressing. The windows are sealed shut and the sharp smell of stale urine lingers, trapped in the air. There is one television in the center of the room. It's off but everyone is huddled around it anyway, as if it's going to magically turn on at any minute.

They sequester my clothing and jewelry and hand me mint-green scrubs and lead me down a narrow corridor to the room I'm going to be sharing with a girl named Tiffany.

Tiffany claims to be a witch. Within a few minutes of meeting me, she tells me she can feel from my energy that I'm a witch too. Naturally, I choose to believe her. Shortly after, she asks me bluntly if I want to be her girlfriend. Tiffany isn't conventionally attractive, but she has an intense gaze. Her eyes are a deep dark brown, almost black, and her pupils are like long black tunnels with no end.

Time seems to drag on forever in the psych ward. Ten minutes feels like an hour, an hour feels like a day. The main room offers limited entertainment options, with little to do besides walking around in circles in the main room or playing ping-pong. All the board games have pieces missing, and all the seats and couches have dried urine caked on them that nobody ever bothers to clean. The TV can only be used on weekends, and the staff are the ones who decide what movies we get to watch.

Tiffany and I spend most of our days hiding in the bathroom and smoking cigarettes a visitor smuggled in for her, blowing the smoke into a vent in the ceiling. We close our eyes, press our palms together, and channel all our energy into each other in an attempt to cast spells.

"Can you feel it?" she asks.

I'm not sure what I'm supposed to be feeling but I nod anyway. She casts her spell on her ex-boyfriend's new girlfriend. I cast mine on Ace.

After a week at the psych ward with no word from Ace, I'm convinced my spell must have worked. Then one day the guy who calls complaint hotlines on every product he can get his hands on yells out to the floor, "Is there a Julia here?"

Fear strikes me as I make my way over to him. He holds out the receiver and I press it to my ear, listening closely before saying anything. I recognize the breathing. It's Ace. He found me.

"How did you get this number?"

"I had to call every hospital in the city! I was so worried about you. I thought you died." I remain silent, finding a brief sense of comfort in his familiar voice. "Are you there?"

"Yeah," I reply coldly.

"Look, I know you hate me but I really want to be a better man for you." His voice trembles. I feel his anguish through the phone. "You have no idea how miserable I am here. I got jumped yesterday. They had to take me to medical, and all I could think about was that I didn't wanna die before telling you how much I love you."

I take a deep breath. The sweat from my palm trickles down the receiver as I twist the cord tightly around my other hand. I start to feel bad for him.

"Please, Julia, say something to me, please! I only have one more minute left on the call."

"Why did you get jumped?"

"I was hogging the phone trying to find *you*," he says.

I smile. "You deserved it. It's your karma."

"I know. Are we even now?"

"No," I say.

The call disconnects and I pass the phone back to the complaint-hotline man, who's been standing over my shoulder tapping his foot. When I go back to playing ping-pong with Tiffany, I can't seem to hit the ball anymore. My hand is shaky. My mind is somewhere else.

The phone rings again.

"If it's for me, I'm not here!" I yell across the room. Complaint-hotline man rolls his eyes and mumbles, "I'm not your secretary," loud enough for me to hear it. I keep one eye on him and one on the game, all the while pretending to be unbothered. I can't hear what he's saying but his body language says it all. He slams down the receiver, and as soon as he does, it starts ringing again. I see him growing increasingly agitated as he repeatedly slams the receiver down. I run over to him and grab the phone out of his hands and yell into it, "Stop doing this to me!!! Just let me go! It's over! You're a cheater and a liar and you hit me. Just leave me the fuck alone!"

I slam the receiver down and run into my room, where I can still hear the phone ringing.

The doctors finally get ahold of my dad. I'm informed that he'll be coming to pick me up Thursday morning. A rush of excitement surges through me at the thought of leaving. I've been here ten days and I'm starting to feel claustrophobic. The food is inedible. I trade my meals for cups of rice pudding. I can't stand the stench that gets caught in my hair and in my clothes. No matter how hard I scrub, it's always there. The hospital no longer feels like a safe space now that I have panic attacks every time the phone rings. But the outside world scares me too. How am I gonna dodge Ace? Who am I going to hang out with? I'm pretty sure Trish is a snitch and is the one who's been telling him my whereabouts.

I decide to call Danny, the friend I used to explore the Ramble with. Hers is the only number I still know by heart. I hesitate before dialing her number. We haven't spoken much since middle school. I feel self-conscious and ashamed of my predicament.

She gasps and drops the phone when she hears my voice. "You bitch! Where have you been?! You had us all so scared. Oh my God! My mom saw your missing poster! She called your dad, and they talked for like an hour."

"I'm actually in the mental hospital right now," I say with a giggle, to keep the mood light.

"What?!" Her tone softens to a whisper. "Are you hearing voices? 'Cause that was happening to me, and I had to take a break from–"

"No! It's a long story but I'm fine. I think I'm getting out soon. We should hang out. I miss you."

"Try to get out by Friday! There's supposed to be a really fun party! We can go together!"

"Yay! I have something to look forward to!" This is the type of normalcy that I crave with every ounce of my being.

"Are you still dating Ace?"

"No. That's over. He's, like, obsessed with me, though. He won't leave me alone."

"I only really know him 'cause I used to cop blow off him. I'm sad he went away, I miss his stuff."

"I gotta go, but I love you. I'll see you Friday!"

"Love you, bitch!"

I hang up the phone and I'm in a good mood for the rest of the day. I think about what I'm going to wear to the party. I daydream about all the people I'll meet and all the friends I'll make, and none of them will know Ace or anything about me.

I wake up early Thursday morning. I shower and pack up all the trinkets I've accumulated during my stay: a notebook, a beaded necklace gifted to me from Tiffany, a protective crystal, a pack of matches, a few loose Newports. I patiently wait in the main room, with a clear view of the tempered glass doors. Time feels extra slow today. I try to distract myself, doodling in my notebook, but my eyes keep darting back to the clock.

"Julia, your dad is here!" I hear someone call out.

I spin around in my chair to see my dad already in a conference room talking with a doctor. "How did he sneak in without me seeing him?" I whisper to myself.

I run up to the glass and pound on the window to get his attention. I wave and mouth, "Let me in," but he just looks away from me. The doctor comes to the door and informs me that I'll need to wait. I start to get a bad feeling. Whatever they're talking about doesn't seem good. My dad looks pissed.

Once they let me in, I eagerly ask, "Can we go now?" The doctor tells me to sit down, then they both pause to look at each other.

"Julia," the doctor says, "we think you could benefit from staying a little bit longer."

I jump up from my chair, and my eyes instantly fill up with tears. "What? Why?!" I yell, looking directly at my dad.

"Sweetie, you need to calm down," my dad says in a controlled monotone, as if he's handling a wild animal.

"No! I've been here two weeks already! Did you know they don't let us open a window or go outside? How are a bunch of sick people supposed to get better sitting under fluorescent lights with no sunshine or fresh air?"

The doctor interrupts me. "We just want you to get better, Julia. My colleagues and I think you can be treated with Seroquel. It's very effective in treating your type—"

"No! I don't need medication! I need to go home. I have to enroll in school. I have plans with my friend tomorrow."

At this point I've already given up. I know I won't be going home. I shoot a look at my dad. "You traitor."

"Can't she just take the medication at home?" my dad asks the doctor.

"We would need to keep her for observation," the doctor says, holding the contract my dad had to sign to agree to have me medicated.

"I'm not a guinea pig!" I scream at the top of my lungs. "I'm a human being! I'm not taking your drugs!"

Two nurses enter the room and escort me away. They put me in a tiny padded room with a plastic bed in it. One of the nurses holds out a little plastic cup with a big capsule in it. I shake my head and cross my arms.

"If you don't wanna take your meds orally, that's fine," he says. "We have other ways." His eyes shift in the direction of the bed, where I notice there are shackles. I grudgingly open my mouth. He tips the contents into my mouth and hands me a cup of water.

"Let me see."

I open my mouth and stick out my tongue. Once he's satisfied, he opens the door and lets me out.

I see Tiffany playing Scrabble and sit down at the table. I start feeling loopy and groggy. I pick up the letters and start placing them on the board.

"Uhh. GLOOP? That's not a word," Tiffany says with a confused look on her face. I start giggling uncontrollably, until my giggle turns into full-blown laughter, as tears stream down my face.

The next morning, I wake up in my bed with little recollection of how I got there. I'm shocked when I discover that I've been out cold for sixteen hours. I run to the phone and call my dad.

"Please, Daddy," I plead with him, "you have to get me out of here. The medicine is too strong!"

"Just do what they say, and they'll let you out," he says.

I slam the phone down and call Danny. "I'm not gonna make it to the party tonight," I tell her.

She seems distracted and in a rush. "It's fine," she says, "I don't think I'm gonna go out anyway."

"Oh, okay," I say with a sigh of relief. "I made such a scene when they said I couldn't leave 'cause I wanted to go so bad."

She doesn't respond.

"Are you there?"

"Yeah. I have a call on the other line. Can I call you back?"

"Yeah, for sure. Don't forget!!"

She hangs up, and I get a strange feeling something is off.

A couple minutes later the phone rings and I immediately answer it, thinking it's her.

"What's this I hear about you going to a party?" Ace asks in a low whisper before letting out a demonic laugh.

"I'm in a mental hospital," I say. "I don't know what party you're talking about."

"Don't forget, Julia, all your little friends work for ME. Your BFFs would sell you out for an eight ball of coke. It's sad, really. I feel bad for you."

My heart races as the rage builds in my chest. I clench my jaw and tell him, "I hope you drop the soap every day for the rest of your life."

I slam the receiver down and call Danny back, except she doesn't answer.

I make up my mind then and there that I will no longer be afraid of him. I'm not going to let him have that over me. I'm not going to give him the power to continue ruining my life. I'm not going to open his letters, answer his calls, or talk to any of my "friends" who keep tabs on me for him. I'm getting my tattoo covered as soon as I get out.

I am no longer his property.

5

AFTERSHOCK

When I finally get out of the hospital, my dad enrolls me in a public high school downtown, and I change my cell phone number. My dad intercepts the letters from Ace and hides them from me. I slowly start to feel free of Ace's grasp. He doesn't dictate my every move anymore. He somehow gets my new number and the calls start coming in. I can screen the ones coming from the Island. It's when he has other people three-way-call me that it gets tricky. It doesn't affect me, though. His threats fall flat. I smoke so much weed and pop so many pills that I wouldn't give a fuck either way. I laugh when he tells me he's going to kill himself. I encourage him to do it, taunting him, screaming, "You won't!!!!!!!!" before hanging up on him. I feel nothing. It's like that part of my brain is shut off.

Going to school is tough. I can't sit still. I can't pay attention. I've been labeled the "weird white girl with a fat ass." I only have two friends, and I spend most of the day in the library reading books about child abuse or in the computer room surfing the Internet. "Cheap apartment Hawaii" is my most common search.

Veronica lives with my mom in her apartment in Italy. She dropped out of school and helps my mom full-time with my three-year-old brother. She's officially a part of the family. She calls me one day to tell me she's coming to visit with my mom for the holidays. I'm thrilled at the thought of having her here. I've reconnected with some old friends from middle school who never liked Ace, and I reconnected with Liana on Myspace. She goes to school nearby, and we meet up and smoke blunts in Tompkins Square Park. I find her crazy outfits amusing. The neon, the leather, the glow sticks, the rainbow hair, the fishnets, the makeup. She's a welcome change from the wannabe Guidettes I've been forced to be around.

I don't tell Liana that I know about the threesome she had with Ace. I never mention his name. I prefer to pretend he doesn't exist, even though I have nightmares and sometimes feel like I'm being watched. I keep the ringer on my cell phone off so I'm not triggered by the dreadful little jingle I've come to associate with his voice.

It starts gnawing at me, and one day, after a few swigs from a vanilla Svedka bottle, I confront Liana. "I saw a photo on Ace's computer of you and a blond girl naked in bed with him."

She looks surprised by my statement but answers honestly. "It was the worst threesome ever," she admits. I can't help but smile. "I swear I had no idea about you," she adds quickly. That's all I needed to hear. "Now that we're on the subject, Ace's been calling me, but I swear I don't answer."

"Why didn't you tell me?" I ask her, my suspicions raised after having been betrayed by my supposed friends before.

Liana shrugs. "He kills the vibe, bro." Fair enough.

I start going out more often and intentionally befriending people Ace always warned me about, a graffiti crew he had dubbed his sworn enemies. It's my silent revenge.

I come to find that aside from sleeping with these guys, I actually have fun with them. We hang out in dimly lit bedrooms permeated with the scent of bongwater and spray paint. Stolen bike parts are strewn about the floor. The walls are covered in paint and crooked canvases. I find comfort in the gritty chaos. We listen to MF Doom, Wu-Tang Clan, KRS-One, UGK, Three 6 Mafia, and Mobb Deep and drink Sidewalk Slammers: half a forty with half a Four Loko. They all sell weed, so the blunts are the fattest. At night, we climb scaffoldings, scale buildings, and throw wild parties in abandoned tunnels underground. I get a rush from spray-painting my name all over the city, and the guys like having me around to be the lookout.

Being introduced to a whole new world downtown is eye-opening. All these guys are LES natives, and they know their way around the shadows. They show me all their local spots like CrowBar, Hanger Bar, Mars Bar, Mama's Bar, Kate's Joint, Max Fish, Lit Lounge, Pyramid Club, Iggy's, Boss Tweed's, and Blarney Cove. They like that I'm crafty and always looking for a come-up, and I like that they're always around.

Everyone I hang out with goes by nicknames, gang names, or tag names. I realize I don't know anyone's real name. But they all know mine. "JULIA FOX!" they yell as they ride past me on their bikes or when they see me walk into a crowded room. My name and likeness quickly permeate the city when I pose semi-nude for a prominent street artist. Soon my painted body is splashed across canvases all over West Broadway. I still can't legally drink but my image is now on display in nightclubs all over Manhattan. It even makes a cameo in a popular reality-TV spinoff show at the Gansevoort Hotel.

On the weekends I go out with my Yorkville friends from middle school. We hit up high school parties in random apartments scattered all over Manhattan, but those parties always get shut down by the cops before midnight. We go to the infamous parties at the bedbug-infested McKibbin Lofts in Brooklyn. We venture to rooftop gatherings in the Lower East Side, we go to punk shows and raves, we sip forties and Four Lokos in community gardens and smoke joints by the river late at night.

During the week, I hang out with Liana and a vast crew of other misfits who don't care to wake up early to go to school. We go to free cribs during the day and drink stolen liquor until the sun goes down. We get our free meal at the Pink Pony and then hit Lucky Cheng's for the cheap booze. We bounce around nightclubs all over the Meatpacking District, ending up in seedy after-hours spots all over the city, with shady characters who have money to spare. The party never seems to end, it consumes me.

Liana and I make the perfect team. She usually finds the party and pushes me up to the front of the line so I can work my charm and get us all in. Her motto is that you can make anything fun with the right crew of people, and soon we become collectors of rejects from all walks of life. After our wild nights out, I wake up the next day with my pockets and bra stuffed with crumpled-up dollar bills and my purse overflowing with cash. Proof of another successful night.

One night as I'm pregaming at my friend's house, I see my mom's name pop up on my BlackBerry. She never calls me. I shut off the music and answer the phone.

"He's dead." Her voice shakes.

I want to hit pause not only on the music but on life and rewind and go back to five minutes ago when I had the option to answer this phone call. Why now? Why did this have to happen now? Truth is, I already knew what she was going to tell me. I knew about my grandpa's health, but I was so consumed with Ace that I didn't want to think about it.

The room is pitch-black except for a light machine spraying the ceiling in all different colors. Red, blue, green, yellow, red, blue, green, yellow. My friends all stare at me, red Solo cups in hand, waiting for me to say something. I hang up, take a swig from my cup, and turn the music back on. I'm drunk and the music is blaring but inside it's dead silent. Just my thoughts bouncing off the hollow walls of my heart.

I leave my friend's house and go to the gay club, doing everything I can to distract myself. I take ecstasy and dance for hours, moving my sweaty body to the music, grinding on strangers. I begin to wonder if he can see me right now. What if when his soul rose to heaven, he caught a glimpse of me at this gay club with my tits out, taking pictures with a coked-up drag queen, surrounded by porn magazines. He was a holy man of strong principles and beliefs. I wonder if he will forgive me. But mostly, I wonder if I'll be able to forgive myself.

My mom holds a small service for just a few people. By the end of his life he didn't have many friends. My parents can't afford to send me to Italy on such short notice. Veronica attends the funeral in my place. I feel slightly envious but I know she's just trying to help. I'm overcome with guilt about his death. I unravel, and I just want to dissociate forever. I want to die.

Liana introduces me to Rick, an ex-associate of Ace's. They're enemies now. Rick is a small-time PCP dealer and cocaine addict who still lives at home with his mom. He's ten years older than me and his girlfriend goes to school with Liana. She's five months pregnant and lives at home with her parents. Rick is not traditionally attractive, but I love getting high with him. And I love the indescribably sweet feeling of revenge that I get every time our lips lock. He lives around the corner from my school, so it's super-convenient for me to hop in and out and get my fix. I smoke angel dust and play my favorite game, where I pretend to be a ballerina and tiptoe on the ledge of his balcony, not so gracefully hopping from one piece of furniture to another, never touching the floor.

On St. Patrick's Day, Liana goes to a bar by herself and ends up meeting a bunch of Irish men, from Ireland, who buy her drinks all day. As night falls, they invite her to get in their limo and go back to their hotel. I'm with Rick and three friends when she calls me and very bluntly demands that I bring drugs and girls to the W Hotel in Times Square. "They have money," she whispers into the receiver. In a matter of minutes, we're all in a taxi on our way there.

I enter the huge suite and notice there's cocaine sprinkled on every surface. The TV, the radiator, the kitchen counter, even the toilet. There are rolled-up fifty-dollar bills scattered all over the room. I go around pocketing them. The girls we came with, Ash and Sara, watch in amusement.

"Have you guys ever tried angel dust?" I yell at one of the guys.

"No, what's that?" he asks as he takes a bump off his hand.

"It's a new designer drug. Everyone is doing it here. My friend has some." I point to Rick, who's been floating around the room with a dust blunt in his hand like a ghost in the shadows.

The Irish guy's face lights up. "I need to get some I need to get some I need to get some," he says maniacally, diving his hands in all his pockets.

"One bag is sixty dollars," I tell him. He pulls out a wad of cash and begins counting it. "Five should be good," I say as he sorts through the fat stack of twenties.

"How much is that?" he asks.

"Three hundred," I say with a smile and my hand out.

After the sale, I smile and lean in to Rick, whispering through my clenched grin, "That's *six* times what they actually cost, so you're giving me some for free."

I hold out my shaky hand, and he drops five bags into it.

The Irish guy and I go into the bathroom and I roll up a dust blunt for him. He takes a few pulls and instantly enters another dimension. He's so high, he thinks he's in outer space. My tolerance is higher, so I roll up another one. And then another one. The Irish guy's running low on coke and I'm starting to feel anxious. I keep hearing techno music in my ears, but I can't figure out where it's coming from. When I come out of the bathroom, I can't find Rick anywhere. I grab my cell phone and realize it's completely out of battery.

I run from room to room, frantically calling his name. "Did he say where he was going?" I ask Sara.

"I think he went to get more drugs," she says.

I relax a little bit. The Irish guy follows me around, proclaiming his love for me over and over again. I'm starting to get repulsed by him as he wipes his runny nose on his hand. His skin is translucent, and I can clearly see his entire vascular network through his clothes. I can barely understand him through his grinding jaw and thick Irish accent.

We run out of coke, and Ash and Sara get up to leave.

"Are you sure you don't wanna come with us?" Sara asks.

The sunrise peeks in through the curtains and an uneasy feeling creeps in the room.

"I think I'm gonna stay with Liana," I say. "I don't want to leave her."

I walk them out and then get on my hands and knees and scour the carpet for cocaine residue, mistakenly rubbing cigarette ashes on my gums. I dig through all the ashtrays trying to find any remnants of a dust blunt. I keep hearing the techno playing in my ears. I stand up and look around to no one. Who the fuck is playing techno?

I hear Liana in the bathroom having sex with one of the Irish guys. I'm starting to grow restless. The Irish guy who's obsessed with me won't stop talking to me, so I run into the bathroom to hide and turn on the hair dryer to muffle the sounds of Liana's naked body clapping against his.

My heart pounds and my stomach is cramping. Only Rick can fix this. I take Liana's phone out of her purse and see that it's six-thirty in the morning. I pretend I didn't see that and go through her contacts only to find she has no numbers stored. I pop my SIM card out with my earring and put it in her phone. I have to see Rick. I call him on repeat until he answers.

"I went home," he says. "Stop calling me. My baby mom's comin' over right—"

I cut him off, speed-talking: "I just need to cop. You don't have to come back here. I'll come to you."

I run out of the suite with Liana's phone and hop on the train downtown. The techno in my ears is getting louder and louder. People's faces on the train morph into demons as they gawk at me in my barely there outfit, a black American Apparel bodysuit and tight spandex pants.

I get to Rick's apartment and his whole family is awake. His mom rolls her eyes at me when I walk past her into the bedroom. I hear her stomping and yelling in Spanish getting closer. "Ma, relax! We not doin' nothin'!"

She pounds on the door as Rick passes me a dust blunt. I take one pull and collapse backward onto the couch. The techno stops and an ocean of black floods my vision. I hear myself think, What is this? Oh my God. What is happening? and then a voice in my head tells me, "Julia, you're dying." I desperately plead with myself to hold on tight and not let go, even though I feel warm and comfortable, not at all high, but finally at peace.

Suddenly I'm transported to an ascending roller-coaster ride of happier times flashing before my eyes. Starting at the bottom, I see my earliest memories. The reel moves fast but I recognize the familiar feeling of being held by my grandpa. I see the tree we planted in the garden. I catch a glimpse of my brother on a bike going up the hill to our mountain house in Italy. As I approach the top of the roller coaster I see myself, where I am, at that very moment in Rick's bedroom. It's like I floated up to the ceiling and I can vividly see a bunch of people crowding around me. I see Froot Loops scattered all around, a puddle of milk surrounding me. I see Rick's mom praying over me in Spanish. I see a pregnant girl going through my purse and pocketing Liana's cell phone. I reach the top of the roller coaster. I clench my fists and prepare myself for the drop, but then a window appears before me in the distance. The rays of light spill into the pitch-black space, illuminating a path for me to walk through.

My eyes remain fixed on the window, which seems to be expanding. I'm mesmerized by it, but whatever consciousness I have left in me tells me to look away. I drop my gaze, and that's when I realize the light is now spilling in through the cracks of the wooden floor. It's so bright and so close that I can feel the heat on my face.

I come to in the ambulance with vomit all around me. Even the paramedics are covered in vomit. One of them goes through my wallet frantically, pulling out my fake IDs and holding them next to my face. "Which one is you?" he asks.

I shake my head and pass out again.

I wake up to the beeping sound of my heart monitor. My vision is blurry. It takes a second for it to focus. When it does, I see my dad sitting in the corner of the room. His eyes are red. He's been crying. I've never seen him cry before.

I feel like I'm drowning in shame. Part of me doesn't want him to care about me, so I don't ever have to feel as guilty as I do at this very moment.

"I'm sorry, Daddy," I tell him softly. "I promise I'll do better."

He struggles to find the words. "Man . . . you . . . you could've died."

I turn my head away from him, trying my hardest to hold back the tears.

The next day I feel reborn. I feel like I've been baptized with the secrets of the universe. I feel energized and invigorated. I call Liana on her house phone to tell her what happened.

"Liana, I saw the other side. I saw God. I know where we go when we die. It's like a black hole with light. An energy vortex." My speech is frenzied and erratic.

She stops me and says, "I was so worried about you. I came out of the bathroom and you were gone and my phone was gone."

"I know, I'm so sorry about that. I'll give you mine."

"No, it's fine. I robbed some bitch and got a new one." I laugh. I'm always impressed by her. "I'm glad you didn't die. Maybe it's time to lay off the pipe."

For the next few months, I stop doing hard drugs and tell everyone I'm "sober," even though I still smoke tons of weed. I have perfect attendance at school. I do my homework. I participate in class. I even win a "most improved" award. It's the first time I've ever won anything. I start thinking about the future. My friends are all starting to look at colleges, so I do too. I dream about fashion. During lunchtime, I wander the streets of the East Village alone, going to all the vintage shops. Fabulous Fanny's for sunglasses. Tokio 7 for designer items. Metropolis for fur coats and leather boots.

My dad brought a bedbug-infested chair into the house, so when Veronica finally arrives, we're made to share a blow-up mattress on the floor. At first I'm thrilled to show off my beautiful blond Italian best friend. I bring her to free cribs and nightclubs in the Meatpacking District. It's so much easier to get in with her by my side. The men find her accent so charming, and she flirts with just about anybody who will give her attention. She can talk about any subject, and when she talks to you, she makes you feel like you're the only person in the room. She's attentive and caring. She makes collages for me while I'm at school. She hangs the artwork on the wall, proudly displaying her adoration for me. She writes me love letters, thanking me for taking her in and how meeting me is the best thing that ever happened to her.

I'm flattered at first, but then it starts to get annoying. She wants to come everywhere with me and she wears all my clothes, carelessly damaging them. One night I walk in on her hooking up with my good friend's boyfriend, putting me in the worst position imaginable.

"Why would you do that?!"

She shrugs and laughs it off. "It didn't mean anything."

The sound of her voice begins to irk me. Things start to bother me that I never paid attention to before, like her wearing my panties, her permanent cough from smoking so many cigarettes, her perpetual runny nose. When she begins acting like me, copying my mannerisms and attitude, I've finally had enough. I no longer feel comfortable sleeping on the same mattress as her and to escape I begin spending more time at Liana's house, wearing all of Liana's funky clothing. But no matter what I do, Veronica can't seem to get the hint.

In my absence she and my dad start spending more time together.

They go to the beach and take long walks through the park. He even takes her sailing on his shitty little sailboat. He buys her weed and takes her picture under the sunset, like I don't exist. Her mom calls our house frequently, begging her to return to Italy.

One night Veronica gets stabbed in a random attack uptown. A masked man crossed the street diagonally, ran up behind her, and put a knife to her neck. She grabbed the blade and was able to throw him off, but not before he sliced through all the tendons in her fingers. She was rushed into emergency surgery. I put my feelings aside and show up for her. When I arrive at the hospital my dad is already there leading the investigation, working to locate security footage.

When she gets out of surgery and comes home from the hospital, she's kind enough to share her pain medication with me. This extends our looming expiration date and helps me tolerate the situation a little longer.

Veronica's mom finds out about the attack and immediately flies to New York. Liana comes with me to a lunch meeting with Veronica's mom and Veronica, who shows up late with my dad. She fidgets with her cast as her mom pleads with her to come home. Veronica and I avoid eye contact when her mom asks me to tell her to go home.

"I don't wanna make it weird between us," I say softly. "I just need my space back."

She shrugs and says, "I'm a guest of Tom's now. He said I could stay. Right?" She glances at my dad to back her up. I shoot him a warning look, but he nods and says, "I'm not going to kick anyone out. If she wants to stay, what can I do?"

The food hasn't arrived yet when I stand up and announce, "Come on, Liana, let's go."

Liana looks pissed that she's missing out on the free meal and grudgingly stands up. As we walk away from the table, Veronica's mom pleads with me in Italian to stay.

When I get back to Liana's house, I lock myself in the bathroom and call the immigration hotline to inform them that an illegal alien from Italy has taken up residency in the U.S. After half an hour on hold, I come to the bleak realization that rich blond girls are not on the U.S. Immigration's deportation radar.

Back at my dad's house, I immediately call my mom. My plan is to tell her that my dad is supporting Veronica financially, knowing that this news will surely enrage her.

And I'm absolutely correct.

"If you don't want her there, then she has to go," my mom says plainly.

I run into the bedroom with the house phone in my hand, my mom still on the line, and stand over Veronica as she paints her toenails with my nail polish.

"You have to go," I tell her, void of any emotion. Her equally dead-pan stare annoys me. "Come on, pack your shit." My dad appears in the doorway. "My mom says you have to go!"

"Fuck your mom," she says.

How *dare* this girl say anything about my mother. I lunge toward Veronica. I grab her by the hair and hit her repeatedly in the head, scratching her face and breaking three acrylic nails in the process. My dad pulls me off her, threatening to call the police on me. I leave her cowering on the floor, crying.

Trying my best to suppress the pileup of tears behind my eyes, I turn to him and say, "It's me or her, or I'm leaving and I swear to God I'm never coming back."

"Calm down, sweetie, just calm down."

I know what this means. "I fucking hate you," I say, my voice trembling with anger.

He pauses for a moment and says, "I love you too, sweetie."

I push him back against the wall, cornering him, shouting, "Give me money! I need money! I'm leaving!" I wave my bloodied hand in his face as he pulls out his wallet and hands me four crisp hundred-dollar bills. The most money he has ever given me. This means goodbye.

I try to remain stoic as I frantically gather my belongings. I wonder if my mother remained on the phone throughout all that. I wonder if she heard me sticking up for her. I hope she would be proud of me. I stuff my bags and clothes into a few small "I ♥ NY" plastic bags. I pick up my cat, Fernando, and run out of the apartment barefoot. I make it to a pay phone and call Liana, praying she answers. She's my only hope.

Luckily, she picks up on the first ring.

"Hey, I have to move in with you," I say.

"Who is this?" she asks.

"Julia!"

"When do you wanna move in?"

"Now."

"Great, can you get a dutch on the way?"

"Vanilla?"

"Yeah."

"Okay, I'm biking over now."

I hop on my candy-colored hundred-pound cruiser and begin pedaling from the Upper East Side all the way to Greenwich Village in the sweltering July heat, struggling to balance the plastic bags on my handlebars and Fernando in my basket. I've picked up some momentum going down Park Avenue when Fernando jumps out of the basket and onto my chest, sinking his sharp little claws into my flesh as we both hold on for dear life. I can't stop or we'll fall over. So we ride the rest of the way like that, as I cry my eyes out for multiple reasons.

Liana's mom, Dina, is an even worse hoarder than my dad. Everywhere there are piles of useless junk that she claims to be valuable. The small railroad apartment off Bleecker Street is so congested that we have to climb over heaps of garbage and inconveniently placed furniture to get to the kitchen and the bathroom. The "bedroom" is a corner of the apartment sectioned off with white poster board. Liana and I share the bunk bed. There are shoe racks on every wall with mismatched shoes that haven't been worn in years. Clothes and costume jewelry litter every surface.

During the day, Dina sells jewelry from a collapsible table on

Broadway. Sometimes I go visit her and bring her coffee and pizza. It's amusing to watch her shoo people away from her table while she introduces me to the other vendors on the block. "This is my daughta Juliana," she yells in her thick ambiguous accent.

I revel in the warm feminine energy emanating from Liana and Dina. It's a stark contrast from the cold, toxic masculine vibes I'm used to. Liana and I start telling everyone we're sisters, and it doesn't feel like we're lying—it's as if we were sisters in a past life. I feel like I've known her since the beginning of time. Her hair is naturally frizzy, but she straightens it and dyes it platinum blond. Her beautiful face is covered by thick glasses and she has a little extra weight on her frame, with stretch marks on her skin, and sometimes her belly peeks out over her miniskirts. Nevertheless, she looks in the mirror and proudly proclaims, "I look fucking amazing" before throwing on a twenty-dollar fur coat from the thrift store. She radiates power and confidence. It's my favorite thing about her. I wish I could be more like that.

When they leave the apartment, I jump at the opportunity to dig through the piles of junk. I find vintage Care Bear posters covered in roach eggs, a Spice Girls lunch box with a ten-year-old banana still inside, and boxes upon boxes of tarnished trinkets. I secretly start discarding the useless items all over the neighborhood. They never notice anything is missing. Instead, they comment on how good the place looks.

I swap our furniture with pieces I find on the street, creating a pathway and making it possible to move around the narrow railroad studio apartment. They love having me and I love living on Bleecker Street, buzzing with electricity in the heart of the Village.

After a few weeks of my dad dodging my mom's calls, she finally gets ahold of him and demands that he kick Veronica out, and he reluctantly complies. I call my brother to confirm she's gone.

"Can you come back now?" Chris asks me in a somber tone. "I miss you and Fernando." My heart breaks for him. He's never asked me for anything before, and as much as I want to show up for him, I can't. I'm relieved Veronica is no longer living as me in my childhood home, but I know I can't go back there. I will never forget this.

I start wondering where Veronica may have gone. I know she's still in New York and my intuition tells me that my dad is still seeing her. I make it my mission to find her.

One night, I'm lying in the bunk bed obsessively going through every possible scenario in my head, when it hits me. She's on his boat! The next morning I wake up early and bike up the West Side Highway, all the way to the 79th Street marina, where Trish and I had gone to hide from the cops a few years before. I wait for someone to leave and catch the gate as it's closing and make my way down the maze of docks until I spot his boat. As I get closer, I get a whiff of the strong Hermès men's cologne she wears and I see articles of her clothing on the deck.

I tiptoe onto the boat and peek inside. There she is, sleeping peacefully on the makeshift bed, completely oblivious to the damage she caused me. Next to her head are five twenty-dollar bills taped to the wall. This infuriates me since my dad never gave me any money growing up. I always had to take it from him.

I spot a bunch of my stuff and decide to steal it back. And while I'm at it, I fill up a plastic bag with some of her designer items as well. As I'm about to step off the boat, I glance over and see her eyes slightly cracked open. I swiftly jump off the boat and run through the maze of docks.

As I pedal down the bike path, the salty wind in my hair, I feel triumphant. I call my mom as soon as I can. "I found her!"

My mom reassures me she's going to handle it and tells me not to worry about it anymore. "I'll have her off the boat by the end of the day."

My elation is short-lived. I still somehow feel like the loser in this situation. Veronica took something from me that I can never get back. I'll never forgive my dad and I'll never be able to go home again and I'm so embarrassed. Everyone knows about it. The boys in the neighborhood, my so-called friends, crack jokes at my expense. I laugh along so as not to cry.

• • •

My dad calls me one morning and informs me my grandmother passed away. I feel nothing. I'm dissociated and numb. I hang up and think about our last moments together. I hadn't visited her since I moved downtown. I'd been so preoccupied with trying to avenge myself that I'd let six months pass without seeing my grandma. The last time I visited her, she was still at home, bedridden and tubed up. She couldn't speak but her eyes lit up when she saw me. I was always her favorite. At heart she was an artist, and she always encouraged my creative pursuits, whether it was building intricate dollhouses constructed of cardboard and newspaper clippings or spending the afternoon watercoloring at the Metropolitan Museum of Art. She always made sure to tell me I was brilliant. I believed it, coming from her, because she never said anything nice to my dad.

As the funeral approaches, I warn my dad that I won't be attending if Veronica is there. I'm still livid that she got to attend my grandpa's funeral in Italy when I was never even given the option. When my dad hangs up on me, I know that he has decided for us. He's going with her. If I hated him before, now I absolutely despise him. I wish he were the one who had died in my grandma's place.

That night, Liana and I get all dolled up as we always do. We put on our sluttiest little party dresses and the highest heels we own and go meet our friend who is a promoter at a nightclub a couple of blocks away. We make our way downstairs and sit at the promoter table, sipping on our watered-down cranberry vodkas, unamused. Liana spots a Dior purse on the floor. She inches closer to it, and with one swift motion she snatches it up and signals to me to follow her to the bathroom. I follow her into the stall and she empties the contents of the purse onto the floor, taking only the woman's wallet back to the table with her.

As I'm texting on my phone, searching for a better party to go to, five undercover officers swoop in and surround our table. Slowly, the people sitting next to us inch away, leaving just Liana and me under the bright beaming flashlights pointed directly in our eyes. The music abruptly shuts off and everyone stops dancing to gawk at us. The victim of our crime, a petite brunette in a Hérve Léger dress, points at us and shouts, "I'm a district attorney! You bitches fucked with the wrong one!"

An officer orders us to stand with our hands to the wall as they aggressively pat us down and dump the contents of our purses onto the floor. A lip gloss, twenty dollars, and a crushed cigarette fall out of mine. I feel relieved that I might be in the clear, but my hopes are shattered when an officer reaches into the back pocket of my jeans and pulls out two fake IDs. Susanna from New Hampshire and Emily from New Jersey, both girls who had made the same mistake a few months earlier of leaving their purses unattended.

"We're gonna run these names," the cop says. "If there's any reports on these, you're in big trouble."

I'm less afraid of going to jail and more upset to be parting ways with my alter egos that had opened so many red velvet ropes for me. "I found them on the street!" I whine.

"Shut up," another cop snaps at me.

They handcuff us and throw us in the back of a police van. At the police station, I manage to reach into my bra and pull out two Vicodins and half a Xanax bar. I pop them all in my mouth at once and pass out handcuffed to the cell.

I wake up to Liana nudging me. "They just interviewed me. I told them it was all me, don't worry."

I let out a sigh of relief. An officer opens the gate, and for a moment I think she might be letting me go.

"Get up!" she yells. "You're going to Central Booking!"

After sixteen hours in a cell packed with hookers and crackheads, only made worse by the sweltering summer heat, a frumpy-looking public defender carrying dozens of loose sheets of paper approaches me and whispers through the bars, "Okay, so, you're being charged with three counts of grand larceny, and they're considering two counts of identity theft, but I think I can talk them out of that."

His clothes are disheveled, his hair is greasy, and he looks like he hasn't slept all night. I look at him through his big foggy glasses and say, "Okay, but when can we go home?"

I glance at Liana, resting her head on a makeshift pillow made of industrial-size menstrual pads. Behind me, two girls are in a heated argument because one of them took a dump in the small toilet in the corner of the room, stinking up the place. Another one is getting roasted for having ramen noodles stuck in her blond weave.

"These are some pretty serious charges," the lawyer begins to tell me.

I cut him off. "Do you think you could get me some water?"

My mouth feels pasty and dry from the pills. My lips are getting stuck to my teeth. He presses his glasses against the bridge of his nose and nods, then scurries away. I wait hours for him to come back, before going back to sleep.

On Sunday morning, my name is finally called. I feel numb as the judge reads the charges. I'm exhausted, and my marijuana cravings make it difficult for me to focus. I wait for Liana, and as we stumble out of Central Booking starving and broke, she turns to me and says, "We need to smoke a blunt."

We trudge through the desolate streets in our high heels and matted club clothes, smelling like a public restroom. Finally, we reach Rosanne's house. She's Liana's neighbor from across the street. She's prescribed pills that are the equivalent of horse tranquilizers and hands them out to us like Skittles. We climb up the five stories and, with our last ounce of energy, climb over the piles of garbage bags in the narrow hallway, until we are eventually greeted by Rosanne with a big blunt hanging from the side of her mouth.

"What mess did you gals get into this time?"

My mouth salivates and my eyes remain fixed on the blunt in her hand as she waves it around. She talks and talks until her daughter, Dawn, pops her head out from her pillow fort on the floor and sees us. "These fuckin' whores?!" she yells. "These whores don't do nothin' for nobody, Ma!"

A clock radio suddenly goes flying through the air in our direction, smashing against the wall. Liana and I are startled but we don't plan on leaving until hitting that blunt.

Dawn is severely overweight and rarely leaves the house but at one point in time her and Liana were best friends and I think she resents me for taking her friend away. Her mom, on the other hand, simply adores me. She gives me her old clothes from the eighties that Dawn can't fit into: a pair of white cowboy boots a size too small that I manage to squeeze my big feet into, a sexy black button-down romper, high-waisted jeans with black lace inserts going down the leg, tube tops, tank tops, and lingerie.

Rosanne loves to tell us stories from her days as the coat-check girl at Studio 54. "You remind me so much of Bianca Jagger!" she says with a smoky exhale. "She had the best style of anyone. When she walked in the room everybody looked at her. She had that *IT* factor." I nod in amazement. "You got what it takes, kid, you got the *look,* trust me, I'd know."

Roseanne lives with the crushing weight of unfulfilled dreams. Her abusive husband didn't want her to work so she gave up her dreams of being a showgirl and now they live in poverty. Despite being in her fifties with jagged teeth and hepatitis C, her beauty still lingers. She has silky blond hair, ocean-blue eyes, and a natural grace in her step.

A few weeks later my dad calls me.

"A letter came. You're being indicted, and you missed a court appearance!"

"It's fine, they're probably just gonna give me community service!"

"No, Julia, this is serious. Get it through your head! They're gonna throw the book at you!"

I don't understand the severity of my actions, and at my next court appearance I show up two hours late, dressed in a sparkly party dress. The night before, I had been biking down Houston Street, with my friend Serena on the handlebars, when a sexy Dominican man pulled up beside us in a white Escalade and rolled his window down. "How are two beautiful ladies like you riding a bike?" he asked.

I stopped pedaling and turned around, almost losing my balance.

"Come on, get in the car, I'll give y'all a ride."

"Should we do it?" Serena asked under her breath.

"Yeah, why not."

I locked my bike up on the corner as he eyed us up and down. We got in his car and before he even introduced himself, he asked, "Y'all party?"

"What do you mean?" I asked, playing coy.

"Smoke, drink, molly, coke?"

"Yeah, why? You got anything for us?"

He chuckled sinisterly. "Oh, do I have something for y'all."

He dug in his console and handed us two plastic bottles filled with an orange-looking concoction. "You ever had a Nemo? It has a little bit of everything in it, every drug, every type of alcohol."

I'm intrigued. I take a sip. It's tangy and sweet with a hint of totally toxic. We drive up the FDR, music blasting, going a hundred miles per hour. He makes a few stops, he picks up his cousin, we go to a Dominican club in Dyckman, we go back downtown and get a cheap hotel room, and that's all I can remember. When I woke up in the morning, I had no clue where I was or what time it was. Serena was naked and passed out in between him and me, and his cousin was nowhere to be found.

When I stumble into the courthouse, my dad is already there, standing outside the courtroom, glaring at me. Before he can say anything, a lawyer ushers me into the room, where my name is called almost immediately. As I stand before the judge, he reads the complaint aloud, and I can still taste the Nemo on my breath. I look down at my dirty fingernails. I wipe my smeared eyeliner from under my eyes. I zoom in on the clacking of the typewriter. I play a game of how long I can hold my breath. I start counting the number of letters in the words the judge is saying. The lawyer nudges me when it's my turn to speak.

"Yes, Your Honor?" I say.

"If you break any of the terms of your probation, you will be sentenced to a mandatory year in prison."

I nod, feeling absolutely nothing. I only start to panic when I discover that some of the conditions of my probation are that I remain sober, graduate high school, and get a real job. I keep hearing the judge's voice echoing throughout my brain: *a mandatory year in prison, a mandatory year in prison, a mandatory year in prison.* I grudgingly accept that I'll need to quit smoking pot.

Liana and I smoke our last blunt. The next day, she goes job hunting, and I take all my Italian high school transcripts to Kinko's and photoshop them by hand to hide the fact that I was left back twice. When I'm done, Liana takes me to the alternative public school she graduated from, called City-as-School. The school is lovingly regarded as the "reject school." It's the last stop before a GED.

"This school is great for kids who like learning in the real world, kids who can't sit still, like us," she reassures me. "Basquiat went here too."

She gives me the tour and introduces me to Toni, the trans principal. She's about six-six in heels and her red padded bra peeks through her low-cut shirt.

"Liana, what are you still doing here? I thought we got rid of you!" She laughs affectionately, holding her arms out. "Come give momma some sugar."

Liana's face lights up as she runs into Toni's arms. After Liana explains my situation, Toni says, "Don't worry, sweetheart, we are gonna take such good care of you!"

I feel the warmth radiating from her and I suddenly feel a sense of belonging, like I'm right where I'm supposed to be. It makes me feel hopeful that I may actually have a chance at graduating high school, even if it's a year late.

Arriving at my first probation appointment, I go through the metal detectors and take a seat in the waiting room, which is packed with people. After hours of waiting, a heavyset Hispanic woman in her mid-forties holding a clipboard opens the glass doors and calls my name. As soon as I sit down in front of her, I turn on the charm but she's not falling for my dumb-and-ditzy act. She slaps a plastic cup on the desk and orders me to go pee in it.

My sweaty hands tremble as I walk down the hall to the bathroom. I quickly calculate how long it's been since I last smoked a blunt: thirty-two days. With marijuana staying in your system for up to three months, I say a prayer and release my bladder into the tiny plastic cup.

The cup is moist with sweat when I hand it back to her. She puts a glove on and holds the little yellow cup up to the light. My heart pounds as she examines the indicator. "Okay, it's a slight positive," she says. "Wait right here."

Before I can offer up an explanation, she's already out the door. I begin to feel faint. I keep hearing the judge's' voice bouncing off the walls of my brain: *a mandatory year in prison, a mandatory year in prison, a mandatory year in prison.*

"Okay, so, I talked to my supervisor, and since it's trace amounts we're gonna give you a drug program. You have to go once a week for three months."

I let out a sigh of relief. "When does it start?" I ask.

"Next week. Wednesday."

That night I go to a random house party in the Silver Towers in Greenwich Village, where I come across a drug dealer named Romeo. Although I can't smoke weed anymore, I can still indulge in anything that leaves the system in seventy-two hours, which is everything else. I catch him making a sale out of the corner of my eye, but I can't see what's in his hand. I impulsively blurt out, "Can I have some?"

"You sure?"

"Yeah, why? What is it?"

He shakes his head and chuckles, pulling out a little bundle of wax baggies. He lifts the rubber band and drops two of them in my palm. I quickly slip them in my bra, unsure what they are but not wanting to embarrass myself.

"Take my number," he says.

"I don't have a phone right now," I say. "Take mine. I'm getting a new phone soon."

Back at Liana's house later that night, I pull out the little baggies and examine them closely. They are each stamped with a blue Nike symbol and "Just do it." I sprinkle a tiny bit of the mysterious brown powder onto a joint and smoke it on the top bunk.

"Can I hit it?" asks Kai, Liana's boyfriend.

"Nah," I say as a warm tingly sensation creeps up my legs and up my pelvis, down my spine, and around my head. I doze off with the lit joint still in my hands. I'm jolted up by Liana shrieking, "What's that smell?! Is the house on fire?!"

I glance down and realize that the joint burned a hole through the tattered comforter. I stomp it out and safely tuck the rest of the joint away on a shelf.

Once the high wears off, I come to the realization that it has to be heroin. *This* is the feeling that Lou Reed sang about in the Velvet Underground. It's what William Burroughs wrote about in my favorite book, *Junky*. It's what Sublime warned about in "Wrong Way." I know I'm flirting with fire, but it's just too damn good to resist. For a fleeting moment, I forgot about all my worries and the voices in my head went away. I felt as calm and serene as a newborn baby tucked away in its mother's arms.

I make a deal with myself that I'll finish out the two baggies and never do it again. Plus, I don't even have Romeo's number. I do the rest over the course of a few days. Soon after, I come down with what I think is a cold. I lie on the bottom bunk in a puddle of sweat too weak to climb up to my usual spot on the top. Despite the humidity, my skin is covered in goose bumps and I'm freezing. I keep yawning, but my mind won't let me go to sleep. Dina keeps yapping in my direction even though my eyes are closed and I'm pretending to be asleep, and Liana's constant fighting with her boyfriend is only making my throbbing headache worse.

It feels like hell. I slowly start to feel like myself again.

I get a new phone and within a few days I receive a call from a random number. I don't have any numbers stored, so without thinking I pick up.

"Hey, it's Romeo, from the party."

"Oh, hey."

"I'm in the area, if you need anything."

"Um . . ." I hesitate, feeling like a puppet being controlled by a foreign entity. I hear myself say, "Yeah," and I'm instantly filled with regret.

"Let's meet on Bleecker and Sullivan in thirty?"

With my last twenty bucks, I buy two more baggies, and lucky for me, he's feeling generous, so he throws in an extra one for free. I rush back home and lock myself in the bathroom, feeling a mix of anticipation and guilt. I cut out a line on the toilet seat and snort it up with a tampon applicator. I fall back on the cold tile floor when the familiar feeling washes over me again, and for a brief moment nothing matters, nothing hurts, nothing bothers me. Even the crusty tile floor feels cool and crisp against my bare skin.

I find that when I'm high, I'm nicer and more patient. I'm hopeful and serene. Things don't bother me and I'm way less likely to start a fight. I know how Liana feels about heroin. It's the one drug she refuses to touch. "Heroin is *not* chic," she says. "It's cheap."

One night, Liana throws a party at Kai's small studio and invites all our friends. The room is packed, and music is thumping. I've had a few too many drinks when I decide I need to do a line of heroin *now*. I stumble over to the bathroom and pound on the door, but it's locked and I'm getting impatient. I walk over to the kitchen counter, and with my back turned to the party, I start to cut up a line on a plate. I'm interrupted by Liana's voice as she charges toward me. "Julia, what are you doing?!"

Everyone turns their attention toward me and the peppery brown line on the plate. Liana's chin starts quivering as her eyes dart from me to the plate. "Everyone needs to get out!"

Nobody moves.

"I said, GET THE FUCK OUT! NOW!"

Her guests grunt and groan and shoot me dirty looks as they're quickly ushered out the door by Kai. Once they're all gone, she looks me dead in the eye. "This is not okay. You cannot bring heroin into our home. I dead-ass won't be friends with you anymore."

She waves her authoritative finger in my face, and I nod, keeping my gaze to the floor, feeling ashamed. The thought of Liana not speaking to me anymore is too much for me to bear.

"I'll stop," I say softly. "I promise."

Her tone is still aggressive when she says, "Dump it out in the toilet."

I hesitate for a moment, which causes her to get even more impatient.

"Now!" she yells.

I drag my feet to the bathroom and empty the rest of the brown powder into the toilet. She flushes it and stomps out of the bathroom as I watch my only reprieve circling the drain.

6

MASTERMIND

I need to get a job. Not only to fulfill my probation requirement but because I have no money. The numbers I had stolen off my dad's credit card stopped working and we can't steal checks from Serena's dad anymore because he threatened to have us arrested and he's totally the type to do that.

I go on Craigslist and I already know where to look. I scroll down to the bottom of the page: "Adult gigs." I scan the job postings—prostitute, stripper, slutty assistant, prostitute, slutty maid, prostitute, prostitute—until I read the words *"Dominatrix dungeon hiring *NO SEX* *no nudity* *no experience necessary.*"*

An image from years ago flashes in my mind. I vividly remember Ella's older sister, Kat, walking into her room to admire herself in the full-length mirror as I sat cross-legged by her patent-leather Mary Jane platforms. I remained transfixed on her, my entranced gaze tracing her body all the way up from her black toenails to her long legs in black fishnet stockings. She was so fucking cool.

I click on the listing and I'm met with instructions.

1. Send in a recent full-body picture
2. Write a quick bio with age, height, weight, and level of experience
3. Describe in detail most sadistic sexual fantasy

Easy. I pull what I think is a good photo off my Facebook page and begin tapping away at the keyboard. I don't have experience as a dominatrix but I certainly have some experience in hating men.

My most sadistic sexual fantasy:

You're completely naked and tied up on your knees. You're scared of what I may do to you but you're also aroused and desire me with every fiber of your being. I'm wearing a black lacy bra and a thong and black leather stilettos. I walk toward you, my panties now parallel to your face. You drool for me. You stick out your tongue, you want so badly to taste me. But you know the rules. Unless you take pain for me, you can only look and not touch. You beg me to let you kiss my big juicy ass. I'll allow it but only if I can step on your cock. You hesitate at first but then you agree, you don't really have a choice in the matter. You're my toy to play with and I can do whatever I want to you. You're trembling. You lie down, face up, and I begin to trample your cock with my bare feet. As you begin to yell and scream, I squat down so that your face is now in between my legs. I then sit on your face with all my weight, muffling your cries and suffocating you at the same time. I untie one of your hands and you begin jerking off until you cum in under ten seconds. The End.

I press send, close the tab, and resume my job search when I hear the familiar "You've got mail." Shocked that I've received a reply so quickly, I open the email, from a man named Ronald. He instructs me to meet him at a café in Chelsea at one p.m.

Until now, all my jobs were in the service industry. I worked at an ice cream shop for seven dollars an hour, forced to wear a fifty-pound cow suit in the sweltering summer heat while my coworkers stole my tips. Then there was the shoe store on 86th Street, where I was relegated to the hosiery section since hardly any customers went there. And Veniero's, the iconic pastry shop by my school that hired me simply because I spoke Italian. I often showed up late and stoned, making a beeline for the basement, where the barrels of cannoli cream awaited me. I would plunge my whole hand into the thick, sweet, creamy goodness and slurp it off my fingers. These minimum-wage jobs offered no benefits except the things I could steal. But this new job posting for this mysterious dungeon said I could make up to a thousand dollars a day.

As I head uptown on my heavy cruiser, I can't help but feel a little nervous. What if this is all a scam and I get kidnapped and sold into sex slavery? I park my bike and carefully scan my surroundings, making sure there aren't any sketchy white vans parked on the block. When I enter the café, I notice it's completely empty except for an older gentleman in dark sunglasses and a black leather trench coat sitting alone in the corner.

As soon as we lock eyes, his face lights up. "Wow, how is it possible that you are even more beautiful in person?"

I smile politely and thank him, even though I don't believe him.

"I was very impressed by the scene you wrote, are you sure you've never done this before?"

"Well, not professionally," I say with a giggle.

"You mean you do this in your sex life?"

I giggle again at the words "sex life." "In third grade my dad used to make me have playdates with the biggest nerds in my class. He said it was because he felt sorry for them. One of the boys was Fabien. I used to force him to strip down completely naked and make him get on his knees. And then I would ride him around like a pony and make him pick things up off the floor with his mouth."

By the look on his face, I can tell he's thoroughly amused.

"How's it possible? You have the face of an angel!" he exclaims.

"It's my best weapon!" I say, giggling yet again.

His expression suddenly turns serious. "When can you start?"

I pause. "Tomorrow?"

"Perfect. I'll let the manager know." He extends his pale veiny hand and I shake it firmly, just like my dad taught me. "One more thing. What is your mistress name?"

"Mistress name?"

"Don't think you can go around using your real name."

I think for a moment and then confidently reply, "Valentina."

"Valentina, great choice."

He watches me ride off on my bike with a cheesy grin plastered across his pasty face.

On the ride back home, I feel invincible, weaving in and out of traffic, taking shortcuts. When I arrive, I call Liana at the leather shop she now works at on West Broadway.

"I got a job!" I proudly exclaim.

"You did?" She sounds surprised.

"Yeah, I'm gonna be a dominatrix! They said I can make, like, a thousand bucks per shift."

There's a brief silence on the other end of the line. "You sure it's not a scam?"

I roll my eyes, annoyed. "No, Liana, I met with the guy at a café. It's legit."

"Oh, wow."

I hang up and start digging through the infinite piles of clothes, pulling out a pair of fishnets and setting aside a pair of black pumps in preparation for my first day as a professional domme.

The next day, I arrive at the discreet building in Chelsea and ring the buzzer for the basement. I hesitate before walking down the seedy, barren steps. I notice the smell—a special blend of sewage, smoke, urine, candles, and Lysol. At the bottom of the stairs, I'm met with a three-hundred-pound Ukrainian woman in her mid-forties sitting at a small desk. She doesn't acknowledge me as I enter the room so I tiptoe over to her, take a deep breath, and hold my hand out. "What do you want?" she says in her thick accent.

"My name is Julia—I mean Valentina—Ronald said to come here?"

She eyes me up and down, then nods curtly. "My name is Greta, I manager here." The buzzer rings and she shoos me away with her hand like a mosquito.

I take a seat on one of the couches in the lounge, trying to blend in with the surroundings. I try to strike up a conversation with a pretty redhead, only to be left hanging midsentence when she turns her back on me. The girls move around the space as if I'm not even there. No one asks my name. No one even looks in my direction. I start to get the sense that they don't like me and this was a bad idea. Just as I'm starting to rethink this whole thing, Greta barges in.

"Valentina, you're up," she barks, jolting me out of my thoughts.

I stand up nervously and stare at her, unsure what to do next but too scared to ask.

"What are you waiting for?!" she yells. "Get dressed!"

I spring to my suitcase and hastily search through my bag. What am I looking for? I'm not sure. A few minutes later, I emerge from the bathroom in a cheap, mismatched black cotton thong and bra and ripped pantyhose and bright red lipstick.

"She looks like a hooker," I hear someone snicker as I leave the room.

"He only likes new girls," Greta says as she logs numbers in a notebook. When she finally glances up to see my outfit, she becomes animated with disdain. I hear the girls' laughter as she makes faces and waves her giant arms around. "Valentina. What de fack are you wearing? This is high-class place, Valentina! You look like cheap hooker!"

She points to a shady locked door behind her desk and orders me to go change. My cheeks sting from embarrassment, and I keep my head down as I walk past the wall covered in paddles, whips, handcuffs, ropes, and chains. When I crack open the door, I find myself staring down an infinite hallway of darkness. All I can see are a few black heavy-duty garbage bags directly in front of me that smell overwhelmingly like latex, lube, and piss.

I take a few cautious steps down the dimly lit corridor, sweat trickling down my forehead as I strain to hear Greta's bellowing voice. "To the left!" she commands, and I hurriedly obey, my heart pounding through my chest. With trembling hands, I push open the next door, flick on the light, and my jaw drops. Before me lies a walk-in closet that's nothing short of a phallic wonderland. Dildos of all shapes, sizes, and colors line the walls from top to bottom. Small and white. Pink and crooked. Black and enormous, bigger than my arm. Thick ones, thin ones, electric ones, two dicks in one. I soon discover that the dildos are stored in the hallway in case the cops decide to raid the place . . . again. "No dildos, no penetration, no problem," Greta quips nonchalantly.

As my eyes scan the cluttered room, they land on the haphazardly hung costumes strewn behind a towering display of dicks, and I cringe. Hastily rifling through the rack, I can sense Greta's impatient energy permeating from the lounge. Everything is either too big or reeks of bodily fluids. I find a cheap plastic nurse's outfit, a nun costume from the Halloween store, and a wrinkled schoolgirl's skirt. None of which works. I finally find a shiny latex catsuit, but as I pull it over my feet I notice a few stains near the ankles which very much resemble crusty jizz. I feel like I'm going to throw up and I start to panic.

I finally land on a black corset and a black tube top that I repurpose as a makeshift miniskirt. I quickly slip on a pair of old, worn-out peep-toe platform sandals, a size too big, and head out to make my debut as Mistress Valentina. It's not exactly the glamorous entrance I had envisioned, but it'll have to do for now.

"Two hours, Xing Palace, his name is Stewart, and he like smoking." Greta points down the hall with her sharp and stubby finger.

I nod, but once again I have no idea what I'm doing.

"First door to the right."

I follow her instructions and make my way down the hall. The clacking of my oversize heels sends echoes down the empty hallway. I walk as slowly as possible to shave even a few minutes off what I anticipate will be the longest two hours of my life. I pause in front of the door to the Xing Palace with my hand on the doorknob. I take a few deep breaths, dreading the moment I will become this stranger's good time.

As soon as I crack open the door, a thick cloud of smoke engulfs me, wrapping itself around me and pulling me in. I squint into the dark room through the haze, trying to locate him. I'm startled when I glance down and find him lying motionless on the floor beneath me.

My heart racing, I nervously blurt out, "Oh my God, I didn't see you there."

"I hope you don't mind," he says. "I hooked myself up to save us some time."

As I inch closer, I realize that he's completely naked, and his balls are tightly bound to a rope that's connected to a torture device hanging from the ceiling.

"I'm Stewart. 'Smoking Stewart.' But my friends call me Stew."

"Nice to meet you," I say quietly.

My immediate assessment of him reveals a man in his fifties, out of shape, with a pasty complexion, and glancing downward I notice he also has a small penis. On the floor beside him are two packs of cigarettes, Camel Lights and Marlboro Lights.

"Those are for you," he says. "I didn't know which you prefer, so I got you both."

I don't tell him I smoke Newports. I don't want to hurt his feelings.

To calm my nerves, I grab a Marlboro and light it up. My hand trembles slightly as I hold the cigarette to my lips, but before I can take a second drag, he interrupts me. "You might want to save that for me," he says, his voice muffled by the black rubber mask he just put on. "You're going to have to do *a lot* of smoking."

I watch in stunned silence as he attaches a rubber tube to the mask's mouthpiece and explains in a distorted voice that I am to chain-smoke the cigarettes and blow the smoke through the tube, which will be in his mouth.

"And if you're up for it, you can spit in my mouth or even pee."

With a deep breath, I take another drag and exhale the smoke through the tube, feeling a strange mix of discomfort and detachment wash over me.

As I kneel over him, dutifully blowing the cigarette smoke into the tube, my curiosity gets the best of me. I begin to examine him, taking in every detail of his body. I've never been this close to an old man before, and it's simultaneously repulsive and fascinating.

I notice the artificial look of his hair plugs, the raised pimples on his arms, the stretch marks on his belly. The smells of Axe body spray and sweat emanate from his body, mixing with the acrid odor of the burning cigarettes. I try not to recoil at the sight of his small, flaccid penis, dangling limply between his chunky legs.

In between exhales, I try to make small talk to pass the time and begin asking him questions about himself.

"Where are you from?" I ask.

He spits the slimy tube out of his mouth and says, "I'm a New Yorker! I grew up in a very beautiful part of New Jersey."

"But you live here now?" I follow up.

"No, I actually live with my mom in New Jersey. She likes having me around," he says with a shrug. "You should come over to the house sometime."

An hour in, he decided he needs a break.

"Hey, do you like the Strokes?" he asks, pulling out a small speaker from his duffel bag.

"They were the first live concert I ever went to!" I reply, excited that we may get to listen to some good music to lighten the mood.

"This is me and my cover band!" he says with a toothy grin. My elation quickly sours when he proceeds to play his rendition of every single song by the Strokes. He sings along, occasionally belting out the lyrics a cappella. It's obvious that he thinks he has a great voice. I force a smile and bop my head to the music, cringing from secondhand embarrassment. "Okay, let's get back to it!" he says, clapping his hands.

He gets back on the floor and I resume my position, chain-smoking and blowing smoke into the tube. As the minutes drag on, I can feel the smoke burning the back of my throat, and my fingers are becoming stained yellow. The terrible music blares, and the man continues to scream, and the smoke and discomfort start getting to me. A splitting headache throbs behind my bloodshot eyes, and my back and knees ache from kneeling for so long. I steal glances at the digital clock on the corner, but time seems to have frozen and the minutes drag on for hours.

After the tenth cigarette, I stop inhaling. My tongue is on fire and I begin to feel dizzy and faint. I can't help but wonder why he doesn't just smoke a goddamn cigarette himself and why he hasn't gotten a boner yet. Am I doing something wrong? I grow increasingly irritated and the urge to kick him in his little dick starts to consume me.

I realize that I have to pee and remember what he said at the beginning of the session. I spot a little funnel in his bag of tricks and stick it inside the tube. I stand up, towering over him, and crouch down, releasing my bladder into the funnel. He gargles and gags as the golden substance trickles down his face. "Mmmm," he begins to moan, and I notice that he's finally getting an erection.

"Do you like porn?" he spits out the tube and asks.

"Yeah, of course, who doesn't like porn?!"

At this point anything is better than chain-smoking on my knees. He gets up, drenched in urine, and goes to get his laptop.

On it, he has a whole queue of saved videos and they are all of older men forcing themselves onto submissive younger-looking men. He jerks off furiously as he maniacally skips from video to video, occasionally asking for my input. I sit next to him awkwardly, as it doesn't really seem like he needs me, but since he's paying for my services I decide to try something.

"I bet you wanna suck that *big* cock like a little slut, don't you?" I say hesitantly, unsure whether he's come to terms with his obvious queerness.

He desperately nods, whipping his head back and forth. "Uh-huh," he says with a little whimper, then his body starts convulsing and he comes all over his hand. I feel a strange sense of triumph and pride. I know what he wants! I realize that part of this job is reading between the lines. I have to know what they want before they've even come to terms with it. I understand the secret to this trade.

He's over the moon when I look him in the eyes and promise him that if he comes to see me again the next night, I'll have a fresh load of jizz to feed him.

The next day, I offer a girl twenty dollars to make her client come into a condom and give it to me. I hide it in the back of the fridge and wait for Stewart. That night, my plan goes accordingly and just like that, he becomes my regular. He comes to see me almost every night and if I'm busy with another client, he leaves. He's loyal to *me*. It's a new sensation. He grows on me. I start to look forward to our rendezvous. He even offers to let me move into his mansion in New Jersey and suggests we have a child together.

"I just know my mom would love you," he tells me.

I become a jack of all trades, adapting quickly is the nature of the job. If a client wants electrical play, suddenly I'm a master electrician. If he wants piercings, suddenly I'm the most experienced piercer there ever was. I never turn down a job. I revel in the fact that I can be anyone at any given moment. I transform into your mean mommy, an evil nun, the bitchy popular girl in high school, all in a day's work. My strong intuition and excellent improvisation skills keep the job interesting and the money rolling in.

"Valentina, you do submissive session with Joe," Greta says to me with a jolly grin. I gulp at the thought. I've overheard the girls talk about how great the money is for submissive sessions. This is when the roles reverse and the client dommes the mistress. One girl got a whopping two-thousand-dollar tip, but she was made to crawl around on all fours and bark like a dog. She even had to pee on a wee-wee pad and drink water out of a dog bowl. Doesn't sound so bad to me. I desperately want to get my own apartment. I'm tired of Dina waking me up at the crack of dawn and I'm over sharing a bunk bed with Liana and her boyfriend.

"He's very nice guy, very easy, you have fun. You have jeans?"

"Jeans?" This is a little strange. I've never been asked to wear jeans in a session.

"In closet." She throws the keys at me, narrowly missing my head. I run back into the chamber of dildos, desperately hoping for a pair of jeans to materialize so Greta doesn't kill me. I finally find a pair of off-brand low-rise bell-bottoms and slip into them, unable to shake the feeling that they've never been washed before. I wipe my sweaty palms on the denim as my heart races from the thought of putting myself at the mercy of a stranger. I'm terrified, but there's a part of me that finds the danger exhilarating. The allure of surrendering control draws me in and I fantasize about relinquishing my power and letting someone take charge, even if only for an hour.

I'm so nervous when I step into the "Medieval Torture Chamber," a dimly lit room with stone walls, a cage, and a padded bench. I've perfected my poker face and without a trace of fear in my voice, I say, "Hi, I'm Valentina."

"So nice to meet you." He stands up and makes his way toward me. "Wow, so beautiful. You are even more beautiful in person. You're so young." He takes my hand and twirls me around. "Wow, your ass is incredible, do you mind?"

Before I can respond, he has both hands cupping my ass. Strangely, I don't really mind being fondled through denim.

"Is this your real hair?" he asks in disbelief as he runs his hands through it.

I don't understand what is happening but I play along.

"Can you sit on my face with the jeans?" he asks. I nod. He lies down on the floor and I squat over his face and begin suffocating him with my ass. He unbuckles his belt and I see white strings fall out of his pants. Then I see curls tucked behind his ears and it all makes sense. He's Orthodox Jewish.

I'm almost disappointed when he's finished a few minutes later. He hastily gets dressed, hands me his business card and four crisp hundred-dollar bills, and runs out the door.

When the session is over, I run to Greta and let her know to start advertising me as a sub. She purses her lips and sighs. "Don't be stupid, girl, they not all like Joe," she warns me. But her words fall on deaf ears.

My second submissive session is nothing like my first. As soon as I step foot in the room, a bone-piercing chill washes over me. The older British businessman barely spares me a glance as he curtly directs me where to stand. He doesn't exude warmth the way Jeans Joe did. I watch in silence as he unbuttons his jacket, revealing an opulent watch and an impeccably tailored suit that scream generational wealth.

He pulls out a fat stack of crisp hundred-dollar bills and hands me one for each article of clothing I shed. Another hundred is offered to hook my arms to the suspension bar, followed by another two hundred to whip me and another hundred to do it hard.

The room we're in is lined with mirrors, and as I stand there, completely naked with my legs apart and wrists tied up and hooked to the ceiling, I can't escape my reflection. I can see myself from every angle. I look so vulnerable in the center of the room, flinching with every strike from the leather flogger. I wonder what people would think if they saw me like this. And then the most forbidden thought of all crosses my mind: What would my parents think if they saw me like this? Cringe.

I'm becoming increasingly popular at the dungeon, often booked back-to-back while some of the other girls sit around for entire days without a session. It's impressive considering I'm only eighteen and the youngest girl to ever work there.

One day, I come into work to find that my cherry-red patent-leather Jimmy Choo pumps, gifted to me by a loyal foot fetishist, were used as an ashtray. I scoop them up and rush into the lounge, demanding to know who defaced them.

Mistress Sadée whispers that a certain Mistress Violet is the culprit.

"And I don't know if this is true or not," she says, "but I wouldn't wear your black leather leotard anymore."

"Umm . . . why?" I ask, as I'm wearing it.

She hesitates a moment. "I'm pretty sure she peed on it, but you didn't hear it from me. She does this to all the new girls."

I do my best to keep my composure but my insides are ablaze.

"I was wondering why it felt damp," I say calmly. "I figured maybe it was the humidity of the basement."

"She broke into a girl's locker and stole everything, and when the girl complained they didn't do jack shit, so the girl just left. And you know how horrible she is to me. She zaps me on purpose!"

I nod with a sympathetic look. Mistress Sadée lives in the upstairs lounge. She wears a long string braided into her long red hair with a ball of tinfoil attached to the end. When she walks, it drags behind her like a can on a car that says "Just Married." She constantly complains about being zapped by cell phones. I tested this theory when her back was turned. I pointed my phone at her and waved it around, but she didn't flinch.

I run to the bathroom and rip the leotard off my body and begin scrubbing at my skin with hand sanitizer. All the while, my heart is pounding. Sure, I'm young and quiet and keep to myself, but she has no idea the levels of rage I harbor beneath my cool exterior. She just unleashed the beast and I'm going to ruin her life. *For fun.*

There's no use telling Greta about my vicious attack, because Mistress Violet is her favorite girl. I know she's a cash cow, even though she looks like a wet rat. She's tragic, but she's a good dominatrix. I look at the schedule and see she's due to clock in soon. Perfect, I'll just wait here for her.

I wait for what feels like hours before I hear it. That noise. Her voice. The unmistakable nasal squeal accompanied by the unmistakable thick Buffalo accent. "Hi, Greta! How are you today?"

I hear her footsteps approaching, and I rise to meet her at the door. As she enters, I quickly shut it behind her, causing her to flinch. With every step I take closer to her, she takes one step back. The color drains from her face, leaving her looking like she just saw a ghost. Seeing her cower fills me with adrenaline, and at that moment everyone else vanishes, all her friends, and it's just me and my prey.

"Now we're having fun!" I yell at her with a maniacal grin. The same one Ace wore when cornering his next victim. I trap her the same way, towering over her since she's shorter without her Pleaser heels on. Looking down at the top of her head, I notice her stringy hair, which has faded to a dingy lime green color, the dandruff, the acne scars and greasy skin, and the dark puffy rings under her eyes.

"What the fuck do you want from me?" she asks, trying to weave past me. I stick my arm out to block her path and shout through my clenched jaw.

"You like pissing on people's shit like a fucking dog?"

"I don't know what you're talking about," she says, avoiding eye contact.

I raise my voice. "Are you incontinent?"

With her back against the wall and her minions frozen in disbelief, never having seen her like this before, she begins to panic. "Get the fuck away from me! I don't even know you!" she screams loudly enough that Greta hears her and comes to the rescue.

"Get to know me, bitch! I'm from here! I'll fucking kill you!"

The door flings open and all three hundred pounds of Greta come waddling toward us as fast as she possibly can.

"Valentina! This is not your shift! Go home, Valentina!" she yells.

She wraps her arms around me and drags me out of the room but I can't control my rage and keep yelling, "Greta can only save you in here, bitch! I'll wait for you outside! You're so tough, right? Come meet me outside! One-on-one! Fight me, bitch!"

Greta shushes me, placing her hand over my mouth.

"She pissed on my shit, Greta! You need to fire her!" I plead with her.

"Valentina, you are new here. Don't make problems for us."

I want to kill Greta too at this point, but then I remember that she has been a dominatrix ever since she escaped Ukraine. This is her entire life. It's all she knows. I make a promise to myself at that moment that I won't get trapped in this lifestyle like so many before me. I'm going to make something of myself, and I'm going to show them.

I storm out of the dungeon, seething with rage and frustration. As I bike down the street, the adrenaline pumps through my veins and I begin to devise an entire plan on how I'm going to exact my revenge.

The next day, I wait for Greta to leave her desk and then I dig through the cabinet where she keeps all our portfolios, which are filled with our best photographs and any excerpts of writing that we feel best represent our specialties. They are essential, since it's what the clients first see upon their arrival and it's how they choose who they want to sample. Kind of like a menu. I flip through the books until I find Mistress Violet's, then I run to the client restroom and rip out her bio and the few decent photos she has in there and flush them down the toilet. This will eliminate any chance of her securing any new clients as walk-ins.

I feel a brief sense of accomplishment but I need instant gratification. I have to ruin her things and it has to be even more vile than what she did to me.

It's a slow Monday night and the lounge is pretty much empty. I sit on the couch, staring at Mistress Violet's locker, waiting patiently for my chance to get her back.

I stand up and pretend to look at myself in the mirror nearby. When nobody's looking, I tug on the lock, revealing a little opening about a centimeter wide. My hand won't fit. Then it hits me. I don't have to take anything out, I can just put something in.

I remember there are enemas in the medical room. All I have to do is fill up a bag with piss and place the plastic tube through the tiny opening and let the contents drip inside. I tiptoe to the medical room and open the disposable enema and pee where one would usually place lukewarm water before hooking one end of the enema to a pole and the other end in someone's butthole.

I assess the contents of the bag and decide this isn't going to be enough. After trying to shit directly into the bag with little success, I put on a latex glove and scoop it out of the toilet. I'm starting to question if all this trouble is even worth it but then I remember my red patent-leather Jimmy Choo's, now burnt and destroyed. I seal the bag and shake it violently, creating a stinky stewlike mixture. I spray myself with the linen Febreze and tuck the enema under my shirt.

As I speed-walk past Greta at the front desk, we lock eyes and I look away. Greta can see directly into the lounge if she scoots her chair back a couple of inches, and Violet's locker is directly in her sight line. I wait for the phone to ring and dart across the room and stand up on a stool, clutching the vile plastic bag. I place the tube through the small opening and watch as the contents of the bag slowly trickle into her locker. Greta hangs up the phone and I squeeze hard on the bag. The room starts to stink but I can't wipe the demonic grin off my face.

That night, I make sure to take all my belongings home with me in preparation for the literal shitstorm that might ensue. But to my surprise, a few days pass and I don't hear a thing about it. A week later when I see Violet's name on the schedule, I strut into the lounge, head high, and plop myself down on the couch, inviting confrontation. She ignores me and continues to do her makeup in the mirror as I glare at her. A few minutes pass and I realize she's never going to admit that I got her back. She won't give me the satisfaction, so I'm going to get it myself.

"Ew, Violet, you stink!" I say as I get up to leave.

The room erupts in laughter.

After the altercation with Violet, the girls start warming up to me. It's as if I proved myself to them while simultaneously removing a tyrannical authoritarian who had been ruling over them, purposely making their lives hell. No one fears her anymore and I'm actually becoming friends with these girls.

Between living at Liana's house with her mom and working at the dungeon every day, I'm overdosing on estrogen. And since I don't smoke weed anymore, I barely hang out with my old crew, consisting of mostly pothead boys from the neighborhood who all stay afloat by selling dime bags to each other. I've come to discover that girls are so much more colorful. The dull and sterile backdrop that had been my life is now this vibrant luminescent force field that guides me when I am lost, protects me when I'm in danger, and nurtures me when I need love. I even tell my fellow dommes about Veronica, and they vow to help me find her and beat her ass all the way back to Italy.

Mistress Olympia used to be a teacher, and she helps me with my homework in the School Room. Mistress Keisha always has a blunt in her mouth and a set of ears ready for our weekly therapy session. Mistress Anastasia went to my high school ten years ago and says I'm her "mini me." She doesn't come in often, but when she does she always pulls me into her sessions and tips me generously. She uses her client to teach me how to use the ropes to tie up a man's cock and balls. Mistress Asia does my makeup and puts my black hair in gorgeous finger waves for photo shoots so I can have better images in my portfolio. Even Greta warms up to me when she discovers we have the same birthday.

I overhear the girls talk about the "pretty dommes" a lot, and how they don't typically last more than six months at the dungeon.

"Why?" I ask naïvely.

"They get plucked up by sugar daddies who don't wanna share them!"

I look in the mirror, examining myself. I wonder if I'll be one of the lucky ones.

Every night before bed, I spend an hour scrolling through Backpage searching for my long-lost sugar daddy. I shut my eyes and pray: "Please, God. Please send me a sugar daddy. I promise I'll be so good. I'll never do anything bad again."

Within the first month of working at the dungeon, I save enough money to move into my own apartment, bringing Liana with me. It's a cozy second-floor studio in the Meatpacking District for fourteen hundred dollars a month, conveniently located between the dungeon in Chelsea and my high school in the West Village. I scour Craigslist for beautiful vintage furniture and decorate it tastefully, keeping it clean and tidy. At night, I lie in my big iron canopy bed, basking in pride and grateful to finally have a place of my own.

I still enjoy clubbing on the weekends, and one morning, as I'm hosting a cocaine-fueled after-hours gathering, I hear a knock on the door. It's six a.m., and the sun is just starting to peek through my ruby-red curtains. I assume it's just another degenerate I drunkenly invited over, so I step over the bodies sprawled across my kitchen floor and, without thinking, I swing the front door open.

I gasp when I see my probation officer standing in front of me as a cloud of smoke pours out of my front door directly onto her. She looks past me at the myriad confused faces staring back at her. "My roommate is having a party," I quickly say, pointing to Liana in the corner. Thank God she doesn't know Liana is my codefendant, since it's technically illegal for us to even be in the same room.

Ms. Cortez nods suspiciously before asking me to step outside. I nod and let the door close behind me.

"Does your roommate throw lots of parties like this all the time?" she asks.

I fidget, not knowing what the right answer is. "Not really."

Miraculously, her phone starts ringing. She looks at it and looks back at me. "I gotta go. This isn't over." She points her finger in my face. "I'm testing you next week."

I step back inside the apartment and fall to my knees, thanking God for another chance. Once I gather myself, I stand up and yell, "Everyone needs to get the fuck out now!"

I learn that Veronica finally returned to Italy after overstaying her visa and is unable to come back to the United States for the next ten years. But even with her gone, I can't regain the image of my dad that I had before. That version of him has been scrapped from my mind. Instead, I find myself wondering what they did and what they possibly could have discussed on their strolls through Central Park while my world was falling apart.

When I finally return to my childhood home after months of being banned for assaulting Veronica, I notice that it doesn't smell the way it used to. It smells like *her*. The strong Hermès men's cologne she wore lingers in the air like a dog that marked its territory. The scent floods me with resentment. I march into my dad's bedroom to find the bottle sitting in plain sight on his cluttered bookshelf. I shudder and immediately vacate the premises.

After her departure my dad goes on tour with a traveling band he meets in Tompkins Square Park.

"We're driving to Alaska on a school bus," he tells me excitedly over the phone. "You should come, it's fun!"

I roll my eyes and hang up.

One day while he's on tour he calls to tell me that Marissa contacted him.

I'm shocked to hear her name after so many years.

"Mia dropped out of college and needs a place to stay in the city. Do you wanna split the rent with her?"

I scan my tiny studio apartment. It's already cramped with me and Liana living there.

"The only place to put a mattress is on the floor in the kitchen," I tell him.

"She said she doesn't care what it is."

My mind jumps back in time and I'm eight years old again, eating Milano cookies on the pullout couch, watching *Romy and Michele's High School Reunion* for the third time in a row.

"Yeah, sure," I tell him.

A few days later, Mia and her mom arrive with two big suitcases and a box of Italian pastries. I've seen Mia around at parties over the years, but I haven't seen Marissa since the second grade when I was practically ripped from her arms. She holds me hostage in a hug for an uncomfortable amount of time.

I sit on my bed quietly watching Mia unpack. She seems pensive and preoccupied. This isn't at all what I had envisioned. A part of me wants to ask her about *it:* our last phone call and what happened to her life after that. I know my life was never the same. I have so many questions but I'm not sure I want to know the answer.

I spend most of my time out of the house. During the day I go to school or my drug program, and I spend most of my nights at the dungeon, sometimes staying there overnight. I'm addicted to making money. I make thousands of dollars a week, most of it cash. I stash it all over the apartment but there's too much of it. I can't keep track of it and I certainly can't count it all. I laugh thinking about how little has changed since I was a kid stacking up ninety-nine-dollar piles.

I decide to put it all into envelopes and give them to my dad to store in his safe. I don't keep a tally, I just assume he will put it away for me. After a couple of months, when I show up at his apartment to retrieve my money, I discover he has spent most of it. After I freak out, he tells me he'll write me a check for the amount that's missing, but I don't know how much there was to begin with. I simply cannot trust this man, no matter how hard I try.

After a few months working at the dungeon, an angsty feeling creeps into my life and I start feeling disillusioned by it all. I'm beginning to find it harder and harder to jump in and out of character all day. I'm exhausted by the easiest of sessions. My go-to move is sitting on the clients' faces and forcing them to jerk off and come within fifteen minutes, to get them out of there faster. I feel drained. I feel depleted. I'm burnt out. I even tell one of my clients he should go to therapy and unpack the trauma with his mom. My soul can't handle it anymore. With my probation officer up my ass, I can't even smoke a blunt to relax.

One snowy night while Mia and Liana are out, I decide I want to trip on acid. I call a dealer recommended by a friend, and he tells me he'll be at my place in an hour. I wait patiently but he doesn't show up. The blizzard outside seems violent, but when I text him again asking to cancel the order, he calls me, begging me not to. "The trains stopped working. I promise I'm on my way."

Two more hours pass before he shows up, completely soaked and shivering in his black leather jacket. I give him the money and he hands me a damp baggy with six little sheets of acid inside.

"Um, do you wanna come in?" I ask him.

"Oh my God, yes, please, my dick is about to fall off."

His crystal-blue eyes twinkle when he smiles. I giggle as I lead him to the couch. He begins to undress. He drapes his wet clothes over the door and I notice the scars on his veins. He tells me he plays drums in a punk band and that he's "sober."

"I'm only drinking beer and smoking weed right now," he tells me.

I confide that I attend a court-mandated drug program, so I don't party as much as I used to.

"Do you mind if I roll up?" he asks, pulling out a pack of American Spirit rolling tobacco. He breaks up a nug of weed and rolls up the tiniest joint I've ever seen. "Do you wanna hit it?" he asks.

"My drug program, remember?"

"Oh, right, my bad. So you're a bad girl, huh?"

"Reformed, maybe?" I say with a mischievous smirk.

Luke is his name. We talk all night, which mostly consists of him talking and me listening. He reads me his poetry off his phone and plays sad songs on my computer. As the sun rises he leans in to kiss me. As our lips lock, I feel sparks traveling across both our bodies. His lips are soft and his kisses are succulent. I take my top off and he suddenly stops and whispers, "I have to go to my methadone program." He gives me a kiss on the forehead and dashes out the door.

The next day I can't stop thinking about him. I keep checking my phone, hoping to see a text from him. I call our mutual friend, Sara, to find out more about him.

"He just broke up with his girlfriend," she tells me. "They had such a crazy relationship."

"Who is she?" I ask.

"She's older than us. She does porn. Facial abuse stuff."

"What do you mean?"

"Like getting her head flushed in the toilet and stuff like that," Sara says casually.

I text Luke again under the guise of buying more acid and invite him back to my apartment. We get to talking and I mention I have some Vicodins in my bathroom mirror. "I've been saving them for a rainy day."

"Does snowy count?" he asks with a devious grin.

I go to the bathroom to retrieve them. I throw him the pill container, and he dumps six pills onto his palm. With one swift motion, he swallows them all down and chases them with a Modelo.

That night we make love and I discover he has the biggest penis I've ever seen. When we're done he whispers into my ear in his raspy voice, "I really like you. Would you date me?"

I feel the butterflies. My cheeks blush. "Maybe," I say.

The next day, he's in a terrible mood. "Fuck, I missed my methadone!" He's pissed.

"Can't you go later?" I ask.

"It doesn't work like that. They shut the doors in your face. They don't care if you're dying!"

I remain quiet as he collects his clothing strewn around my room.

"You don't understand the severity of my addiction! You shouldn't have given those pills to me!"

I feel like the biggest piece of shit in the world. "I'm sorry. I really didn't know."

"It's fine. I shouldn't even . . . You know what, never mind."

He storms out and I don't speak to him for a few days. I try to distract myself but my mind keeps going back to our revolutionary sex.

I call Sara again, pleading with her to tell me anything she knows about where he might be.

"I think he's using heroin again," she says. "I forgot who told me."

"Fuck, it's all my fault."

"No, babe, he's back at his ex-girlfriend's house, shooting up with her."

My sadness instantly morphs into anger. I'm fuming. I hang up the phone and type out a text to send him. I have to lure him back and show him what he's missing.

"Hey Luke, I have some H I wanna get rid of. Let me know if you can come over later to pick up."

I press send and not even a minute later my phone rings. He's coming over tonight. I hang up and call Romeo.

"Long time no see!" he says excitedly.

"I need a bundle, it's a literal emergency."

"Aight, I'll be there in an hour."

My heart races at the thought of doing heroin again. I haven't touched it since Liana yelled at me at her and Kai's party and made me flush it.

Later that night when Luke arrives I'm sprawled out over the bed seductively, wearing black sheer pantyhose without panties and a black lace bra with a short silk robe wrapped around my shoulders. "She's Lost Control" by Joy Division plays in the background. He keeps his gaze low as he talks to me, purposely not acknowledging that I dressed up for him. I begin to feel silly. The sparkle in his eyes has faded. He looks sickly and disheveled. Before he can say anything, I blurt out, "I want you to shoot me up."

He pauses, examining the veins on my arm. "Have you ever done it before?" he asks. I shake my head no. He thinks about it for a moment before getting up to go to the kitchen.

He pulls a spoon out of a drawer and bends it. He drops some water in it from a water bottle and sprinkles the brownish powder over it. He then takes a little piece of cotton from a cotton swab and rolls it into a little ball, drops it in, and pierces it with a syringe that he brought. My heart pounds as I watch the tainted water rise in the syringe. I'm mesmerized by his skill.

He ties my arm with a belt. Smacks my largest vein with his hand. "You have great veins."

I look up and force a smile. I know this is a bad idea.

I flinch as the needle pierces my vein. My eyes remain fixed as I watch my blood get sucked back into the syringe. It looks so pretty as it swirls around in there for a brief instant before he pushes it all back inside me. I feel a warm sensation creep over my body, more intense than anything I've ever felt. Pure bliss. And then there's nothing. Only blackness.

I wake in my hallway half naked with my neighbors towering over me. Paramedics kneel over me with an oxygen mask. They shot me up with Narcan to counteract the heroin. I scream for Luke. I hear my neighbor telling the paramedics, "A guy dragged her down the stairs and pounded on all our doors to call the cops."

I cry as the paramedics strap my nearly naked thrashing body to a stretcher. "I don't wanna go! Please! I wanna stay here!"

When I arrive at the emergency room, I call Luke on repeat, cursing at him. I glance down at my wrist and notice my bracelet is gone, the one that was placed on my wrist at birth. I figure it must have fallen off at my apartment and shift my attention back to him. "How could you have left me like that? Did you steal all my drugs?" I yell into the hospital phone when he finally answers. He hangs up and turns off his phone. A few hours later I walk home from the hospital in my pantyhose and bra, cursing him all the way.

The next day, when I've calmed down, I call him to ask him what happened.

"I know I shouldn't be telling you but I almost was just gonna leave when you started foaming—"

That's all I need to hear. I hang up the phone and vow to never speak to him again. I tear my apartment apart looking for my bracelet, my most prized possession in the world. In searching for it, I realize more of my jewelry is missing: the bracelet made of charms that my grandma and I had collected over the years. It feels like a stab to the heart. How could I have been so stupid to allow this to happen? Why does something inside me want to kill me?

My mind goes back to the overdose, the infinite pit of blackness I saw. I didn't see a light or a window or a tunnel like the last time. There was nothing for me on the other side.

Liana is the only one who seems to care. She calls my mom, pleading with her to save me. "She's your daughter, and she's going to die!" she screams into the phone. But I know my mom all too well. I'm not surprised when she hangs up on Liana.

I can sense the heartbreak and frustration in Liana's voice as she yells to no one in particular, "What kind of mom doesn't care about her own kid?" But I know the answer all too well. I never had a *real* mom.

One night Marissa and Mia invite my dad and me out to dinner to thank us for allowing Mia to move in on such short notice. Since my dad agreed to give me his urine for drug tests, we're on speaking terms, so I decide to go. When we arrive at the restaurant and wait for my dad, I can sense Marissa's nerves. She reapplies her lipstick in the reflection of her glasses and fixes her hair. It feels a little awkward. She looks different now, with years of a painful life beginning to show in the cracks of her tanned skin, her teeth darkened from years of smoking and her eyes tired and droopy. It's a stark contrast to the vibrant and vivacious Marissa I once considered a surrogate mother. Now we make small talk as we sit anxiously awaiting the missing piece of this fucked-up equation.

He finally arrives, and for a brief moment I glimpse what our lives could have been like, allowing myself to imagine what it would feel like if *this* were my family. It feels surreal but I'm quickly brought back to reality by my dad's behavior. He starts drinking and I know this isn't going to end well. Marissa keeps trying to catch his eye, but he avoids her gaze like the plague. I can sense her frustration while he makes himself as unlikable as possible. It's as if he's doing it on purpose to spare her feelings.

After dinner I just want the night to end, but Marissa insists we take a walk down Bleecker Street. We end up in a bar, and not even a few minutes later my dad gets on the floor and starts doing the worm. My jaw drops as I watch my dad behave like a lunatic. I've never seen him do this before. I grab him off the floor and before I can scold him, he darts out the door without saying bye. The rest of the night feels like a blur except for the clear look of disappointment and heartbreak on Marissa's face. A few weeks later, Mia informs me she will be moving back to Italy with her mom. I can't help feeling a little disappointed that this wasn't the *Romy and Michele* happy ending I had always envisioned, but at least it's closure.

7

BILLION-DOLLAR BABY

After six long months at the dungeon, I wake up one morning and decide today's my last day. I'm going to quit. I've amassed enough regulars I can see at my apartment, and I can always be a stripper if all else fails. At least it wouldn't require the same amount of mental gymnastics as BDSM.

I've arrived at the dungeon, strutting into the lounge confidently, prepared to say my goodbyes, when Greta yells out, "Valentina! You have outcall. Classy guy, rich guy." She winks and warns me, "Dress elegant, Valentina. No hooker."

I've never done an outcall before, but they're known to pay well, so I nod and run back to my locker. Rummaging through my collection of Sixth Avenue sex-shop lingerie, I find a Victoria's Secret maxidress with a hideous floral print that I like to lounge in and throw it on. I pack a big bag of tricks and hail a cab and head uptown.

I arrive at The Union Club, where I'm stopped at the entrance and instructed to enter through the service door. Looking down at my quite modest outfit, I can't help but wonder if they think I'm a prostitute, even though I'm wearing a floor-length dress.

I get upstairs and take my time walking down the long corridor, carefully examining the endless rows of portraits of old white men. This place is the antithesis of sexy. It feels eerie and haunted. The musty smell, peeling wallpaper, and stained carpet make it clear that the place is in dire need of a makeover.

As I stand outside the door, my sweaty palm clutches the rickety brass doorknob. I take a deep breath, trying to expel some of my nerves. The dungeon is a controlled environment and the manager checks in frequently. This place feels abandoned and I'm here alone.

I hear the sound of glasses clinking and someone shuffling around inside the room. I muster up the courage to knock on the door. It swings open, revealing a gentleman in his late forties with tan skin, jet-black hair, big brown eyes, and a warm smile stretching from ear to ear. I extend my sweaty hand and he pulls me in and kisses me twice on each cheek. He introduces himself as Rohan. His accent is unique, Indian with a twang of something else I can't quite place, but it sounds rich.

I excuse myself and run to the bathroom, where I reapply my MAC Ruby Woo red lipstick, let my hair down, and put on my little black dress and heels. When I emerge, I find him standing over a tray of strawberries and whipped cream. He offers me a glass of champagne, and we toast to "new friends." His gaze lingers on me long after I'm done talking, but somehow, he's quite disarming.

I take a seat on the couch, and Rohan pulls a chair next to me. He starts talking about how he came across my photo and was reminded of his childhood girlfriend, who he claims was the love of his life. "You remind me of a young Sophia Loren!" he exclaims, his excitement palpable. When I tell him I'm Italian, he grows even more animated. "I could move to Italy with you tomorrow!" he proclaims dramatically. He's theatrical in his mannerisms, exaggerated, and passionate. He's a natural storyteller and a visionary.

After an hour of talking, I start to wonder when we're going to get this show on the road. "So, what's your fetish?" I ask bluntly.

Rohan pauses, then admits, "My ex-girlfriend, we just broke up not long ago. She confided in me that she had been a dominatrix before we met—"

"So basically you're trying to find her again." I cut him off, feeling emboldened by the drinks. "Like a new version of her, her but not *her*."

"That is a brilliant analysis, I must admit. You are so wise, young girl." Rohan is clearly impressed with me. I blush, realizing that I often receive compliments for the way I look, but no one ever tells me I'm smart.

"Do you mind if I smoke a cigarette?" I ask him.

"Please, make yourself at home."

Rohan stands up to get me an ashtray, and I find myself captivated by him. I've never felt so safe and at ease with any man. Our conversation knows no limits. We cover it all. He seeks my advice on his children, two daughters who are closer to me in age than he is. He says they're acting out and I tell him not to punish them, they are clearly struggling with something deeper. He values my opinion as if I'm his equal. I can tell by how intently he listens to me and by the fact that he remembers everything I say. He's a welcome change from the insecure American men I'm forced to be around.

I don't check my phone for six whole hours as we talk and laugh without pause. When I finally do, I see fifty missed calls from the dungeon.

"I have to go," I say with a sad look on my face.

He seems disappointed too. "May I drive you back downtown?"

"I thought you'd never ask."

During the ride, he plays loud opera music and occasionally belts out lyrics in broken Italian. I laugh uncomfortably, but the truth is I'm both amused and intrigued by this strange eccentric man.

When we arrive at the dungeon, he puts the car in park and we sit in silence, both unsure what to say next.

"You should take my number, 'cause I'm quitting this place," I tell him.

He hands me his iPhone, and I save my name under Valentina/Julia.

A few days pass, and I don't hear from him. I don't think much of it. It's not unusual to forge a connection with a client, but they will usually talk themselves out of pursuing beyond the business transaction. After all, I'm just a sex worker. At night, I still pray for a sugar daddy to rescue me from this life of servitude.

He finally calls me and we make plans to meet for lunch the following day. I'm so nervous that I spend the entire night picking out an outfit. I don't have anything that screams "classy" or "sophisticated." All my clothes resemble things a high-class escort might wear. I try on dozens of outfits before settling on a white knit tank top that lands low enough to expose my hefty load of cleavage, tight jeans, and a pair of Roberto Cavalli wooden platform wedges I thrifted.

He's already seated at the table when I arrive at the restaurant. As soon as he sees me, he stands up and doesn't sit back down until I do. I blush as his eyes move around my body, absorbing every detail. He showers me with so many compliments that while I'm with him, I feel like the most beautiful, brilliant girl in the world.

"I love the way you speak," he says. "It's so Italian. It's like a song." He's so impressed that I speak Italian fluently. "You must teach me!" he says excitedly. He finally asks me how old I am and I lie and tell him I'm twenty, even though I'm really nineteen. I decide not to tell him that I'm still in high school. I can sense that would be a red flag for a man of this caliber.

As I eat my lunch, I can't help but notice the judgmental stares and dirty looks from the hostess that only I seem to be getting.

"So, what's your plan now that you're no longer working at the dungeon?" he asks.

"I don't know. To be completely honest, I really just wanna buy a crappy car and drive across the country and see all the things."

He nods, amused. "But what are you going to do for money?"

"I'm not sure. I was thinking I could work at Scores since it's nearby."

After lunch, I'm tipsy. He walks me to his car, pulls out a checkbook from the console, and hands me a check for seven thousand dollars. "This is to hold you over until you figure it out."

I've never had this much money before. Without thinking, I kiss him right in front of my building, on the street for everyone to see. It's a long, passionate kiss with lots of tongue.

I begin to wonder if God finally answered my prayers for a sugar daddy. But this doesn't feel transactional, and I don't feel like a sugar baby. This feels real.

Rohan and I have lunch again a few days later, this time at a restaurant in the Financial District, where he works. He introduces me to the waiters and the maître d', and unlike the previous restaurant none of them seem bemused by the teenage girl dining with the older man. At lunch, I can barely get a sentence in. Dozens of people come to our table to greet him, as if he's the Godfather.

"This is my dear friend, the lovely Julia," he tells them. "She's from Milan."

I nod and play along.

Out of nowhere, he asks why I haven't cashed the check yet. I hesitate a moment. "I don't know, I don't want you to think I'm only here for your money," I explain.

He immediately shuts it down. "I'm leaving for India for a couple of months and I don't want to worry about you."

He sticks his hand in his jacket and pulls out a thick wad of cash and casually drops it into my purse under the table.

I can hardly contain myself when I glance over at the table beside us and realize Jerry Springer is sitting less than five feet away. I vividly remember a time when Jerry Springer was my only escape. The comforting chant of "Jerry! Jerry! Jerry!" from the audience members drowned out the endless chatter in my mind. He seems so different when he's not on a dingy stage, orchestrating people's drama.

Rohan notices my reaction and teases me, "Are you starstruck?" I nod, feeling embarrassed. "Do you want me to ask him for an auto-graph?" he jokes, grinning mischievously. He's shocked when I nod my head. A few moments later, he returns with a cocktail napkin with Jerry Springer's signature on it.

After lunch, he sends me back to my little studio in a long stretch limo. I thumb through the crisp bills, ecstatic. I count ten thousand dol-lars.

I charge through the front door, waving the cash screaming, "We're rich! We're rich!" I throw Liana a few hundred-dollar bills. She springs out of bed and jumps up and down with me, screaming, "Oh my God! We're rich!"

Later, she asks me, "What kind of car does he drive?" as we lie side by side on the canopy bed.

"Um, I'm not sure. It had a letter B on the steering wheel, I think."

"Bugatti!"

"No."

"Bentley?"

"Yeah! That's it, I think."

"When do I get to meet him?"

"He's leaving for a month. When he comes back!"

We squeal with excitement.

Rohan and I text sporadically in his absence. A lot in the beginning and then gradually less and less. I graduate high school and celebrate by getting high. I complete my drug program with my dad's help and now I only have to report to probation once a month, just to scan my hand.

This newfound privilege causes me to spiral, especially now that I have money to burn. Liana and I go out every night until dawn, chas-ing Xanax bars with unlimited shots of promoter tequila and blacking out on purpose. We do lines of coke off each other's feet for the viewing pleasure of older graff heads. We even go to the Box and take our clothes off onstage with the performers.

One evening at Mama's Bar in the Lower East Side, I go to the bathroom to pee. When I pull down my pants, I find something strange on my panties. It looks like a ball of wax with veins running through it. I examine it closely and flick it into the toilet. As I flush, it dawns on me that I just had a miscarriage. I scramble and try fishing it out, but it's too late. I watch my embryonic sac circle the drain and disappear into the New York City sewage system. I feel bad that I couldn't give it a more dignified arrangement. I wonder for a moment who the father could be and truthfully I have no clue. I sigh and shrug and go back to the bar to finish my drink.

One particularly tumultuous drug-fueled night, Liana slaps me in the face and gets kicked out of our friend's house. When she wakes up alone at her mom's house covered in vomit, she decides she's had enough and is ready for radical change.

A teacher in middle school once told Liana about A.A. meetings and how they had saved her husband's life. Liana tucked that little bit of information safely away in her mind, and on one cold winter night she drags her limp body to the Midnite meeting of Alcoholics Anonymous, where an old eccentric man named Nicky finds her and invites her back to his home in Queens. She could either go back to her mom's hoarder house or take a chance. And she does, she stays at his house for the entire week. During this time, she barely texts any of us and she doesn't answer our calls. When I finally get in touch with her, she tells me about Nicky and the meetings and I'm surprised to hear that she actually sounds *good*.

"You should come with me, J," she says.

I remember how my mother detested Alcoholics Anonymous, and though I don't feel the same way, I think that I'm different from them. "I can stop whenever I want. I just don't want to right now."

I can sense Liana's disappointment since we always do everything together, but by now she has the wisdom to know that this is a journey she needs to take on her own.

· · ·

I continue blowing through Rohan's money, and by the time he returns there's none left and I'm a completely different girl. I've gained twenty pounds, and I'm undeniably unrecognizable.

"Wow, you look so different," he says to me in amazement as I nod out at the table. He doesn't seem to be bothered by my behavior, nor does he judge me. He finds it amusing that I wake up in the afternoon and that I never know what day it is.

"I've never met anyone like you before, it's so refreshing!" he says as I down six glasses of wine in a row.

"Am I your girlfriend?" I ask him, slurring my words.

He pauses. "I would love that," he says.

I'm constantly blown away by Rohan's kindness, but I also feel guilty for hiding my addiction from him. He doesn't seem to notice, or maybe he chooses to ignore it. Whatever the case may be, I can't understand what this *good* man sees in me. He's like a guardian angel to me. His energy is so intense that I feel his presence even when he's not around. It's like I can feel him thinking about me. We often text each other at the same time or have similar dreams. It's like we are bound on a cosmic level that's beyond my level of comprehension.

We spend hours talking and he'll drop anything in a heartbeat to spend time with me. He rents me a new apartment in the East Village and never comes over. I suspect he knows the living conditions would tarnish his perception of me. I appreciate that he protects his love for me. He sends me flowers and a brand-new Chanel bag when we move in, and I cherish every gift he gives me. My favorite is the four-leaf clover he picked on the day we met. I keep it stored safely among the rest of my jewels. When I'm with him, I hide the tracks on my arms with long-sleeved shirts, but when I come home I have a spoon on my nightstand waiting for me.

I can't help but wonder if the only reason he shows so much interest in me is because we haven't had sex yet. It's a well-known fact that most men lose interest once they get a taste and I refuse to let that happen to me again. I'm so anxious that he will disappear from my life that I with-hold sex for months before I eventually concede.

The thought of having sex with Rohan sends a rush of excitement through me, yet at the same time, it feels wrong. I pop a Xanax in my mouth as I head to the hotel, and when I arrive he has a shiny red Cartier box on the table. He hands it to me and I pop it open, revealing a beauti-ful platinum diamond ring. It's not an engagement ring, but it's all the confirmation I need that he's in it for the long haul. I put the ring on and he kisses my hand all the way up my arm and into the nape of my neck à la Gomez from *The Addams Family*. I giggle, trying my best to be sexy and not seem nervous.

I chug two glasses of champagne and the angst slowly begins to melt away. I turn off the light and begin to undress. He turns it back on and watches me from across the room, his eyes oozing with lust and desire. I sit at the foot of the bed in a black La Perla lingerie set he gifted me as he stands before me and lifts me up and we fall back onto the mattress. He slowly pulls my panties down, spreads my legs, and dives into me. I'm in ecstasy as his tongue slides across my body. I glance down at his face completely glazed in a layer of my fluids. I've never been touched by a man with this much experience and I think to myself that he really knows what he's doing.

After about thirty minutes, I begin to feel drowsy. I try my best to stay alert, but it's too late. Between the silence and the Xanax, I doze off. He's so engrossed in every crevice of my body that luckily he doesn't seem to notice. I'm so tired and I just want it to be over, so I decide I'm going to finish the job. I climb on top of him and turn around, sixty-nining with him. I wrap my hands around his penis. It's thick and girthy and covered in veins. I envelop his penis with my lips and suck it for three minutes that feel like three hours. I crack open my eyes and steal a peek at his naked body.

He's in good shape for his age.

•   •   •

On a routine visit to the probation office, I scan my hand and get an unexpected notification that I've been randomly selected for a drug test. Luckily, my dad gave me his pee, which I had warmed up in the microwave before biking over, so I'm not worried.

But my confidence wavers when an officer comes over and informs me that they've run out of urine tests. "Sit here, I'm going to get an oral swab."

I couldn't have anticipated this. As I wait for them to call my name and begin saying a prayer, a young guy next to me offers me a Listerine strip. Without thinking, I accept the strip and place it on my tongue. Moments later, my name is called, and when the officer swabs my mouth it comes back negative for everything. I feel as though I just went skydiving, except I'm not jumping from a plane in the sky, I'm walking on a tightrope over the fiery pits of prison without a parachute or a safety net.

As I speed-walk out of there, I still can't believe I tested clean. I realize that the antibacterial agent in the Listerine strip must have killed any trace of drugs lingering in my saliva. That guy saved my life. I wish I could thank him.

On my twentieth birthday, I return home after a long lunch with Rohan, clutching the bundle of heroin I've been saving in my pocket. As I step through my front door, the lights come on and all my friends jump out, yelling, "Surprise!" I'm touched by the gesture and I want to seem appreciative, but the truth is, I just want to get high by myself.

I entertain my guests for a few minutes before excusing myself to go to the bathroom. I run the water in the sink and start setting up a shot. I sprinkle the powder onto the spoon and watch it get sucked up into the syringe. I put a hair tie around my arm to make the veins bulge and stick the needle inside. As the warm sensation travels across my veins, I pull my sleeve down and open the door. But before I can take more than a few steps, I fall headfirst into a box of pizza.

I wake up briefly to paramedics surrounding me and the sound of Liana sobbing in the distance before passing out again.

• • •

When I regain consciousness, I find myself in the emergency room again. This time, Liana is by my side, and by the look on her face she's just about had it with me. I reluctantly agree to accompany her to the Midnite meeting of Alcoholic Anonymous, the same meeting she got sober at.

The moment we arrive I can't wait for it to be over. I can't sit still. My leg shakes uncontrollably while my eyes keep darting toward the clock on the wall. I feel hot and cold, my eyes are watery, and I keep yawning. All I can think about is getting high.

An Australian man at the lectern begins speaking. I turn to Liana and roll my eyes, zoning out, lost in thought, until something he says sparks my attention.

"Drugs will give you wings to fly, but it'll take away the sky."

I feel like I've been soaring through the infinite abyss for so long and I finally see a glimmer of hope. Liana nudges me to raise my hand. In between ugly sobs and hiccups, I tell the room how lonely I am and how stuck I feel. When the meeting ends, I'm swarmed with people asking for my number, and in no time, I'm transported to the proverbial pink cloud that all the sober folk speak about. After that, I start attending meetings every day and stop hanging out with anyone who isn't sober.

Rohan seems a little disappointed when I tell him I don't want to drink anymore. Like my mom, he thinks A.A. is for Americans. "But I *am* American!" I whine. "I want to get my life together and go to college and become a real member of society," to which he replies, "Julia, you will never have to work a day in your life!"

His statement comforts me and scares me at the same time. I yearn for purpose and I so desperately want to make something of myself. There's a reason I didn't die, and I have to figure it out.

I'm worried I won't be able to hang out with Rohan sober. I don't even know who I am without substances. Downing bottles of red wine and sneaking to the bathroom was the norm, it's how I got through it. How am I going to go at this alone?

The first few dates are tough. I don't laugh as loudly at his jokes. I catch myself zoning out and checking my phone uncomfortably. I struggle to be present and in the moment. But eventually, I get to know him as my genuine self, and he gets to know the *real* me. To my surprise, this is when he falls in love with me. I can let out a sigh of relief, as I was terrified he wouldn't like me anymore if I wasn't enhanced by the drugs.

I start taking care of myself. I cut my long stringy black hair into a chic bob with bangs and dye it back to a cool brown. I quickly start losing weight and go back to a size 2/4 from an 8/10. I get rid of all my trashy rags and start dressing in designer clothes. I make an array of appointments with doctors and dentists and aestheticians, all on Rohan's dime.

For my twenty-first birthday, he gets me a cherry-red Mercedes-Benz that I drive without a license while still on probation. When I get pulled over, I always manage to charm my way out of it. He upgrades our cramped Lower East Side apartment to a spacious loft in Soho, and Liana has her own room now. Viki, who was once an after-hours friend of ours, comes to stay with us on the weekends, and when she graduates college she moves in with us permanently. Having them with me takes the pressure off me to perform, and quickly we become a little family unit in which we are the cute little parasites and Rohan is the generous host. "I got three for the price of one," he jokes.

He exposes us to a world of luxury and culture, inviting us to the opera, the ballet, and front-row seats for shows like *The Book of Mormon* and Charlie Sheen's drug-fueled theatrical debut. We even sit courtside at Knicks games, even though I find sports so boring. He takes us on shopping sprees at Bergdorf's and Saks, and it becomes tradition that we all spend Thanksgiving and Christmas Day together at Cipriani. I always order the gnocchi and he always gets an arugula salad with olive oil and lemon.

I even introduce him to my mom and they become fast friends, exchanging numbers and having lunch if she's in town. My life is so enmeshed in his that I start to lose myself a little bit. His larger-than-life personality eclipses me. I try so hard to be the perfect girl for him that I don't ever have the chance to get to know myself.

The more he starts to like me, the higher his expectations become. He wants me to dress more conservatively, so I do. He tells me to stop biting my nails, so I do. He says my arms are too hairy, so I get the hair lasered off. He's the painter and I'm the canvas, and he's painting his greatest masterpiece, so I better not interfere.

His nickname for me is *"poupée."* It's French for "doll." And I'm starting to feel like just that: a doll that he can dress and play with. Or a caged animal, but the cage is platinum and encrusted with diamonds and nobody feels any sympathy when I complain about it.

He starts becoming more needy and possessive, and I live in constant fear that he will take everything away from us. It's a different kind of fear than I felt with Ace, a different kind of possessiveness, but no less damaging. I begin to feel trapped and dependent on him for everything. My friends depend on him now too, and the pressure overwhelms me. He gives me just enough money to keep me asking for more, and I've completely adapted to this new lifestyle as his princess. But the weight of his affection is too heavy for me to carry. It's bringing me down. I'm miserable, but still, I can't let him go. When did he become both the hero *and* the villain in my story?

I can sense him overanalyzing my every move. If I look at my phone at dinner, if I don't laugh at one of his jokes, if I tell him I want to have a night with my friends without him, something switches inside him. He's too polite to just tell me how he feels. Instead, I'm forced to read between the lines of his passive-aggressive gestures.

The man who gave me freedom now judges me if I wake up as late as ten a.m. He begins to judge my friends, telling me, "Those people don't care about you. I do." A part of me knows he's right but I can't suppress the growing desire to just be *normal.*

Our bond is doomed when Rohan offers to invest in a fashion line for Liana and me, which is a dream we never even *allowed* ourselves to dream. Things like this only happen for heiresses, not girls like us. I accept the offer while realizing it will render me even more dependent on him. But I take the chance, telling myself that if the line does well, we'll have our own money. And that's all I want, my own money so Rohan won't have so much power over me. I just wish we were equals.

Without telling Rohan, I throw a party at my apartment and a bunch of old friends come over, among them a guy named Shane. I've known him for a few years and dated one of his friends in high school but was always under the impression that he hated me, so I'm surprised to see him on the roof of our duplex.

He's even more strikingly handsome than I remember, with dark shaggy brown hair, green eyes, paint-splattered clothing, a tattered skateboard in one hand, blunt in the other. Shane is from Alphabet City, where his family squatted in multiple apartments in the eighties, resulting in them becoming the owners. I make my way through the crowd and tap him on the shoulder. When he turns around, his eyes widen and I can tell he likes what he sees.

"Wow, you look so . . . healthy?" he says.

He goes to hand me the blunt and I shake my head. "It's a gateway drug for me," I say with a smirk. I can tell he's impressed and it makes me feel good. "I think we all know by now it's better if I stay sober."

"Yeah, I was always afraid you were gonna rob me!" he says, laughing.

"You're not wrong, my friend."

We lock eyes, feeling the electricity buzzing between us. We spend the next hour talking in my bedroom and when a fight breaks out on the first floor, Shane regulates and yells at everyone to get the fuck out. He even stays behind after his friends leave to help us clean up.

I feel giddy around him, but I can't get Rohan out of my head.

"Do you wanna sleep over?" I ask him, as he scoops red Solo cups into a trash bag on the floor.

"Fuck yeah! I'd love that." He says this with the same enthusiasm of a child on the way to Disney World. I roll my eyes and blush.

Later, we have the messiest, sweatiest, raunchiest unprotected sex of my life.

I even come. Afterward, as we lie in bed, he says, "May I ask what the deal is with your sugar daddy?"

"Is that what people are calling it?" I ask coyly.

"Oh, I don't know, that's just what I heard."

"It's not like that. He doesn't fuck me and leave me money on the nightstand, he actually loves me."

"Isn't he married?"

I let go of him and turn over on my back.

"For what it's worth, I think it's pretty cool that this billionaire guy is, like, in love with you and does so much for you. I think it's fuckin' badass."

"Yeah, and that's why he will always come first," I warn him.

"That's fine. I won't fuck it up for you."

I cut him off by kissing him hard and slow, savoring every drop of saliva. Sober sex is a whole different beast. My endorphins can't get enough of him.

The next day at dinner with Rohan, I text Shane anxiously under the table. I excuse myself to the bathroom to answer his calls. My pussy tingles at the mere thought of him inside me. I rush through dinner to get back to him.

I lie to Rohan, telling him I'm sick, and spend the next ten days with Shane. Rohan sends me care packages and flowers that I stash in the closet, pretending he doesn't exist so I can immerse myself in Shane. He fulfills everything I yearn for. He helps me feel like a regular girl. We take long bike rides to Brooklyn and dangle our feet over the East River. We climb up the Williamsburg Bridge and graffiti our names in a heart. We climb up on billboards and break into abandoned buildings. Our fun is innocent and simple and dumb. But it's so fucking refreshing.

By the time Rohan insists on seeing me, Shane and I have already exchanged "I love yous," and he doesn't take it as well as he promised he would. He punches a hole in my wall before grabbing my phone and threatening to call Rohan and tell him everything.

I try calming him down. "I'm not gonna fuck him! It's just dinner. I'm going to go. I hope you will be here when I'm back, but if you're not, I understand," I say, kicking off my dirty Air Forces and sliding into my platform Louboutins.

When I see Rohan, I'm so mean to him that I get up from the table and cry in the bathroom until I throw up. I call Shane on repeat, begging him to be there when I get home. When I come back to the table, I can barely look at Rohan. I feel guilty and selfish, but I need to do this. I can't help my cravings, I've never been able to. When he kisses me goodbye, I keep my lips pressed together to ensure he doesn't leave his scent on me.

I'm relieved to find Shane lying in my bed watching a movie when I get home. I quickly disrobe and climb into bed, eager to make love again, but he recoils at my touch. "You smell like him," he snaps.

Shane becomes my new addiction as I pour all my time and money into him. He works odd jobs while I allow him to crash at our place for weeks, until our fights become so explosive that he disappears for a few days. Liana and Viki see the bruises on my arms and feel the walls shaking at night. Concerned for my well-being, they attempt to stage an intervention that goes horribly wrong, and I shut them down.

"I'm the captain of this ship," I remind them dismissively. "You guys have no idea the pressure I'm under and I just need you guys to let me get this out of my system."

They have no choice but to accept.

I choose drama over sobriety. I stop going to A.A. meetings and focus all my free time on Shane. I barely ever go into the office, leaving Liana to shoulder the bulk of the workload. Even our achievements pale in comparison to the thrill that being with Shane provides for me. "Joan Rivers put one of our skirts on her head and it ended up on *Fashion Police*—" Liana tells me excitedly.

"Can I call you back?" I ask, cutting her off.

Shane loves to party, so I often find myself driving around late at night searching for him at nightclubs. It's not uncommon for me to pop up at a bar at closing time and drag him out as he yells in protest, slurring his words. Pretty soon I start drinking again. At first it's just a harmless glass of champagne, but it quickly spirals into shots of Fireball and going out every night. I rationalize my behavior by telling myself that as long as I'm not doing heroin, I'm doing great.

Shane is a tempest in disguise and the dynamic between us is volatile. When we're in sync, it's like I'm on a rocket ship soaring through the cosmos, but when we clash, it feels like I'm drowning in quicksand with no way out.

I start coming to the realization that there's something wrong with this. It can't be normal to feel everything at such an elevated state. I see how people compartmentalize their lives, not allowing the drama to envelop the rest of them. I begin to wonder why I can't seem to do that too.

Rohan rents a house for us in the Hamptons, as he does every summer. I decide to invite Shane out on a weekday, when Rohan is usually in the city. We're swimming naked in the pool when I hear the familiar voice: "*Poupée,* where are youuu?"

Shane and I both freeze. The color drains from my face as my eyes dart around the pool, searching desperately for a way out. It feels like I'm having an out-of-body experience, watching Rohan in slow motion as he walks onto the deck, until he's standing right above us. I wipe the horror off my face and smile as I leap out of the pool and wrestle a towel around my naked body. "Rohan! What a nice surprise!"

I lean in to him and kiss him on the cheek, trying my best to act normal. I see the confused look in Rohan's eyes and blurt out, "This is Marcello, my gay hairdresser!"

Shane smiles and does a little wave. Rohan nods in his direction, still examining the scene. I can tell he isn't convinced. And frankly neither am I. I loop my arm through his and quickly lead him away from the pool and into the yard.

"He doesn't look very gay to me," Rohan says.

Shane's farmer's tan, tattoos, and gold chain are a dead giveaway, but I gasp, "Go ask him if you don't believe me!" My voice trembles.

"Is it just you two here?" he asks.

"More people are on their way. Liana and Viki are coming with a few other friends—"

"No, you've been acting differently. Something is up, Julia."

I get defensive. "I just wanna be a regular girl sometimes! Being your 'poopy'—"

"It's *poupée*," he corrects me.

"Okay, well, whatever it is, sometimes I just wanna chill with my friends, like right now! I can't believe you're getting mad at me for that!"

After thirty minutes of debating back and forth and talking ourselves in circles on the front lawn, Rohan finally gets back in his Bentley and drives away.

I run back inside and tell Shane, "Pack your shit. We're leaving."

The ride back to the city is quiet. Shane reaches over and places his palm on my bare knee, but I flinch at the feel of his touch.

"It's gonna be okay," he says.

"You don't know that," I snap back.

The next few weeks I'm on my best behavior. I stop seeing Shane, I finish probation, I graduate from community college, and I'm accepted as a student at the New School. I focus on the fashion line. If I can make some money on my own, then I won't be tethered to Rohan anymore. Liana and I cold-call buyers and send our line sheet to any email address we can find online, rarely receiving a reply. On the weekends we drive around the tristate area with mountains of samples in our trunk and hustle them to high-end boutiques. Even with all this effort, we don't break even. After a while, I begin to feel discouraged that I'll never find a way out, and relapse on my favorite drug of all: Shane.

Shane teams up with some power players in the art and hospitality world to open a nightclub and asks me to invest in it. Without much thought, I empty my savings, twenty-five thousand dollars, and pour it all into his business.

Rohan becomes suspicious after noticing two charges for massages and a pricey dinner at the Versace mansion on his credit card statement. He decides to hire a private investigator in Miami to go to the same hotel where the massages were purchased, and that's where he gets the photos of me straddling Shane in the pool, topless. I'm so engrossed in Shane that it takes me a few days to realize Rohan hasn't texted me back. I call him on repeat but he refuses to answer. The rest of the trip is ruined as my mind races, consumed by fear of the impending consequences. I'm terrified of losing everything and sending myself and my two best friends into homelessness. The brand is already struggling to stay afloat and we are hemorrhaging money. This is going to make everything even worse.

Liana calls me frantically from the office to tell me she spoke to Rohan and confirms my suspicions that he knows about Shane. I struggle to understand her through her frenzied speech.

"He fucking asked me if I knew!"

I feel terrible for putting her in this position. "What did you say?"

"Of course I said I didn't know, are you crazy?"

When I hang up the phone, I collapse on the floor of the hotel room, hopeless and defeated, tears forming in my eyes. I can sense Shane getting frustrated.

"Don't act like this is my fault," he tells me.

"I didn't say that! I just need to go home and clean up this mess."

"No. You need to choose. It's him or me!"

I stare at him, hatred burning through my eyes. "If you really loved me, you wouldn't put me in that position. You knew what it was."

The plane ride back to New York is quiet as I pensively stare out the window. Shane gets annoyed when I tell him it's best if we take different cabs from the airport.

As I walk through my front door, I feel a wave of relief wash over me when I find that Viki and Liana are already crunching numbers, brainstorming, and doing damage control.

"Don't worry, we have each other, and we're gonna get through this," Viki comforts me.

I let out a sigh of relief. I don't know what I would do without them.

. . .

I distance myself from Shane, constantly fighting the urge to text him. Rohan barely speaks to me but I accept his silence humbly, as I know it's what I deserve. I feel awful for hurting him, he doesn't deserve that. When he finally calls me, I beg for a second chance. After much convincing, he concedes and agrees to have lunch with me, but only with my mom present. I find it strange, but I know they've been in contact and she's been helping him deal with his heartbreak.

When I arrive at the restaurant, they're already there and by the empty glasses and plates, I can tell they've been there quite a while. As I sit down, I feel like a child being reprimanded at school and I'm already annoyed.

"Look, I'm not seeing him anymore, okay?" I say bluntly.

"Well, then you wouldn't mind showing us your phone," Rohan says calmly.

My hands begin sweating. Rookie move, not concealing the evidence.

"Okay, fine!" I say, sounding like an angsty teenager. I unlock my phone and flash it before him, making sure he can't catch a glimpse of the screen.

"Can I hold it, please?" he asks.

"No, you cannot hold it." I go off, yelling at him. With one hand, I discreetly attempt to select Shane's entire text thread to delete it.

"You're erasing something!" He turns to my mom for help. "She's deleting something!"

My mom remains frozen too stunned to speak at the scene unfolding before her.

"You're not being honest with me, Julia. You're throwing your whole life down the drain." His words cut through me.

"I told you it's over!" I yell. "Why can't you just take my word for it?!"

My mom looks around the restaurant at the few patrons attempting to enjoy their meal. In Italian, she tells me to lower my voice. I can't select the thread and keep eye contact, so I impulsively chuck my phone across the restaurant. Everyone stops at the loud crash. I cross my arms with a satisfied look on my face. "See what you did!" I tell him.

"Me?! You did all of this!"

My mom yells at me in Italian, and when the waiter brings back my phone, the screen is completely shattered. I run out of the restaurant and go straight to the Apple Store.

As I stand in line, the situation sinks into me and fear takes over. I'm going to lose it all: the apartment, the fashion line, the money for college, everything. His words echo through the walls of my brain the same way the judge's words once did. *Your whole life down the drain, your whole life down the drain, your whole life down the drain.*

Later that night, Viki and Liana sit anxiously in our ten-thousand-dollar-a-month loft on Centre Street as I tell them what happened. I can see the worry written all over Liana's face.

"We have so many people to pay, J. The seamstress, the factory, the PR company. They're harassing me."

"Well, he's not answering me at all, so what do you want me to do?" I snap at her.

"Do you want us to try to call him?"

I shrug, defeated. Suddenly, my phone lights up with a text: "I miss you."

"Oh my God!" I yell. "He texted me!"

"Thank the Lord!" Viki says, throwing her hands up to the sky.

"It's Shane," I say. Viki and Liana exchange a look and roll their eyes. They don't like Shane, and Shane doesn't care for them either. I get up and run to my room, locking the door behind me.

An hour later, Shane is at my doorstep. When he steps out of the elevator that opens directly into the apartment, I jump on top of him, wrapping my legs tightly around his torso. He walks me into my bedroom and places me on the bed. He tears off his clothes as I push my panties to the side and he climbs on top of me and we have the most exhilarating sex ever.

Afterward we lay on the damp comforter, entangled in each other, in silence.

"What are you thinking about?" he asks.

My mind keeps going back to Rohan but I can't let him know that.

"Let's watch a movie," I say as I reach for the remote. A few minutes in, my phone lights up. I'm relieved and terrified when I see Rohan's name appear on the screen. I grab my phone and run into the bathroom and open his text: "I'm outside your place, can you let me in?"

"Fuck!!!!!!" I yell as I run naked into Liana's room that she shares with Viki. "He's here! He's here! I don't know what to do!" Liana and Viki look up from their phones, visibly confused. "Rohan is here!!"

Shane appears in the doorway and Liana snaps, "You need to get the fuck out!"

"He can't," I say. "Rohan is literally downstairs right now. He'll see him!"

"You told me it was over with him," Shane says.

"I thought we were!" I plead with him.

Shane starts grabbing his clothes and I snatch them out of his hands.

"What do you think you're doing?!" I yell.

"I'm outta here. I don't wanna deal with this shit anymore!"

I shush him, pulling him away from our floor-to-ceiling windows. The buzzer rings and Liana's phone lights up.

"It's him!" she says.

"Pick up and tell him you're not home!" I yell at her.

She hesitates. Her hand holding the phone trembles. It stops ringing and a text appears. She reads it aloud: "Liana, I know you are home, please let me upstairs."

"How the fuck does he know everything?!" Viki complains.

"He has a spy," I say.

Eventually, the buzzing and the calls stop. Shane falls asleep as I lie in the bed next to him, wide awake, filled with torment, unable to shut my brain off.

· · ·

The next day, Shane is quiet and it fills me with dread. I don't want him to disappear again.

"What's wrong?" I ask.

"Nothing, just stressed about the soft opening tonight. I'll see you there?"

"I wouldn't miss it. It's technically *my* club too."

He winks and kisses me on the forehead before strolling out the door.

As soon as he's gone, I rush to my window, looking down at the snowy street below, examining each car, trying to figure out which one is the one that's been watching me. I'm interrupted when Shane calls me.

"Uh, I don't mean to alarm you but there's a van following me since I left your place."

My phone beeps and I see Rohan on the other line. I rush Shane off the phone and swap the call. Before Rohan can speak, I casually say, "Hey, sorry, I was sleeping when you called."

He cuts me off. "Stop lying to me, Julia. If you don't want to be together anymore, just let me go."

I can feel the desperation and heartbreak through the phone. "I'm sorry," I say. "You weren't speaking to me. I thought it was over. I don't want it to be over. I just want to feel better."

"Will you have dinner with me tonight?" he asks.

Fuck. The opening.

"I'd love to, but can you please stop having me followed?" I ask with a giggle, trying my best to keep it light and get my point across.

I decide that I'll have dinner with Rohan first and head to the club after. I'm anxious on the ride to the Carlyle. At dinner, I try my best not to pick up my phone or look at the clock as Rohan spirals. When I try to change the subject, he brings it right back to: "I'm so good to you. You want to go on vacation, I send you all over the world with all your friends. You want to start a business, I invest in it. Anything you want, I give to you! Where did I go wrong?"

I put the blame on myself. I look him dead in his glassy, blood-shot eyes and tell him, "I'm an addict. I have mental problems. I'm sick."

I come up with dozens of excuses, dancing around the uncomfortable truth that I am simply too young and he is just too old.

It's almost midnight and I'm already exhausted. I yawn extra loud, hoping he'll get the hint that I'm ready to leave. He ignores it and continues lecturing me. I start to get antsy looking at the clock. Shane's event started hours ago. I worry I'm not going to make it.

I excuse myself and run to the bathroom, where I'm surprised to find zero missed calls or texts from Shane. My mind spirals as I imagine him surrounded by artists, supermodels, and heiresses, his usual type. I hear his voice in my head: "You should've gone to art school, it would make you more interesting." It's like I'm not good enough.

I know he flirts with other women, and I can't help but feel like he's ashamed of me. I don't fit the mold of the rich girls he seems to be enamored by, the ones with tons of Instagram followers, who cosplay as artists and DJs. When I'm with him, I hide the scars of my past. I bury myself so far down that I start to forget who I am.

When I strut back to the table and bravely announce that I'm leaving, Rohan stares at me, bewildered. "You're making a mistake," he says, shaking his head. I shrug and turn around.

"I give up," he mutters as I walk away, leaving him alone in the empty dining room.

I hop on the train and run the rest of the way to make it to the club. When I arrive, I step over the velvet rope and canvass the venue, my eyes scanning the room for Shane. I bump into a friend and ask her where he is. "Haven't seen him in a while, actually," she says.

An uneasy feeling looms over me as I scurry downstairs to the dark unfinished basement. I bang on the bathroom doors, yelling his name over the music and calling him on repeat.

After thirty minutes, he magically reappears on the dance floor. Our eyes lock and I sense that he's not thrilled to see me. I march up to him and before I can speak, he holds out his hand and says, "Jules! You made it!"

I stare at his hand for a moment. "Where were you?"

He shrugs, wiping the droplets of snot dripping from his nose on his sleeve as his wide, bloodshot eyes dart around the room.

"You're coked up."

"I don't have time for this," he says. "If you're not enjoying yourself, you should leave."

He whips around and skips away from me, joining a group of gorgeous people chatting at the bar. I watch him, laughing and cracking jokes, completely indifferent to my predicament. I storm out and text him to find somewhere else to sleep, demanding my keys back, as he's no longer welcome at my place. I'm livid when he replies with a thumbs-up emoji. I walk the rest of the way home in the cold, feeling so dumb for having left Rohan, telling myself this is my karma. It's what I deserve.

The next day, I go meet Shane to retrieve my keys at a friend's house he's crashing at. The elevator opens up directly into the living room, where I see two of his friends sitting on the couch, stoned, playing video games. From the chaos, it's clear they've been up all night blowing lines.

"Where's Shane?" I ask, looking around for him.

A door creaks open, and I hear footsteps coming from down the hall. As Shane comes into view, I notice how awful he looks. He's pasty and bloated and obviously still drunk. Without saying a word, I impatiently hold my hand out in his direction, waiting for him to produce my keys.

"I have to look for them," he says nonchalantly.

I stand by the elevator, my patience wearing thin as I watch him clumsily rummaging through the scattered clothes on the floor, checking every pocket.

"Can you hurry the fuck up, please?" I ask.

He shoots me a look and throws the keys in my direction, narrowly missing my head. "You're such a little bitch," I mutter as I call the elevator to leave.

Next thing I know, Shane's arm is draped over me, and he has me in a headlock. Acting on instinct, I quickly bend over and pick up a Windex bottle off the floor. I begin slamming it onto his head repeatedly until he loosens his grip. With one swift motion, I knee him in his stomach, right where he recently had hernia removal surgery, and he releases his grip and drops to the ground. As he's curled over in pain, I frantically press the elevator button. When the doors finally open, I run inside, relieved to be escaping. As the doors close, I steal a glance at his friends, who remain seated on the couch, speechless. I'm shocked and disappointed neither of them came to my defense.

Luckily, I can fend for myself.

I examine the damage in the elevator mirror. My hair is disheveled, the collar of my sweater is torn, and my neck and face are covered in red marks. The surge of adrenaline wears off and I begin to feel the extent of my injuries—my head throbs, and my body aches all over. Despite this, my feelings for Shane don't disappear, they just get more complicated.

I refuse to stop seeing Shane, and I'm always looking over my shoulder to make sure we aren't being followed. I figure out that if I enter Bloomingdale's at one entrance and sprint through the store as fast as I can to the other entrance, I can lose whoever is following me. For my plan to work, I make sure there's a car already waiting for me on the other side, and once I'm inside, I lay flat on the seat until we are far away.

One night, after months of being followed and having my whereabouts reported back to Rohan, I notice a man tailing me closely on foot with his phone to his ear. I enter the gelato shop on Mulberry Street and buy myself an ice cream cone. When I leave the shop, I see that he's still behind me. I spin around a few times to get a better look at him. He avoids making eye contact and quickens his pace, walking ahead of me and into a nearby hotel. This time, *I* follow *him*. He gets in the elevator, still on the phone, as I plop down on one of the couches in the lobby. I watch the numbers on the elevator go up and then quickly come back down. The doors open and there he is. When he sees me in front of him, casually licking my ice cream cone, the color drains from his face. He scurries out of the hotel and I follow closely behind.

"Stop fucking following me!" I yell at him.

"I don't know what you're talking about, lady, you're the one following me! You're crazy!"

"I'm gonna call the cops and have you arrested for stalking!" I warn him.

A few minutes later, my phone rings and it's Rohan.

"Do you know that this guy, in his thirty-year career as a private eye, has never been made? And you managed to do it. You never cease to amaze me, young girl."

In the past, Shane would apologize profusely after hurting me, but now he doesn't even bother. When I try to explain how I feel, he dismissively says, "Hit me up when you're not mad anymore," adding insult to injury.

Things only get worse once Shane's promoted to club manager and he stops coming home altogether. "The club closes at four!" I yell into his answering machine. "There's no reason you should be out until eight a.m.!" I stay up the whole night waiting by the door for him to stumble in.

"I'm not high!" he yells as I grab his head and stick my tongue up his nostrils.

"My tongue is numb!" I yell back. "You fucking liar!"

In the morning, I notice a phone number scribbled in Sharpie on his hand. I dial the number while he's sleeping and to no one's surprise, a girl answers.

"Who the fuck is this?" I ask.

"Umm, who the fuck is this?!" she yells back in a thick French accent that cuts through my eardrum like glass.

My hand trembles with nerves as I take a deep breath, trying to remain calm. "You wrote your number on my boyfriend's hand."

There's a brief pause. "He didn't say he had a girlfriend," she says.

I hang up, pounce on top of him, and beat him in the head with the phone still in my hand. He jumps out of bed and starts putting his clothes on, blood leaking from his head.

"You're fucking crazy, you know that!" he yells as I chase him out into the hallway half-naked.

"I put my whole fucking life on the line for you! For nothing!" I yell at him as the elevator doors close.

I walk back into my apartment sobbing, stepping on the droplets of blood with my bare feet.

After this, I start acting erratically and Liana begs me to get help. At first I'm defensive. "I'm fine, what do you mean?" I say with wide eyes and a half-assed smile.

"You have fish in your bathtub, and you think someone made a voo-doo doll of you!" Her chin quivers as she pleads with me, desperately trying to convince me that I'm losing my mind.

I look around my room with a sense of detachment. I've rearranged my furniture so many times this week that I barely recognize it. The graffiti on my wall, which I've convinced myself is art, resembles the scribbles I used to draw at the mental hospital. And there are, in fact, a dozen large freshwater fish in my bathtub.

She's right. This is *bad*.

I book an appointment with the first psychiatrist who pops up on Google and within a few days, I'm prescribed a mood stabilizer. As a teenager in the psych ward at New York-Presbyterian I was diagnosed with bor-derline personality disorder and placed on lithium and Seroquel. I hated the way the medication made me feel. It sedated me, but not in a fun, euphoric way.

While this new doctor doesn't explicitly tell me I have bipolar disor-der, he doesn't deny it when I suggest it. He listens closely as I describe the excruciating level of self-awareness that plagues me. I admit how I dread going to bed at the end of the day, fearful of what mood will greet me the next morning. I can usually tell within the first few seconds of opening my eyes what my day is going to be like, and I'm completely powerless to it. It's paralyzing and it's only getting worse.

I decide I'm ready to get off this treacherous roller coaster of volatile emotions I've been riding all my life. "It feels like I'm in the passenger seat and this demon inside me is at the wheel and as I yell for it to stop, it slams on the pedal and next thing I know, I'm in a terrible predicament." He scribbles on his yellow notepad as I shift uncomfortably on the maroon leather sofa, tattered and worn by the many lost souls before me. "The only reason I'm not homeless in a ditch is because I'm attractive."

"Well, you're also very smart too," he assures me.

"Being smart never got anybody anywhere," I tell him bluntly, my words coated in cynicism. "Look at how happy stupid people are!"

As the medication takes effect, I feel the suffocating weight being lifted off me. It's as if all the lost pieces of myself are slowly returning, and I'm starting to recognize traces of the person I used to be. The clouds of depression that once enveloped me are beginning to clear, and I feel a sense of peace. "I feel like I can finally be the person I always knew I was," I tell the doctor with a hopeful smile. "I'm not sad anymore."

I make a conscious decision to distance myself from the negative forces in my life. I stop going out and hanging out with the neighborhood goons, instead spending more time at the office, helping Liana with the day-to-day chores that I had always ignored. I keep my mind occupied with arts and crafts, movie nights, and sleepovers with my friends.

I make an effort to show Rohan my progress. We spend hours on the phone and I send him pictures of my latest paintings and links to articles about our fashion line. His encouraging words give me the motivation to keep going and it's rewarding to know that he's proud of me.

I'm shocked that he still supports me. After everything I put him through, it seems like he's willing to give me another chance. But all this comes crashing down one day when I get an email from ABC Carpet & Home. Since Rohan's credit card is linked to my account, any purchases he makes get sent to my email. But this order—an overpriced console table—is for a girl named Sabrina on the Upper East Side.

At first I think it might be a mix-up, until I search her name on Facebook and see what she looks like. She looks more Italian than I do.

She has dark eyes and olive skin, her hair is thick, and she has the most perfect toned abs. She's rough around the edges, but she certainly has potential. And Rohan loves himself a fixer-upper, as we already know.

My heart races as I call Rohan and ask him who she is.

"What?" he asks, bewildered. "How do you know her name?"

"My, my, how the tables turn," I say in a chilling tone. "I'm coming to you now," I tell him and hang up.

Liana and Viki stare at me from across the room.

"What's going on?" Liana asks.

"He has a new girlfriend," I say.

"Who does?" Viki asks.

"Rohan."

Their expressions sour. I can tell they're anxious. After all, they depend on him too.

"Don't worry," I assure them. "This is good. I can leverage this. I have a plan."

I arrive at Rohan's office, armed with a very long list of demands. "You have to continue to pay for my apartment, car, school, and business. I want a weekly allowance and you have to keep paying Liana's salary."

"Absolutely not," he says. "Why should I?"

My eye starts twitching as I suppress my rage. Through my clenched jaw, I manage to say, "It's called spousal support! I was with you for five years! I gave you the best years of my life and if you don't take care of me, I promise, I will make your life a living hell!"

He looks afraid now. "Okay, okay, fine."

Despite Rohan's continued support, I can't shake the feeling of impending doom. I can't even remember my life before him, and it scares me to imagine my future without him. He's been my confidant, my mentor, and my guardian angel for so long that I feel lost without him. I regret not getting on medication sooner and I hate myself for the pain and suffering I inflicted on him. And it was all for nothing.

8

HEARTBURN

It's only a matter of time before Shane and I rekindle our tortured romance. On the day before Valentine's Day, I take a pregnancy test, and it comes back positive.

I want to tell Shane in person, so I get in my car and drive to the club, my heart racing as I speed through stop signs. Once I arrive, I realize there's a private event going on. I watch from my car as a slew of tall, beautiful people line up at the velvet ropes. I look down at my outfit: scuffed sneakers and baggy paint-stained sweatpants.

I walk up to the club, greet the bouncers, and step over the rope, as I always do. Once inside, I scan the room for Shane. When I spot him, he's talking to a few blond models in the corner. I run up to him and tap him on the shoulder. He quickly looks me up and down before trying to dismiss me.

"Does this look like a good time?" he asks as his eyes dart around the room manically.

"Can you pay attention, please? This is important!"

"All right, all right, what is it?"

"I'm pregnant."

He pauses to think for a moment. "Um, congratulations? Look, I'm super-busy right now, let's talk about this later." He leaves me standing alone in the stuffy room and disappears into the crowd.

I get back in my car, humiliated. "Congratulations?" I mutter to myself. "What the fuck?"

I fall asleep anxiously waiting for him to come over. When I wake up at six a.m. to an empty bed, I snap. I shoot out of bed and start getting dressed. It's 19 degrees outside, below freezing, when I get back in my car and drive back to the club. Once I arrive, I realize the gate is down and the club is closed. I call Shane repeatedly and hear his phone ringing from inside, so I bang on the gate until he finally comes to the door.

"What the fuck are you doing? Are you trying to get me in trouble with the neighbors?!" He's agitated and defensive, his pupils are dilated, and he looks wired. I shake my head no. "Go home, Julia!" he says before trying to step back inside.

But I don't budge and quickly jam my foot in the door, stopping him from locking me out. "What are you hiding?!" I yell as he wrestles with me for a moment. Suddenly, my vision goes blank. I'm startled by a loud thump on my face and I stumble backward.

When I regain my vision, I see him standing in front of me, his face twisted in anger. "You punched me!" I yell hysterically, gripping my face. "You fucking punched me!"

He doesn't answer, but I can see the shame in his eyes. It's then that I realize I can't do this anymore. He didn't just hit *me*, he hit my baby. On Valentine's Day. How can I ever forgive him?

Later in the day, as I lie in bed watching *The Real Housewives* surrounded by cupcakes I ordered for myself, I hear the sound of the buzzer. I hope it might be Shane coming to apologize, but I'm disappointed when I see a courier holding a shiny red bag. My disappointment quickly turns to elation when I peek inside the bag and see a big red Cartier box. I reach for the note, and my heart breaks a little.

"Thinking of you this Valentine's Day. Love, Rohan."

I open the box to find a beautiful necklace with three interlocking hoops. I pick up my phone and think about calling him. I want to tell him how badly I fucked up and how desperately I need him right now. I want to tell him how sorry I am and beg him for forgiveness. But I don't. I stalk his new girlfriend extensively enough to know that she drives a Porsche and spends her weekends at the Hamptons house I once called mine. He's moved on and I need to let him go. I'm lucky enough as it is that he agreed to continue to pay our rent.

I block Shane's number as soon as I realize I won't be receiving an apology and schedule an appointment to terminate the pregnancy. After the operation, I begin to spiral again. I lose twenty pounds and start going out every night, drowning myself in sauvignon blanc and fueling myself with advances from men.

My friends who work at the club keep me updated on Shane's escapades.

"He's dating a Norwegian model," the bartender tells me. "But I don't think it's serious 'cause he had a cocaine orgy in the bathroom last weekend with, like, ten people."

I pretend it doesn't bother me, but it does. It isn't fair that he can move on so fast while I'm left to do the emotional labor of picking up all the pieces. To make matters worse, I crash my cherry-red Mercedes and when I take it to the dealership to have it fixed, they refuse to give it back. It was leased.

One night, I'm at 1 Oak with my friends when a bouncer taps me on the shoulder. "A-list actor would like you to come to his table."

I peer over his shoulder at the handsome man in a baseball cap and immediately recognize him. I grab my friends and head over to him. Sparks fly as soon as our hands touch. We spend the rest of the night yelling in each other's ears over the loud music.

"Wanna get out of here?" he asks.

I think for a moment and nod.

We all go back to his hotel room, where, for the first time in a long time, I'm able to laugh and dance and not worry about Rohan finding out or Shane cheating on me. As the sun comes up and the booze wears off, I announce that I must go home. We exchange numbers, and he insists on seeing me again before going back to L.A. I salivate at the thought of Shane finding out. I start plotting my revenge.

The A-list actor texts me that evening and invites me and my friends out to dinner for the following night. I suggest a cool little club in Chinatown with a great chef that I just so happen to be an investor in. He agrees, and I make a reservation. My friends and I all get ready at my place. We chug bottles of wine to calm our jitters and try on dozens of outfits. I'm having a particularly hard time getting dressed, since I've shed so much weight and none of my clothes fit me anymore.

I settle on a plain white American Apparel bodysuit and white Gucci pants. I'm already tipsy by the time I arrive at the club. I spot the actor and his friend at a big round table in the back. He stands up to greet my friends and me with a big smile, giving me a kiss on each cheek. I sit down next to him and he places his hand gently on my thigh under the table. I look around the room. I don't see Shane, but I know he's on the schedule tonight.

As the night proceeds, my desires intensify. I lean in and nibble on the actor's ear, sliding my tongue over it and kissing the nape of his neck. I see a bulge rise in his pants as he grabs my face and kisses me ferociously. At this point, all the patrons in the restaurant have noticed the actor's presence. Some even come up to our table to ask for selfies, and he graciously obliges. I can feel the room grow quiet as they watch us in awe. I crawl on top of him, straddling his lap and grinding against him. As I come up for air, I catch a glimpse of Shane standing in the doorway, frozen, staring at us, and I hear the bells of victory sound off in my head.

On our way out the door, Shane grabs my arm in passing and yells something about me embarrassing him. I shrug and pretend I can't hear him over the music. I yank my arm out of his grasp and continue walking out the door. I don't look back but I can feel his inflamed eyes burning holes in my back.

A few weeks later, I return to the club with my friends for an event. As soon as I arrive, I sense that Shane is irritated by my presence. He finds excuses to walk past me and I catch him staring at me multiple times throughout the night. I decide that, for the sake of both our peace of mind, we need to squash our beef.

I wait for him to finish with a patron before I walk up to him and apologize.

"Why are you talking to me?" he asks dismissively.

"Look," I say, "I don't want any problems with you. I'm sorry for being crazy but I was really upset. I just want you to know that I forgive you and I hope you can forgive me too."

"Are we done here?"

"Yeah, sure. I just wanna be able to come to my club and not have any weirdness."

"Okay," he replies coldly before storming off. As the night progresses, the room starts to fill up with people, and I decide it's time for me to leave. On my way out, I bump into an acquaintance of mine: an annoying short rich kid with a persistent Adderall problem and a Napoleon complex who has a crush on me. I've grudgingly stopped to talk to him for a minute when I feel a big hand swoop over my shoulder and put me in a headlock.

I freeze. My eyes widen as I desperately search the room for my friends. I make eye contact with a few people, and I know they can see me, but nobody is doing anything to help. Shane drags me into the kitchen by my hair and throws me up against an industrial metal rack. My head smacks against the steel, causing a loud ringing noise to echo in my ears, and I start crying. I'm so embarrassed. I pull my phone out to call the police, and he grabs it out of my hands, snapping it in half, obliterating it with his rage. Suddenly, the bouncer appears and pulls him off me.

I run out of the club with my dress torn, neck irritated, hair disheveled, and phone in pieces. Outside, I become belligerent, screaming at the bouncer, "Tell him he better get me a new fucking phone or I'm calling the fucking cops!"

One of Shane's friends, a rich French girl with an indie fashion magazine no one reads, raises her eyebrows and whispers loudly to her friend, "If he's so bad, then why doesn't she just leave?"

The bouncer can tell from my facial expression that I'm about to go off on her. He steps over the rope and walks me down the block. "I know you're mad but you can't be screaming in front of the spot," he says.

"What would you do if you were me? You've seen him attack me multiple times—"

"I would call the police," he whispers softly before scurrying away.

The next day, Liana and I have a meeting with the accessories director at *Vogue*. The whole time we're there, my mind wanders to last night. I keep seeing all the blank stares and expressionless faces of all the people who pretended not to see me get attacked. I hear the judgmental whispers replaying in my mind. Liana is left to steer the meeting as she does the brand: alone.

After the meeting, I text Shane from Liana's phone and ask him to please replace my cell phone.

"Get Rohan to get you a new one," he replies.

"Liana," I say, "I need your phone for a few hours."

"What's going on?" she asks, but I'm already halfway down the block on the phone with him.

"Meet me at the club," Shane tells me.

I arrive ten minutes later, trying my best to remain civil. As I spot him approaching, I brace for confrontation. However, he walks right past me and heads into the building next door, where the office is located. A few minutes later, he emerges with a cracked iPhone 4, which he hands me before strutting off without a word.

I grip the phone in my hands, wanting so badly to bash it over his head, like I did when I found that French girl's number written on his hand.

"Um, is this from the lost and found?" I ask him.

He keeps his back turned and ignores my question.

Frustrated, I chase after him. "It's locked! I don't want this shit! I want the same model I had before!"

He doesn't acknowledge me, which only fuels my rage further.

"If you don't replace my phone, I'm calling the cops!" I take out Liana's phone and start dialing 911. "Hello," I say loudly, "I'd like to report an assault that happened last night at a club."

Shane stops and spins around, this time paying attention to me. He pleads with me to hang up, but it's too late. The cops are already on their way.

He sits down on the stoop and begs with tears in his eyes, "Please, Jules, don't do this."

I look down at him, seeing him for the pathetic little boy he is.

"I feel no sympathy for you," I say. "I gave you a chance to make it right. You wanna treat me like shit when we're together, fine, that's on me. But you're not gonna do this shit to me now. You're nothing to me now."

His demeanor suddenly changes and he's back to being an arrogant prick. "It's not gonna end well for you," he says before running away.

When the cops arrive a few minutes later, I go with them to the police station to make my statement. An Irish lesbian officer takes particular interest in my story. She crosses her arms and assures me, "Don't worry, we're gonna get this bastard."

Later that night, two squad cars and eight cops swarm the club and drag him out in handcuffs. I hear all the details from the bartender who works there.

"He's definitely getting fired," she tells me. I feel relieved, vindicated, but only for a brief moment.

Word starts spreading about the arrest and I sense allegiances slowly begin to form. I get dirty looks in the street. One guy tells me they're calling me a "single white female." I discover that Shane is telling people I was jealous of his new girlfriend and started the fight. The majority shareholder of the club calls me and assures me that Shane won't be allowed back, but unfortunately neither will I.

"Why?" I ask.

"For fighting," he says.

I didn't fight anyone. I was attacked. Why is he treating me like this? I try to remain cool. "Well, can I have my investment back?"

"Um, yeah, I'm sure that's doable. Let me get back to you on that."

I try to ignore the passive-aggressive jabs and gossip until one day, when I'm getting a massage in Little Italy, I hear my phone vibrating. I ignore it and let it go to voicemail. It vibrates again and again until I finally answer it.

"Julia! Check your texts *now!*" Liana yells into the phone.

I click on a screenshot of an Instagram account impersonating me. The handle is @MistressValentina and the bio is a list of all my specialties, including ass worship and golden showers. I feel like I'm about to faint. I scroll through my domme photos from years ago and click on the "following" tab. This account follows my employees, people I work with professionally, acquaintances, and even family members.

"Everyone is seeing this!" Liana yells.

I leap up from the massage table and head straight to the Instagram office in the East Village. I run through the lobby, panicking and sweating, begging to please speak to someone upstairs. After thirty minutes, a guard comes down with a small slip of paper. "You can write your complaint here and we can have a look at it," he says to me.

I lodge the complaint but hours later the account is still up. Hundreds of people message me about it, asking if it's real. Whoever did this must have gotten these photos off the dungeon's website years ago. There's nothing I can do. I've been exposed.

That night, I'm forced to go out for a friend's birthday at the Jane Hotel. Multiple people approach me about the account. I can't escape it.

Liana and Viki are right there with me, feeling the secondhand pain and humiliation.

"I try so hard to put the past behind me, and here it is again, making its way into my future," I tell them with tears in my eyes.

"Why don't we do a story about this?" Viki asks.

I look up at her, confused. "A Mistress Valentina story?"

"An ode to the past but incorporating the brand, and maybe you can talk about cyberbullying," she says. "My friend at *i-D* will run it on their website."

"Will you let me tie you up?" I ask with a hopeful smile.

The photo shoot is a success. I do Viki's hair and makeup, style her in the clothes I designed, and dangle her from the ceiling. *i-D* loves the images and they run the story a few weeks later. I'm not going to let the haters ruin my life. I'm owning my history and I feel closer than ever to Viki and Liana, who keep supporting me no matter what I do. It starts to feel like we are on our own deserted island as we start seeing who our real friends are.

I find out from my bartender friend that Shane still frequents the club on a nightly basis, so I call up the owner and threaten legal action.

"As far as I'm concerned, I was attacked by one of your employees and then I was punished for it, while he remains free to do whatever the fuck he pleases! It's not fair!"

"Okay," he says, "let me talk to the other owners and we'll remedy this."

But I have no faith in them anymore.

That night, I have a little too much to drink at a fashion party and impulsively decide to go to the club. "If Shane can go, then I can go!" I say to Liana and Viki, who nod in agreement. I'm surprised when the bouncer opens the red velvet rope and lets us all in. I head straight to the bar and kiss the bartenders hello. I order a glass of wine then feel a hand grab my arm tightly. It takes me a moment to realize what's happening as one of the majority shareholders drags me down the long corridor toward the exit. He throws me outside like a pile of trash and yells, "And don't you ever come back here!"

At that moment, I decide I'm going to take them all down.

This particular owner also owns a few other mediocre establishments in Little Italy. He's an old bitter man who failed as a musician and often insisted on DJing at the club, to everyone's dismay, since he only played cheesy disco songs from the dark ages. I go on Yelp and start writing scathing reviews for all his establishments about how he supports woman beaters, but this isn't enough. I order two hundred hissing cockroaches from Madagascar and convince my old friend Serena to release them in the club in exchange for a hundred bucks. But before the cockroaches arrive, a reporter from Page Six calls me from a private number. I pick it up and start singing like a bird.

The next day, the story goes to print. I run to the corner deli and pick up a copy. As I skim through the pages and read the article, I stop at the word "allegedly." There is nothing alleged about this! They are all guilty! Back home, I slam the paper down on the desk. "It feels like I have to prove myself at every turn," I whine to Viki and Liana. The article gets reblogged hundreds of times and the news spreads fast. I start getting prank calls and hateful messages on my social media from complete strangers calling me a liar.

The article only creates a bigger wedge between *us* and *them*. I bump into a mutual friend on the street who whines, "You're breaking up the friend group, Jules."

"Um, no," I say, "he did that when he put hands on me."

But my words are ignored. Everyone seems to see him as the victim and me as some kind of feral pathological liar. We are blacklisted from every club downtown and we stop being invited to parties. Viki and Liana often find themselves defending me in public when people make snide remarks. A British socialite named Georgina invites both Shane and Viki to her birthday party, and when Viki sees Shane waiting on line to get in, she pulls Georgina aside and expresses her disappointment.

Georgina responds by shrugging and saying, "Well, I've never seen him act like that." Everyone turns on me. Even the bouncer who told me to call the police denies ever seeing Shane abuse me.

So many people saw the attack, and yet I have no witnesses. I always heard about stuff like this happening to women who came forward. I just never thought it would happen to *me*.

Soon after the article is released, I get a certified letter in the mail from a law firm issuing me a cease and desist from speaking to media outlets or posting about the scandal on social media.

I start isolating myself from the outside world, refusing to go out or answer the phone. I spiral deeper into the pits of my mind, turning inward to escape the chaos.

A friend informs me of their plans to drag me to court and tarnish my reputation further. They intend to create an untraceable website in Switzerland, where one of the club owners is from, featuring all my dominatrix photos and divulging my past encounters with the law, sex work, and drugs.

I decide I'm going to take control of the narrative and beat them to the punch. I will put together a book about my life. For the title, I take a line from one of the club owners' public statements about the assault. He said that our squabble was "symptomatic of a relationship gone sour."

I climb up to the loft and search for my secret box of artifacts, where I find Ace's inmate ID tag, nude Polaroids I tried sending him while he was in prison, photos documenting the drugs and the bondage and the abuse. I even find my missing person poster and various other newspaper clippings. I dedicate the rest of the night to cutting, gluing, and scanning everything into book form, fueled only by the burning desire to avenge myself.

A friend hooks me up with a printer in New Jersey and I place an order for a hundred copies. I don't think anyone is going to buy them, but I have to give it a shot. I can't be ashamed of myself. I can't let them win.

I show the book to my friend Andrew Richardson, and he loves it.

He offers up his booth at the New York Art Book Fair to sell them, and to my surprise, crowds of people line up to buy it. We sell every single copy at twenty dollars a pop. A few boutique bookstores even place orders for more copies.

The next day, my inbox is flooded with inquiring journalists eager to write about it. *Dazed* does a feature on it and the article crashes their site. The journalist texts me, "I'm not supposed to tell you this but you broke the record for the most clicked article on our site!"

I feel a fleeting sense of redemption, but mostly I just hope that people will believe me now. Even with the book being received well, the damage is done. I have few friends left. And with the book's obscene imagery now online for everyone to see—I didn't expect it to get so much attention—I feel exposed and vulnerable. I start rejecting everything around me. I lose interest in New York entirely. It no longer feels like home. New York betrayed me.

I decide to give up my share of our fashion line. "I can't do it anymore," I tell Liana. "There's more for me to do."

"Well, I don't wanna do it if you don't," she says, a little defeated and a little relieved. The line has been eating more money than it's bringing in and we can no longer support it alone.

One morning, I get a call from an acquaintance of mine asking if I'd ever consider posing nude for a spread in *Playboy*. "It's kind of a big deal 'cause it's the last nude issue. It's not confirmed but if Hugh likes the photos, they'll put you in the mag." She pauses. "But obviously, he will." I think for a moment. When I was with Rohan, I never could have done something like this. Something about that makes me want to do it even more. Plus, I've already pulled the curtains on my deepest wounds in my art book. What do I have to lose? I agree to do the shoot, and a few days later, I sell the Birkin bag Rohan bought me for my twenty-third birthday. With the money, I buy a vintage Mercedes-Benz off a friend for five thousand dollars and call the only person I know who will drop anything in an instant for a fun adventure: Harmony.

9

PTSD

I drive through pouring rain in the dark with broken windshield wipers to Harmony's house upstate, where she's been living with a drug dealer for the past year.

When I arrive, all her things are packed in garbage bags on the porch. She laughs and rolls her eyes when she sees my car. "Whose grandmother did you rob?!" Harmony yells out the front door.

"I got a good deal!"

I help her load the endless boxes of loose sheets of paper, photo albums, and trinkets into the trunk as she awkwardly whispers to her ex-boyfriend.

"Do we have to bring all this shit?" I ask her when she comes back to the trunk with the last bag.

"I don't trust him," she says quietly.

"What's his deal?"

She shushes me when his silhouette appears in the doorway. She gives me the look and I immediately change the subject. He retreats back inside and locks the door while we pack the rest of her junk in the driveway.

"Um, what's his problem?" I whisper to her.

"I'll tell you when we're in the car," she says under her breath.

Once we're on the road she confesses to me, "It was getting really bad between us."

"What do you mean?"

"He threw me on the ground and twisted my arm."

"Why are you even with him? What happened to you being a lesbian?"

She laughs. "Yeah, I don't know. Just got lonely. So, where are we going?"

"I have no fucking idea!" I say with a devilish grin.

"Okay, sounds fun," she replies.

We drive through the night and make it all the way to Tennessee when smoke starts seeping up through the hood of the car. I do my best to veer to the side of the road when the engine starts to mimic the sound of gunshots.

"Oh, that's it, the engine seized!" Harmony says, peering into the smoky hood.

"Fuck!!" I yell. We pause to look at each other and start hysterically laughing.

We sit on the railing of the highway in the drizzling rain, shivering, waiting for the tow truck for hours while entertaining ourselves. We spook each other out with stories of serial killers. We come up with an elaborate story about us being cousins through an adoption in the family. She practices the stand-up routine she's been working on in her Notes app.

"I haven't laughed like this in so long," I tell her, my pants damp from having peed in them already a few times.

"Me too, dude." Her tone changes. "You have no idea what I was going through."

"Can you stop being so secretive? What the fuck was going on?"

"Okay, you have to promise not to tell anyone."

She holds out her pinkie, and I interlock it in mine. "I promise."

"I started shooting up again," she says. "I'm better now, but we were selling it."

"You were selling heroin?!"

"He was! I was just helping him but someone snitched and called the feds and they've been following us for two months."

"Harmony! Who are you?!"

"They even came to the house looking for guns but luckily we buried them in the lot next door." I listen to her in disbelief. "I really think you coming to get me out of the blue is like God or something. You really saved my life."

I wrap my arms around her, tears forming in my eyes. "I love you," I whisper.

We spend the next few days holed up in a motel waiting for the car to be repaired. I'm informed that the vintage part necessary might take weeks to source, and even then it might be faulty. We decide to ditch it and rent a car to continue our journey. I suddenly remember that my friend Brian recently moved to Louisiana from the Midwest.

"Let's go visit him!" I say.

Harmony doesn't seem too thrilled.

"He's gay, don't worry."

"Fine, but you're driving."

After nine hours of nonstop driving, we end up on the bayou of Louisiana. It's more than a thousand miles from Manhattan and I love not being reminded of anything. It's the middle of the night and Brian's already asleep when we creep inside the tiny house. It's a humid night and the house doesn't have air-conditioning, but I find comfort in the sweltering heat. Every time I step outside it feels like I'm being wrapped in a warm hug, which I so desperately need.

When I wake up in the morning, I'm startled by a tall, lanky figure standing awkwardly in the doorway, waiting to be invited in.

"Umm, do you wanna come in?" I ask.

He smiles and nods his head like a little kid. He glides into the room and plops down at the foot of my bed. His pupils are the size of an ant, and he seems nervous and jittery.

"You're so pretty," he says. "I'm Eric."

He holds out his shaky, frail hand, adorned in permanent scribbles. His face looks sunburned and greasy, with poorly drawn tattoos all over it. His tank top is covered in holes and stains, he has mosquito bites all over his body, and his arms bear the scars of a painful life.

I shake his hand and he places a crystal in my palm. Suddenly, I feel the shield of ice that guards my heart melt away.

"This will protect you even when I'm not here."

I offer to drive him to the gas station to get a pack of cigarettes. Once we're in the car, he reaches for the aux cord. He plays "Lay Lady Lay" by Bob Dylan for half the song then switches to Russian death rap, and ends his set with "Clair de lune" by Claude Debussy. I can tell by how excited he gets that he loves everything. We drive past a slowly sinking shrimping boat covered in broken furniture and garbage bags.

"Wow, that's so beautiful," he says with a sigh.

I glance back at the boat. "Yeah, I guess it is." I notice the sunset behind it, the contrast of the water swallowing up the boat and how poetic it all is.

"This little boat that worked so hard is gonna meet its fate, and there's nothing we can do about it," he says.

I love being around Eric. Every day I eagerly wait for him to wake up in the room next door. There isn't much to do on the bayou but Eric makes even the most mundane activities fun and exciting. We race crabs, we barbecue, we practice our aim shooting cans with Brian's guns. We explore the abandoned houses wrecked from years of hurricanes.

One day as we venture out in the canoe, we paddle farther into the Gulf than we intended. The sky is overcast, the wind picks up, and the current starts pulling us farther and farther from land. When Eric sees the fear in my eyes, he instantly transforms into my protector. His gentle voice grows deep and serious. He calmly takes the paddle out of my hands and gets us to shore safely.

Doing things with Eric feels like the first time again. It's exciting. He introduces me to the world through a brand-new lens, where everything, even the ugly, is nothing short of breathtaking.

I feel so lonely when he retreats into his room for hours to get high. He gets that glazed, vacant look in his eyes, the familiar hollow gaze that most heroin addicts have.

A part of me wishes I could float on the cloud with him and feel what he's feeling but I know how slippery that slope is for me. I try my best to abstain as long as I can.

I have to force him to take care of himself. He hates showers because they remind him of the blood that leaked down his legs and swirled into the drain after he was raped by a stranger as a child. He was just a boy and didn't know any better. He believed it was his "gay punishment." This was only enforced by his Catholic upbringing. Due to this, he never told a soul. So instead, we take baths. He loves when I get in with him, lathering up his back and massaging shampoo into his hair. I even buy some rubber ducks from Walmart for him. It feels like we're brother and sister, giggling like two little kids. It also feels like I'm his mother. And sometimes it feels like he's *my* mother. But he loves most being my sis, when I let him wear my lingerie and take photos of him. He loves posing provocatively as I egg him on.

I'm in awe as I listen to his heartbreaking stories.

"I shot heroin for the first time when I was twelve in the back of a trailer with my friend's older brother. He was my first love. He was nineteen and he took my virginity. I was so devastated when he said, 'I ain't no faggot,' and stopped talking to me. I started tricking after that, behind the IHOP, but when I got older and my voice got deeper, they didn't want me anymore."

I act as a therapist to him, encouraging him and comforting him. "None of that is your fault, you know that, right? You have to stop punishing yourself."

He nods. "I know, you're right."

At night, I read to him from our favorite book, *The Outsiders*. I affectionately call him Ponyboy, and he says I'm his Cherry. We even tattooed it on each other using a syringe. I did a stick and poke on his arm, and he put a cherry on my butt. Brian got really mad about that. He yelled at Eric not to ruin me.

Brian and Harmony resent our relationship.

"Eric, Eric, Eric. Everything is Eric!" Harmony complains.

"You can hang out with us if you want," I remind her. "You don't have to stay in your room sniffing pills by yourself!"

She rolls her eyes and continues microwaving her fish-flavored tofu sticks.

After a month on the bayou, Harmony and I outstay our welcome at Brian's house and move into an old house on stilts at the end of a long narrow road that stretches far out onto the Gulf. When the wind blows, the whole house sways back and forth. We purchase a Lincoln Town Car for fifteen hundred dollars from a neighbor who has fire ants crawling on his toes and blood leaking down his legs during the sale. We meet all the locals, and our neighbors invite us over for shrimp dinners. We spend Thanksgiving with a guy we meet at a bar and his family. We go fishing off the coast of Mexico with complete strangers and proceed to have the tastiest barbecue of our lives.

Harmony regularly hitchhikes to the nearest bar, where I often find her later playing pool with the senior citizens.

"I could honestly live here forever," she tells me with a smile.

"Me too," I say.

It's just another ordinary afternoon as I turn the corner on the long windy road surrounded by water, headed for the laundromat twenty minutes away. I'm singing along to Fleetwood Mac's "The Chain," bobbing my head to the music, when the big old Town Car I am driving loses control, spinning in circles and heading straight for the water. I close my eyes and grip the steering wheel as the car wraps itself around a massive wooden telephone pole.

The impact is intense, and the sound of metal crushing against wood echoes through the air. The little plastic cigarette cup with the remnants of last weekend's vodka soda goes flying, spraying the entire backseat. The smell of alcohol and ashes fills the car, and my clothes are covered in debris. Panic sets in as I try to escape the car, but the door is jammed shut. I have no choice but to climb out of the passenger side door and quickly change my clothes by the side of the road.

I call Harmony, who is too far to make it over on foot. I have no choice but to call Brian and tell him what happened. He's been getting annoyed with me for interrupting his and Eric's music sessions, and I feel bad calling him now, but he doesn't hesitate. In just a few minutes, I see his big green truck coming down the road.

When Brian gets out of the truck, he cracks a joke and puts me at ease. Despite the weirdness, I know I am lucky to have him. And I'm certainly lucky to be alive, because if it weren't for the pole, the car would've dived straight into the bayou and I would have been alligator food.

Eric moves into our house and Harmony eventually submits to his charm. They bond over their love of Adderall, Xanax, and Suboxone and often swap pills. We become a little deranged family. We spend our time doing arts and crafts and listening to music. We take down all the fishing ornaments around the house and redecorate with paper chains and watercolors. Eric is a musical wiz and one day he comes home and plays a song he composed for me. I'm moved to tears by the gesture. When my twenty-sixth birthday rolls around, he gives me a beautiful portrait he painted of me.

Our relationship intensifies and I start to develop feelings for him.

"Babe, he's SO gay," Harmony teases me. "You're losing your mind!"

"I know but read this poem he wrote for me!" I hand her the torn sheet of paper.

She reads aloud: "'You are so beautiful to me, like the song I'll sing you while we're driving in the Lincoln Town Car. I'll look into your eyes and get hypnotized. I imagine I'm a lounge singer singing true and sincere like they used to, but my voice will crack because I'll cry but I'll try to hide it, like a man should. Because the love I have for you is so strong my body doesn't know any other ways of feeling when I see you. And I'll sing "You Are So Beautiful to Me" again, and I'll stop because unlike the lounge singer, so pure and true, I'll be high and my eyes will close and we'll drive into a house or a river but I'll be so happy because I'm dying with you.'"

"Isn't it beautiful?" I say.

"This is so gay," she says, shutting me down.

One December night, Liana calls me with an invitation I can't refuse.

"This billionaire with a private jet wants to take us to Art Basel in a few days!"

Her voice shakes with excitement. I've been missing my friends and was already planning a trip back home for the holidays, so a few days later I pack my bags and hop on a plane to New York.

The next day, we meet at Teterboro Airport and pile into a sleek private jet. As soon as I board, I'm handed a glass of champagne by a waiter. I sit down, and Liana snaps photos of me in the luxurious surroundings. Our host arrives, an intoxicated rich guy babbling away and hungry for attention. I think how lucky I was that my prayers for a sugar daddy were answered with Rohan rather than some jerk like this. I try to ignore him, but he won't stop looking at me.

"You have such a beautiful aura," he tells me.

"Thank you, it's 'cause I've been in Louisiana for a few months—"

I lose his attention as he shifts his gaze to the other twentysomethings boarding the plane.

I notice a mysterious man with dark sunglasses sitting alone. I can't tell if his eyes are open or not. His mouth hangs open and he occasionally jolts up when he catches himself dozing off. As soon as we depart, he taps my shoulder and asks to take a photo with me. I find it odd, but I agree anyway. When he tells me his name, I immediately recognize it, as he's known to be quite the troublemaker in the press. Typical trust-fund-kid behavior. As the flight progresses, I have more and more champagne. A few passengers go to the bathroom to do bumps of coke and ask me to join. Instantly, I start to feel strange. Like I'm not in my body anymore.

Everything goes black.

I wake up in a hotel room, lying naked next to the mysterious billionaire in glasses. I shoot up in bed, clutching the covers over my bare breasts. He cracks his eyes open, and I leap off the bed.

"Where is everyone?!" I scream. "Where is all my stuff?!"

He points to the closet, where all my belongings have been neatly unpacked.

"What's going on? Did we have sex?" I feel a wave of shame wash over me.

"You wanted to pee on me," he slurs. I notice drugs on every surface of the room. I quickly grab a few Roxy's off the commode and throw them in my purse.

I frantically grab all my stuff and run out of the lavish room. Unable to reach Liana, I call Harmony and Viki. They meet me at a Walgreens on Collins Avenue, and I get a douche for my vagina, using it between two cars. I can't shake the feeling of violation and disgust as I try to piece together what happened on that plane. Was I drugged? Was it just a reaction due to the air pressure?

Liana finally calls me back asking me where I went. I hadn't noticed she was asleep on the couch when I sprinted out of there.

"What the hell happened?" I ask her.

"I don't know, you wanted to go. You were possessed. You were so fucked up."

She packs up my stuff and meets us at our little one-bedroom Airbnb, far less extravagant than the billionaire's suite. Once inside, I leave my bag unattended to take a quick shower. When I come out of the bathroom and reach inside my bag for the Roxy's, I notice one is missing. I confront Harmony. "I know you took it!" I yell at her.

She doesn't deny it and shoots me a devious smirk. I can tell she's been drinking. I want to go off on her but after the night I've had, I don't have it in me.

"You're not coming out with us," I tell her coldly.

"Well, then, I'm taking the key to the Airbnb," she snaps back.

"Umm, no, you're not."

Viki and Liana roll their eyes at our bickering.

"You guys sound like an old married couple!" Viki complains.

"I'll meet you guys there," I tell Viki, and they walk out the door.

I finish getting ready as the argument escalates. Harmony reaches for my bag, trying to get the key. I push her off me. The fighting continues out onto the street as I walk in the rain to the club. Harmony trails behind, shouting after me. I ignore her until I feel a sharp ringing in my right ear and see my diamond hoop earring go flying through the air. It takes me a second to realize that she sucker-punched me. I turn around and see Harmony disappear around the corner. I start frantically looking for my earring in the puddles of rainwater. A homeless man who saw the whole thing picks it up and hands it to me. The back is missing, so I put it in my pocket and keep walking. Then Harmony comes at me again. This time I fight back. I grab her by her hair and punch her repeatedly in the head. We've been rolling around on the wet ground for a few seconds when the homeless man returns and tries to pry us apart.

I stand up and begin shouting at her, "You just had to come back!"

Her nose is bleeding, and as I storm off, I catch a glimpse of my reflection in the glass. I look horrible. I decide to skip the party and head back to the Airbnb, where I pass out immediately.

The next day, when I wake up, I search up and down for the earring and realize it's gone. At the same time, the billionaire texts me, asking how I'm doing. I tell him I got attacked and lost my diamond earring, and he offers to buy me a new pair.

"Be there in five," I text him.

I'm hoping once I have the earrings, I won't feel as bad about what happened on the plane. In my mind, this will even the score and make it okay.

He takes me to a fancy jewelry store in a fancy area of Miami. He does key bumps out in the open as I browse the shiny glass cases, looking for the perfect pair of earrings. I point to a pair and ask the clerk how much they are.

"These are sixty-five hundred," the clerk says.

I look at him and he nods, then drops his black Amex on the glass, making a loud clinking noise. I look at the greasy billionaire, groaning and grunting from being so bloated. I feel filthy even being in his presence. Once I put on the earrings, I realize I don't actually feel better. However, I'm no longer mad at Harmony.

I go meet her, and as I show off my shiny new diamonds, she lifts her sunglasses, revealing the damage from our fight.

"I don't feel bad for you," I remind her.

"I'm ready to go home," she says.

"Me too."

We decide to set off on a road trip through the southern states with our friend Matt. As soon as we walk into the car rental agency in Miami, Harmony charms the clerk, as she always does, and convinces her to give us a top-of-the-line vehicle at a fraction of the cost. We blaze through Florida and make it to Georgia, where Matt gets pulled over for reckless driving on the highway and is hauled off to the local jail. We spend the rest of the day bailing him out, and once he's back in the driver's seat we continue on the open road ahead of us.

We discover hidden gems in small mining towns. We stop at seedy bars and sketchy motels and of course we befriend all the locals. I try to enjoy myself, but I can't shake the feeling that something about me has changed. My mind keeps going back to the plane ride and the drinks they gave me. I think about pursuing charges for rape, since I was definitely too fucked up to consent, but then I remember what happened last time. Nobody believed me. Everyone would just call me a liar and say

I'm doing it for attention. I look at my earrings and remind myself that at least I got a consolation prize.

I'm relieved when we make it back to the bayou. I missed Brian and Eric and our wobbly house on stilts. I never want to leave again.

We all decide to get high on pills one evening.

"My friend sent them to me!" Eric says excitedly, gripping the small blue Roxy's in his hands. He uses his pill crusher to pulverize the handful of pills. He sprinkles the blue mountain onto the table and we all gather around it. Eric uses his EBT card to cut the powder into thin blue lines. He pulls a crusty dollar bill from his pocket. Harmony snatches it out of his hands. "We don't use singles, boo, that's nasty."

She comes back with a rolled-up crisp hundred-dollar bill, swoops in to do the first line, and then passes it to Eric. I'm practically salivating when it's my turn. I inhale the synthetic heroin and immediately feel the warmth enveloping my body.

The light machine I bought for the house sprays blue and purple waves on the ceiling. *Harvest Moon* plays in the background as the house subtly sways back and forth, as it always does. The room vibrates with electricity.

For Christmas, Viki sends me a vintage camera in the mail and tells me to start taking photos. "I'm so inspired by the photos you post on your Finsta," she says excitedly. "My friend has a space and said I can use it to curate an art show!"

"Umm, I'm not sure," I told her. "I never wanna go back to New York."

Viki brushes me off. "Just take the photos. We can think about the rest later."

I take out the camera and start snapping photos of Eric and Harmony.

I lean in to kiss him for a photo. He's gentle, I'm more aggressive. I feel him get an erection through the comforter and we make love. It's short and unsuccessful, but it's so meaningful to me.

"You're the only girl I've ever gotten a boner for," he says proudly.

. . .

One evening, on our weekly Walmart run, Harmony looks over at me from the passenger seat and declares, "I think my mom is dead."

"No way," I say. "She's an alcoholic. She just disappears sometimes. You know how she is."

I've been friends with Harmony long enough to know all about her mother, Mindy, and how Harmony had to give up a full scholarship at her dream school to stay in Florida and drive Mindy to jail on weekends. I know about the drunk-driving accident when Harmony was five years old that left her with a broken leg. I know about the lawsuit Mindy filed to try to get Harmony's grandmother's inheritance taken away from her. Harmony nods and we drive the rest of the way in silence.

The next day, a detective calls Harmony's phone and confirms her suspicions. She puts the call on speakerphone so I can hear everything. "Your mother was found unresponsive in a hotel."

Harmony remains composed on the phone, calmly asking questions and gathering more information. "What do you mean? Like she drank herself to death, or she was murdered?"

"Well, by the looks of it, it looks like alcohol poisoning, but we aren't ruling anything out."

There's a long pause. We all remain frozen until the detective breaks the silence.

"We're gonna need you to come pick up her dog. He's been trapped here a couple of days."

"Teddy! Yes, of course, I'm on my way."

Harmony pauses to look at me.

"I'm coming with you," I say. She pops an Adderall and we load up Eric's car, since ours is no longer safe to drive. Harmony doesn't speak for the entire ride. She focuses on the road, driving a hundred miles per hour across the southern states.

I pass out, and when I wake up we're already in Florida. We pull up to a sketchy apartment complex, where a short little man with terrible sun damage greets us with an overweight Chihuahua at his feet.

"Which one is Harmony?" he says. I point to her and he lunges into her arms, tears streaming down his face. "I loved your mother so much. I can't believe she's gone. My world, my life, will never be the same."

Harmony nods sympathetically and scoops the dog into her arms. He then leads us up to his apartment, where we're met with dozens of boxes and plastic bags, all belonging to Mindy.

"Please take whatever you want, it's yours," he says.

We sort through it all. I pull out a vibrator from the eighties and show it to Harmony to make her laugh.

"Where are the minks?" she asks.

He seems caught off guard by the question and starts acting suspicious. "Minks? I don't know about any minks. Maybe she sold them."

Harmony and I exchange a glance. We aren't convinced.

After a couple of hours of sifting through Mindy's junk, we pile anything worth saving into the car and check in to a hotel for the night. Surprisingly, Harmony doesn't cry about losing her mom. "I lost her a long time ago," she says, seeming almost relieved.

We drive through a hurricane all the way back to New Orleans and arrive a few hours before Harmony's birthday. Brian and Eric meet us at a fancy restaurant in the city. None of us are dressed appropriately and Eric's face tattoos always draw snickers from the waiters, who talk about us behind our backs. That night we get absolutely shitfaced on Bourbon Street and check in to a fancy hotel. The next day I run into a bridal party in the elevator. I overhear their conversation. They're sorority sisters in town for their best friend's wedding. I close my eyes and imagine what that must be like.

In the lobby, Harmony approaches me and mumbles, "I need to get high."

"Me too," I say and follow her out of the hotel. We get in the car and drive around aimlessly, asking any junkie on the street for the plug. They all shake their heads and shoo us away.

"They think we're cops," she says. She takes her phone out and googles "Where is Lil Wayne from?"

"Ok we have to go to the Ninth Ward," she says confidently.

We drive through the impoverished section of New Orleans in Eric's shitty car.

"We couldn't look more like cops if we tried," I say with a giggle.

Harmony remains serious in the driver's seat. "Don't worry, I've done this before. We need to find a liquor store."

I nod at her logic. We pull up to the liquor store and park in a lot near the entrance.

"Now we wait," she says, reclining her seat and putting her feet up on the dash as she lights a cigarette.

After a few minutes we see a group of boys in baggy clothes, covered in tattoos, approach the store. Harmony lowers her window and pokes her head out inconspicuously. "Pssst, you guys got any dog food?"

I can't help but burst out laughing. "Harmony, nobody says 'dog food'!"

"Shut up, I know what I'm doing!"

The leader of the crew struts over to us and glances inside the vehicle. "How do I know y'all ain't the police?" he asks.

I pull up my *Playboy* spread on my phone that just came out—and flaunt it in his face. "Would a cop be in *Playboy*?" I ask smugly.

He takes my phone out of my hands and carefully studies the photos, occasionally glancing back at me. "Aight, follow me."

We get out of the car and follow them down a sketchy block in the Ninth Ward. As we walk past the rows of dilapidated homes and crumbling buildings, Harmony befriends all the guys while the leader of the crew and I lag behind.

"What's your name?" I ask him.

"You can call me Coke."

He keeps his hand on the pistol in the waistband of his jeans as we talk. His face is covered in tattoos and his cologne smells sweet and musky. He seems paranoid as his eyes dart around.

"I have eyes at the back of my head. Motherfuckers out here shoot to kill."

He relaxes once we're inside the dilapidated trap house. The windows are boarded up and there's no electricity. There's a space heater, a TV and a video game console hooked up to a tiny generator in the living room, and a few mangy couches scattered around. I sit down and feel something hard stab me in the butt. I push the blanket over to reveal a 9mm Glock. I pick it up and examine it. I notice that the serial numbers have been scratched off.

"You got any rigs?" Harmony asks.

Coke disappears into the back room and returns with a fresh box of sealed syringes. "I'll throw them in for free, but y'all gotta do it here in front of me."

"I can't believe you think I'm a cop, I'm actually flattered," Harmony says.

"Trust me, we both can't hold down a job," I say.

Nobody laughs.

"Bundle is a hundred, but I'll do sixty for you," Coke says, looking in my direction.

Harmony pulls her wallet out of her back pocket and hands him three crisp twenty-dollar bills. "You owe me thirty," she says to me.

"I got us the discount!"

"Y'a'll sisters or something?" one of the guys asks.

"Cousins," we say in unison.

"That explains it," Coke says. "So are y'a'll on the run or something?"

"Kinda," we say in unison again and break into laughter.

Harmony hands me a baggie and starts loading up her syringe. I follow her into the bathroom, where there's no running water and the toilet is overflowing in caked-up shit. The smell is nauseating, but we both decide to ignore it.

"You wanna go first?" She takes off her leather belt and hands it to me. "You have such good veins," she says, eyeing the big bulging blue vein on my forearm.

"I know," I say, as if it's a burden.

My heart races as I wrap the belt around my arm. "I haven't done this in so long." I take a deep breath and stick the pointy needle in the vein. I watch the blood shoot into the syringe and push the murky brown water back into my arm. I rip the belt off and stumble back against the wall. I catch my balance.

"Oh, it's good," I tell her.

"Okay, good, I just wanted you to go first in case it was spiked," she says deviously.

"You bitch!" I say, slapping her on her shoulder.

We start driving to New Orleans more often and spending more time at the trap house. The boys hate going outside but they agree to take us to a bounce club, where we are the only white people. The boys tell everyone, "Nah, they're cool," but it doesn't help.

"I don't think they like you," Harmony says after an ice cube flies through the air and hits me in the forehead.

"Fuck off, Harmony."

One night we get wasted on Hurricanes and march up and down Bourbon Street. We taunt the religious fanatics spewing insane crap about the devil.

"Take a photo of me!" I yell as I shove my camera at her and pull down my pants in front of one of them.

"Strippers love me," Harmony brags. Thirty minutes later, I find her blowing lines of cocaine in a dressing room with a bunch of naked girls surrounding her. I snap photos as she does karaoke with the bartenders and smokes cigarettes with the bouncers. Everywhere we go, everyone loves her. She's my muse and I love capturing her in all her glory.

At the end of the night, we drive by the trap and realize it's boarded up and covered in yellow police tape. We frantically call Coke, who informs us it got raided the day before.

"They came in with guns, broke the door down and everything," he says. "Everybody got locked up. Y'all are lucky you weren't there. I got another spot, though. I'll text you the address."

We head over to the new trap and climb the rickety stairs to the second-floor motel room, where Coke is alone and seems preoccupied. "I just got out of jail, man, I ain't trying to go back," he says.

He seems different. His eyelids hang heavy over his glazed, pinned-out eyes. "It's on me," he says, dropping a few bags on the TV stand.

I'm still buzzed from our evening on Bourbon Street, but I manage to draw up a clean shot. I tie off my arm with my hair scrunchie and stick the syringe in my bulging vein. I feel the surge of euphoria travel up my spine, then suddenly my vision goes blank.

I regain consciousness on the floor with my head in Harmony's lap as she slaps the life back into me.

"Relax, what the fuck, just chill," I mumble.

She lets out a massive sigh of relief. "Dude! Your lips turned blue and you did the death rattle, do you know what that is? You're so lucky I brought my Narcan with me."

I look around the room. "Where's Coke?" I ask, confused.

"He got so shook, dude. He started flipping out and bounced."

I get up and run to the toilet, vomit spewing from the corners of my mouth. I cradle the toilet seat in my arms, regurgitating my insides until there is nothing left.

"Dude, I can't believe I saved your life! I was slapping you mad hard too." Harmony's voice is so loud, her words are like daggers in my ears.

"Okay, I get it!" I snap at her. "We're even now!"

This event has a sobering effect on us and we stop going to New Orleans. A few days later, we discover Coke got arrested and sentenced to eight years in prison for possession during a traffic stop.

I stop doing drugs and focus on my photography, taking thousands of pictures of Eric and Harmony and anyone else we meet on the bayou. Everyone in our parish knows me as "the *Playboy* model from New York." I wear the title proudly. One man even brings a copy of the magazine to the bar for me to autograph.

Harmony tells me she's always dreamed of going to the film school at UCLA, so I help her write a screenplay and we send in an application. A couple of weeks later, she's accepted to the film program, and we both decide that after six wild months, our time on the bayou has come to an end. She books a ticket to California and I book one to New York. We spend the next week packing all the trinkets we've accumulated and removing our art from every surface of the house.

On our last night, we hang out near the water's edge.

"Remember when we met?" she asks me.

"How could I forget?! I came home from school, and you were in my living room with a duffel bag!"

Harmony leans over, laughing. "It's not my fault!" she says. "Danica should've told me she was leaving for the summer before inviting me to New York!"

"I can't believe she dumped you on me like that." I shake my head.

"Shut up, you loved it," Harmony says.

"Oh my God, it was the best gift she's ever given me! It was love at first sight."

"You didn't even let me hang out with anyone else!" she says.

"We spent every single day together."

"And nights!"

As we look up at the infinite star-studded sky, she says, "I can't believe we're leaving this place."

An anxious feeling washes over me. She's my comfort person. We fight like hell, and we're not above throwing a few punches, but we always hug it out. And strangely, it only reinforces our bond. Our love is unconditional and never judgmental. She sees me through my lows and never holds them against me. Another thing we have in common is that we are both prescribed the same mood stabilizer, Lamictal. Same exact dosage too. It feels as if we've known each other forever, even in a past life.

"I'm gonna come to L.A. right after the art show," I say.

Harmony flicks her Camel Crush into the bayou and we go inside to finish the last of our packing.

Eric can't stop crying. "Please don't leave," he says with tears in his eyes. My heart breaks, but as much as I love him, I know our time is coming to a close. Besides, Eric met a guy on Instagram and I flew him to Louisiana and they fell in love. There's no room for me anymore.

In the morning, Eric drives us to the airport. The sky is gray and the ride is quiet. I'm sitting in the front seat when I start smelling smoke. I close the window and it only gets worse. I turn around and the whole backseat is in flames. Harmony is passed out with her sunglasses on. The hoodie on the seat next to her is engulfed in flames. I start screaming as the car swerves. I shake Harmony and grab the hoodie, swiftly chucking it out the window. I examine the damage and notice the shotgun shells on the charred seat.

"You could have killed us all!" I yell at Harmony.

"It wasn't me!" she yells back. "Eric's cigarette probably flew back in the car!"

Once we get to the airport, Harmony quickly gathers her things and her dog and disappears inside while I say bye to Eric. "I love you, Pony-boy," I whisper in his ear.

"Don't forget about me in the big city, Cherry girl."

I clutch Eric's crystal and silently sob throughout the flight. I finally open the window shade and realize we're directly over the New York City skyline. Despite having seen it from every vantage point, including Rikers Island, I had forgotten how spectacular the view was. We fly over the bridge and past the Chrysler and Empire State buildings and over Central Park, where I'm flooded with memories that I blocked out of my mind.

Returning home after a long time away should feel comforting, but for me, it's not that simple. While a part of me is relieved to be back, I'm not ready to reintegrate myself into my old life. Mostly because my old life no longer exists. The once familiar streets feel foreign and strange, and the sting of betrayal lingers. The loss of so many friends has left me feeling bitter. I envy the sense of routine and foundation among the few friends I still have here. I feel like I'm just floating along without any roots to anchor me.

I keep thinking about Louisiana. I miss Harmony and Eric. I miss the comfort of them always being around. It's hard to come back to a place that has gone on without me. So much has changed, and I'm not sure how I fit in anymore.

Being back home is haunting. I sleep on the couch at night to avoid my bedroom, but I can't escape the ghosts of my past. Traces of violent fights serve as painful reminders, like the hole in the wall I sloppily patched up, the dent in the steel lamp, the shattered picture frame, and a few specks of hardened blood.

I focus on my art show and decide to call it *PTSD*. I find that very fitting. I get the hundreds of rolls of film that I amassed on the bayou developed and start putting together the show under Viki's guidance. We spend a week in the gallery reconstructing my bedroom in Louisiana, filling it with the souvenirs of my time there: the portrait Eric painted of me, teddy bears, a snow globe, and a vial of holy water Eric gave me.

The little gremlin voice inside my head tells me no one will come, no one will show up for me, everybody hates me. I start sniffing Roxy's secretly to quiet the noise in my head and ease my discomfort. I get anxious every time I leave the house. I feel the judgmental stares. I hear the familiar faces whisper and laugh as I pass them on the street: "That was Julia Fox!" "Was," not "is." The tense choice bothers me. They can see me only in their misconception of the past, and I fear I'll be trapped there forever.

The opening is on a rainy Sunday night. I think surely no one will show up in the monsoon-like downpour. I'm thrilled when Harmony walks through my front door unexpectedly. I sprint across the living room and wrestle her to the ground.

"You didn't think I would miss your first art show, did you?!"

My anxiety intensifies with every step as we walk arm in arm down Canal Street toward the gallery. I fear that my artwork won't be well received and everyone will hate it. The fear of failure looms over me like a dark cloud, suffocating any glimmer of hope. But as we ascend the five flights of stairs, the murmur of voices grows louder until it's a deafening roar. To my surprise, the show is packed. People spill out into the hallway and line up to congratulate me. As I scan the crowd, I see lots of familiar faces, old friends, and even some complete strangers. I notice my books flying off the shelf and I feel a brief sense of accomplishment. I know I should be happy. But I'm not. I still hear the nagging voices in my head. I grab Harmony and slip out of the event undetected. Then I call our old dealer and we proceed to lock ourselves in my bedroom and get high for the rest of the night. It's only then that I feel calm and at peace.

The next day, we hop on a plane to L.A., and I practically move into Harmony's house. She lives with a roommate who doesn't appreciate me crashing in their living room, leaving cookie crumbs and weed in the crevices of the couch. I find us a pill dealer through a mutual friend and we start getting high every day, spending hundreds of dollars on drugs. Time is a blur. The weeks go by in a daze.

Harmony joins a kickball league to try and make some friends and meets a nice Jewish girl named Rachel. They quickly fall in love, and I start feeling like the third wheel in their relationship. Between her roommate wanting me out and her girlfriend's suspicions around her drug use, I make the decision to pack my bags and go.

I get in my rental car and start driving toward the desert. I have no idea where I'm going, but I follow the calling. I listen to Beach House with the windows down and smoke dozens of joints as I drive through the mountains toward Arizona. The warm, dry air smacks me in the face and I feel free. I see signs for the Grand Canyon and decide to go check it out since I've never been.

Once I arrive and peer over the edge at the magnificent valley, I feel angry that no one ever thought to take me here sooner. I can't believe I've been missing out on this for so long. I'm blown away by its grandeur. It's comforting to feel so small sometimes. It makes my problems feel smaller too.

I spend the next few nights in deserted desert towns, sleeping in trailers I find for cheap on Airbnb and befriending the hosts, who tell me all the folklore surrounding the area. I entertain myself by exploring ghost towns and searching for artifacts from the Manson Family, who, legend has it, hid out in the caves. I enjoy going to the mineral hot springs in the middle of the night, outdoors under the shooting stars. I love the sounds of the desert. The hissing and the chirping create a soothing song. And around three a.m., when the full moon is directly overhead, the entire desert lights up. It's the longest I've been single and I've never been alone for this long. I'm just now getting to know myself.

I've been driving on the fine line between ultimate freedom and complete and utter loneliness. Some nights, if I'm too tired to drive, I pull over on the side of the road and watch the shooting stars from my sunroof until I fall asleep. My phone doesn't have service out here, so I often have only the compass app to navigate. I get lost time and time again, but somehow I end up exactly where I need to be.

I reconnect with my good friend Sara from middle and high school. She's since moved to L.A., and I reach out to her while I'm there. We go on crazy secluded hikes and hop from trailer park to trailer park in the middle of the desert. On one particular journey, we take mushrooms in New Mexico and pick up a Navajo hitchhiker who leads us to a sixteen-hour peyote ceremony in Arizona.

When I start running low on cash, I get a job dancing at a few strip clubs in Vegas. On my first night, I make fifteen hundred dollars and move out of my car and into an Airbnb. Stripping is nothing like being a dominatrix. I hate having to grind and give the customers massages. I only last a couple of weeks before I quit in the middle of my shift and never go back. I decide that I'd rather be broke.

Once summer is over, I pack up my car and drive all the way back to New York. Immediately when I arrive, I start getting antsy and decide to drive to Michigan to visit Eric, who I haven't seen since I left the bayou. He's been calling me a lot lately, complaining about being back in his parents' basement.

"There's no H here at all," he tells me frantically on the phone. "I've been hanging out with this really annoying girl 'cause she gives me pills 'cause all my dealers, the two dealers in my town, are all out. I feel so sick, I look so disgusting. You would not think I was sexy."

"I'll get you some and bring it to you," I say. "Don't worry."

Fueled by my desire to please, I set out on the hunt for the best-quality china white in the entire city. It's not hard to find. With a full bundle in a rubber band and a half ounce of marijuana, I throw some clothes in the backseat and hit the road.

Two hours into the drive, I'm smoking a blunt through Pennsylvania when a state trooper emerges from a wooded area and turns on his sirens. I put the blunt out in an old Coke can and stash it under my seat as I pull over on the side of the highway. As I dig my license out of my Mary Poppins purse, I see him in the rearview mirror, stepping out of his car and walking toward me.

"You were going eighty in a fifty-five. License and registration, please."

I roll down the window a couple of inches and hand him my information. I figure he's just going to write me a speeding ticket and send me on my way.

He examines my license as he walks back to his car. I suddenly remember the bundle of heroin in my cupholder. I quickly grab it and stuff it in my bra and take what's left of the weed and crumple it up, shoving it deep in my pants. As soon as I'm done, I look up, and he's at my window again.

"Ma'am, I can smell marijuana in your vehicle. In the state of Pennsylvania, that's probable cause for me to search you. Please step out of the car."

I keep a smile on my face, trying my best to charm him, as I do most cops, but this Pennsylvania cop is not falling for my shit. He starts performing a sobriety test on me, which I fail.

"Recite the alphabet backward."

"Z, Y, X . . . umm, I have ADHD. It's hard for me to—"

He cuts me off. "I'm gonna have to take you down to the jailhouse."

I nod but I feel like I'm going to throw up. I'm not getting out of this one. Each step I take, I hear the crinkling plastic in my panties and smell the strong odor of weed wafting through my clothing. I keep talking to mask the sound when he instructs me to stand with my legs and arms apart.

"I have to pat you down."

I clench my butt cheeks as he gently pats me over my clothing, thankfully avoiding my crotch and breasts.

"Sorry, I have to do this," he tells me as he puts the handcuffs on my wrists.

I sit in the back of the cruiser as he searches every crevice of my vehicle. I keep my eye on him as he examines an empty Ziploc bag covered in marijuana residue. I see him sniffing my glass pipe I thought I had lost and my grinder. He places everything inside an evidence bag.

"Have you smoked marijuana?" he asks me sternly.

"Not in the car, I swear," I plead with him.

Ten minutes later, I'm in a jail cell in the middle of rural Pennsylvania, praying that they don't find the drugs in my bra and panties. I close my eyes and beg under my breath: "Please, God, I'll get sober. I'll never do drugs again if you get me out of this."

I open my eyes to find a lady cop standing at the gate, holding a bag. This is it, I think, she's going to make me undress and put me in a hideous orange uniform like the ones on TV. Instead, she opens her kit, pulls out a syringe resembling a medieval torture device, and draws my blood. I give her the arm I don't use to shoot up so she won't see my scars. She doesn't talk to me and I'm too afraid to ask any questions.

Thirty minutes after this horrible encounter, another cop opens the gate again, makes me sign a bunch of documents I don't read, and hands me back my phone.

"I can go?" I ask in disbelief.

"Yup," he says.

I jog away from the jailhouse before they change their minds. I google a local car service and thirty minutes later, I'm back in my car. I pull out slowly, keeping the speed limit. Once I'm in Ohio, I take the bundle out of my bra and wrap it in tissue paper and shove it up my vagina.

I call Eric to tell him what happened. "You don't understand, I had the drugs on me in the cell, I prayed to God, and they let me go!"

"You still have the H, right?" he asks.

I sigh, disappointed. "Yes, my GPS says I'll be there at midnight."

When I finally arrive in northern Michigan, I'm exhausted, and after having had ten hours to think about my life, I can't ignore the deal I made with God. I dig the heroin out of my vagina and pull out the moist bundle. Unfortunately, the sweat from my vagina juices penetrated the tissue paper and the wax baggies, turning the powder into a thick tar, but this doesn't stop Eric, who scrapes them with a razor blade and dumps the brown goop into a spoon.

"Do you want some?" he asks.

I pause. I miss getting high with him so much and it takes everything in me to shake my head. "I think I'm gonna stick to weed," I say as I roll up a fat blunt.

He shrugs and slurps the gunk into his rusty syringe. "I kinda like that your pussy juice is on it," he says.

My mouth waters as I watch his trembling hand poke around his body for a vein.

"Let me do it," I tell him, taking the syringe out of his hands. I empty the contents into a vein in his neck and watch his eyes roll to the back of his head. The rest of the night is dull except for the noise coming from the TV. He nods out as I zone out, thinking about how much this promise I made with God is going to cost me and if it was really worth it.

When I get back to New York, I delete all my dealers' phone numbers. I even start attending A.A. meetings again. One morning at the Living Now meeting, I spot Shane sitting in the audience, cozying up to a girl who bullied me on Instagram after the release of my book. This is the first time I've seen him since the phone incident. The adrenaline starts pumping through my veins as my eyes fixate on them. I don't hear a word the speaker is saying, and when he's done sharing, I raise my hand and let the room know: "There are two people in this room who do not make me feel safe."

When I finish my rant, the girl sitting next to me starts clapping. She sticks her hand out and whispers, "I'm Gianna." I can tell by the way she looks at me that she already knows who I am, but we both play along. I crack a smile but I'm too worked up to engage with her. As the meeting proceeds, I examine her pretty hands and perfectly manicured nails. I think to myself that she could be a hand model. Her auburn hair is thick and healthy, and her skin is tan and smooth. She smells sweet too, like flowers and hair products.

Outside after the meeting, she marches up to me and orders me to take her number. I don't have much of a choice, so I pull out my phone and hand it to her. "What you just did there, that was the best thing I've ever seen. You have no idea how many times—"

I feel a tap on my shoulder. I turn around and see Shane, arms crossed, with a disapproving look on his face.

"Jules, you can't do that."

"I can do whatever I want!" My voice gets louder as the blood rushes to my head. He leads me away from the crowd forming and escorts me down the block.

"I turned my life around, and by the looks of it, you should too," he says, eyeing me up and down. I glance down at my outfit. My stained off-brand puffer coat is a far cry from the colorful shiny fur coats I used to wear. "You look like *white trash*," he says under his breath in a concerned yet playful manner.

I catch myself laughing and straighten my face. "Well, you *are* white trash!" I say in my brattiest voice and storm away.

An hour later, I get a text on my phone from Shane, and we plan to meet up on a bench down the block from the same apartment we once lived in together, that Rohan still pays for. He's much less confident this time. He avoids looking me in the eyes and his posture is hunched. He seems defeated, desperate.

"You ruined my life," he tells me as his chin quivers.

"You ruined your own life."

"Do you know what it's like having everyone think you're a piece of shit?! Nobody wants to work with me."

"Do you think it was easy for me? You got to stay here. I had to go!"

"No, you ran away! And I stayed here and dealt with my problems."

After we debate for a while, I invite him upstairs. He hesitates but I can tell he misses me. There's something strangely comforting about this situation. It's like I finally have the confirmation I always needed, that our bond can withstand anything and everything. However, it feels a little too late.

Once we're upstairs, it's only a few minutes before we are both undressed on the same mattress we once shared, having explosive sex. But as soon as we're done, an unmistakable cloud of guilt hovers over the room.

"You can't tell anyone about this," I say, waving my finger in his face in a threatening manner.

He looks at me like I'm crazy. "Do you know how many people would disown me if they knew about this?!" he says.

"Me too!"

We laugh, ignoring our recklessness, disregarding the fact that we tore this city in half with our love.

The next few weeks, we see each other every day. I sneak him in and out of my apartment, avoiding Viki and Liana, who still live with me. We have the best sex of our lives while agreeing to keep our relationship platonic.

"We can't be together," he constantly reminds me when it starts to cross the line.

Everything is going fine until one night I'm scrolling on Instagram and a photo of a naked girl pops up on my feed. I immediately recognize her, and when I see who posted it, my heart breaks again. She was my friend. How could she fuck Shane and let him post a nude picture of her? I stare at her bronzed skin and perky tits. She looks hot, and that makes me feel even worse. She's a typical good-time girl, a sunny Malibu heiress with a shallow head and an even shallower heart.

She's everything I'm not.

I'm flooded with familiar feelings and decide that I can't allow him to make me feel this way again. As much as I want to curse both of them out, I decide not to. Instead, I text my new friend Gianna and we make plans to go to a meeting together.

You'd think I'd be upset at the ultimate demise of Shane and me after having given him another chance, but I'm actually the happiest I've ever been. I quickly learn that Gianna might be the funniest person to have ever lived. We start spending more and more time together. In the beginning, we go to A.A. meetings every day, but we slowly stop going and immerse ourselves in our own little world filled with sweet treats and prank calls and the never-ending echoes of our laughter. I spend almost every night at her parents' lavish apartment at the Carlyle, and it's not long before we both start smoking weed and popping the occasional Percocet.

We swap partying with the rest of our friends for movie dates and midnight shows at the Comedy Cellar. She tells me her dream is to be a stand-up comedian on *SNL*.

"You should do it," I tell her.

She shrugs and looks away. "I don't know," she says softly.

"Well, my dream is to attend my own funeral, so I think I got it a little worse."

She laughs.

"I'm serious!" I tell her.

"You should do it," she says.

I call the show *RIP Julia Fox*. Viki again finds a gallery and helps curate it. Liana helps with the memorial installation. Gianna comes to the space every day to help set up. She prices my books at sixty dollars and appoints herself my book salesman, charging people twenty dollars just to flip through it. That same night, she single-handedly recoups all the money I invested in the show. Hundreds of people show up to mourn me. Some people bring flowers, some people wear black.

When a journalist asks, "What does *RIP Julia Fox* mean to you?," I tell her, "This chapter of my life is over. She's dead. It's an ending but it's really a new beginning."

10

STARSTRUCK

My phone starts vibrating loudly on the table. When I glance down, I see Josh Safdie's name pop up on the screen. It's been over five years that Josh has been telling me about this movie he's writing called *Uncut Gems*. He swears up and down that I'm perfect for this part: the lover and coworker of a Diamond District jeweler played by Adam Sandler whose gambling problem grows increasingly dangerous. "You *are* Sadie," he tells me. His confidence starts to rub off and I actually start believing him. He sends me script after script, and each time I read over it carefully. I know how important my notes are to him and I want to give him genuine, thoughtful feedback.

Unfortunately, the last time we spoke, he sadly informed me that even though my screen test with Adam was incredible, the studios want someone with a "big name," like Lady Gaga or Jennifer Lawrence. Sure, I'm somewhat of a hood celebrity here in New York, but I'm nobody in Hollywood.

"I'm going to try my best to get you the part, but I can't make any promises," Josh reassures me. I cling to his words like a life vest. I *need* this.

I feel a sense of impending doom as I watch my phone light up, debating over letting the call go to voicemail. What if he tells me something I don't want to hear? I think back to what the nurse said to my mom the day I was born: "With eyes like this and a name like Julia Fox, she's going to be a movie star!" It feels like this is my destiny but I'm so afraid to be wrong. I'm so afraid of not being chosen. I put all of myself into this character. Josh and his cowriter/director brother, Benny, even renamed her Julia, since Adam's daughter's name is Sadie and it hit too close to home. How will I go on with my life if someone else can play *Julia* better than Julia?!

As I replay the scenes from the screen test over and over in my head, the belief in my destiny begins to change and the lens through which I view myself grows hazy and distorted, causing me to conclude that girls like me don't get opportunities like this. I try to quiet the voices by telling myself that the chemistry was undeniably there. But then that creeping little gremlin voice in my head asks: "But was it?" I could have done the karaoke scene better on the second day. But it was raining and I had to take the train and my hair got messed up and I couldn't sleep the night before from the jitters of the first day and I was cranky and in a bad mood.

But the first day of the screen test was magic. My hair was perfectly coiffed and Gianna graciously lent me a half-million-dollar choker that's been in her family for centuries and I felt like a real-life princess. I arrived at Barney's shoot location, and the moment I saw those lights and the cameras, a switch went off and I was Julia Motherfucking Fox. I was quick and witty. I was funny and charming. I was able to keep up with fucking Adam Sandler! And not just keep up but challenge him, push him, bring out the best in him. It was as if all the planets and stars in the cosmos were all perfectly aligned and a star was born. ME.

My friends watch my phone vibrate around on the table for a few more seconds before Gianna opens her eyes real wide and yells, "Pick it up!" I take a deep breath, say a quick little prayer, compose myself, and answer.

Before I can even say a word, Josh yells, "You got the part!"

His excitement hits me through the phone and I start shouting, "No, no, no fucking way!" I'm in awe. I'm in disbelief. I feel like I'm dreaming, like I just hit the life lottery and he's the one betting on me. "Thank you! Thank you! Thank you!" I say over and over.

I think about how the night before Ace turned himself in we stayed up watching Adam Sandler movies. Now I'm going to be in a movie with Adam Sandler. I have a permanent smile on my face for the rest of the evening as I think about what this means for my future.

"You're going to be a movie star!" my friends cheer me on.

Later that night, I decide to call Shane and tell him the news. Partly to rub it in his face and partly because he always told me I should be an actress.

"I got the part," I say.

"I knew you would," he says. "You're a star."

I feel the anger and resentment I'd been harboring leave my body, and I quietly forgive him for everything he's done to me: the nights alone waiting for him to come home, hooking up with my friends, cheating on me with prostitutes, abandoning me when I was pregnant, telling me I would be more interesting if I had gone to art school, and just always making me feel like a piece of shit for the things I couldn't change about myself.

For so long, I looked to him to validate me. I wanted to prove myself to him, that I was better than the nepotism girls he always compared me to. I don't desperately crave his approval anymore. I've just validated my-self. Getting this role is all the confirmation I need, and I got it by being my most authentic genuine self, by unapologetically being the person he was always so ashamed of.

When I hang up the phone, I'm aware this is the last time I'll ever call him. I won't be taking him with me to the next phase of my life, and I'm not the least bit sad about it. Instead, I revel in my victory.

I call my mom to tell her about the movie and it becomes immediately clear that she doesn't really understand the magnitude of this
opportunity.

"I'm going to be famous," I tell her, and she laughs. I have a flashback
to when I was ten years old and she asked me why I wanted to learn to
play the guitar. "I'm gonna be a rock star," I said to her confidently. She
laughed at me then too. Well, I guess this time I'm just going to have to
show her.

The months before filming are filled with anxiety. I have to get in shape
but it's hard when all I do is smoke weed and eat cupcakes at the Carlyle.
I practically move in with Gianna any time her parents are out of town.

Whenever my manager calls me, I hold my breath, convinced he's
going to tell me the studios changed their mind about me. Even after
the contracts are signed, I still can't believe it. I live under the paranoid
delusion that it's going to get snatched from right up under me. I'm so
used to things aligning to perfection and then disintegrating just as fast.

It's only when I'm on set for the lighting test that it dawns me. I call
Gianna. "Holy shit! This is not some small indie movie! This is fucking
Hollywood!" I tell her from my own personal trailer. "There's so many
people here! And all this heavy machinery. They even have a fucking
crane!"

She feels my excitement buzzing through the phone. "Should I
come?" she asks.

"Yeah, I need you to help me memorize my lines! I literally don't
know any of them!"

Once Gianna arrives on set, she doesn't help me rehearse. Instead
she starts making her rounds and charming the crew with her wit. She
even introduces herself to Adam and makes him laugh.

"If you play your cards right, he might get you on *SNL*," I tell her
with a wink.

Pretty soon she becomes an unofficial crew member. She doesn't
leave my side. She stays for the late shoots, three in the morning, thirty

degrees outside. She runs lines with me and carefully watches me from the monitor, throwing me the occasional thumbs-up and mouthing, "You're doing amazing, sweetie," a tribute to Kris Jenner on Kim Kardashian's first ever *Playboy* shoot. In between takes, she brings me water and my favorite assortment of candies from crafty. When my eyes are red from being too stoned, she rushes over with eye drops. When I'm in a bad mood, she's always ready with a bend-over-crouch-down-pee-in-your-pants-funny pep talk to hype me up. When my feet hurt, she gives me her UGG slippers right off her feet. Any time I turn my head, she's always right there, always in the way and always being yelled at to "Get out of the shot!"

On our way home each day, I make her do impressions of the crew members talking about my performance by the monitor. She changes her voice to a British accent: "You know, I hadn't heard of her before, and at first I had my doubts, but she's not bad at all!"

I can tell the crew find it hard to believe that a girl with no prior acting experience could land a movie of this magnitude. But I slowly start to win them over. Every morning, when they hand me the call sheet, my eyes scan the page for my name, checking to make sure I'm still number two, right below Adam Sandler and right above Kevin Garnett, the NBA legend who plays himself in the film. I'm in awe that little old me is sandwiched between these two masters of their craft. This means something to me. I stare at the paper a little longer and tell myself, "I cannot fuck this up." The pressure is on.

Over the course of filming, the stage becomes our home, and the cast and crew become our second family. We get close to Kevin Garnett when we discover he has weed on a day we didn't bring enough. We start hanging out in his trailer, burning down blunts in between scenes. We invite him back to our hotel room after work and get high listening to music. He's into conspiracy theories and I fall down the rabbit hole listening to his wild takes as Gianna rolls her eyes. "This is the dumbest shit I ever heard," she groans.

We don't want him to leave, so we convince him to sleep over with us in our hotel room. He's too tall to fit on the bed with the both of us, so he has to lie on it diagonally while we curl up in the corners. Once we fall asleep, he creeps out of our room quietly in the middle of the night and bumps into Josh Safdie in the hallway. And what are the odds of Josh believing that we were literally just having a slumber party?

We play basketball with Adam at lunchtime and listen to his old-school jams on his boom box. We invite all our friends to set, where we sit around and gossip about the rest of the crew with the hair and makeup team. We gasp at all the secret affairs happening on set. Gianna has eyes in the back of her head, always ready to divulge the not-so-furtive flirting she witnessed.

But there's always an underlying layer of darkness beneath the thin veil of glory. Gianna and I are drug addicts. The night before the first day of filming, I get sick from some bad pills and throw up all night. I get forty-five minutes of sleep. Luckily, the scene we are filming is the one where Howard comes home to find that Julia has been out all night partying. When I tell Josh I haven't slept, he refers to it as "Method acting." He always knows how to spin my antics into a productive contribution to the creative process. I love him for that. The hair and makeup team doesn't have to do much work that day. I looked like absolute shit, but once again I got lucky.

The night we shoot the scene in which Julia surprises Howard at their fuck pad wearing lingerie, I'm so nervous about having to be half-naked and make out with Adam that Gianna and I sniff a whole bunch of Roxy's right before, causing her to nod out and projectile-vomit in the same bathroom where I'm getting touch-ups all night. Every time I watch that scene, I'm transported back to that agonizing moment of wanting to stop everything to hold her hair back and comfort her. Instead, I tell everyone she ate some undercooked chicken.

One morning, as I doze off in the makeup chair while Mia the hair-stylist twirls my hair into perfect bouncy curls, my phone starts vibrating in my hand. I see it's Liana and answer it immediately. She's choked up and can barely get a word out. Between the muffled sobs, I hear the words "Katharine overdosed, she died." The tears well up in my perfectly made-up eyes as I hang up the phone. Everyone in the room senses something is amiss. Gianna rushes over and I tell her what happened. She stares blankly at me.

I had known Katharine as a teenager, but we didn't get close until we were both sober. I met her when she took my friend's purse at a party and stole all her birthday money. I got it back but not without a very humiliating fight on the street in which I grabbed the Chanel bag off Katharine's arm and emptied the contents. The money was gone, and in its place were two untouched vials of cocaine. She stared at me hopelessly with those big blue puppy-dog eyes as I paused to think for a moment. I pocketed one of the vials and let her keep the other out of pity.

I didn't see her again until years later when we were adults and she was a different person. She had blossomed. She had dug herself out of the hole her life sank into, but the scars of her past were still so visible. She relapsed on heroin often, putting herself in dangerous situations with shady characters, but she always came back to the rooms and kept trying to get better.

We went to meetings together, and eventually she even became my writing partner. We spent hours writing, locked away in the storage closet in my building, as it was the only quiet place I could think of. She loved reading my work and I loved reading hers. She wrote candidly about her time on Rikers Island. After a string of drug-related arrests, she'd been sent to jail for stealing a candy bar from a pharmacy.

During her incarceration, she almost died from a staph infection that was left unchecked even after she complained to the guards about it. When she called her mom from the jailhouse phone to ask for a few dollars for her commissary, her mom hung up on her.

This wasn't supposed to be her life. Her mom was one of the first women to land a job on Wall Street and got pregnant late in life by a married man who wanted nothing to do with them once Katharine was born. It didn't matter that Katharine had the bluest eyes or that she was tall and thin with thick blond hair. She never felt like she was good enough. So she got boob jobs and lipo, and once her mom got diagnosed with Alzheimer's, Katharine ran up her credit card on mountains of Chanel bags. But none of that could fill the void that not being loved properly had left her with.

I decide to stop using drugs for the remainder of the film. But not Gianna. As my problem with drugs improves, hers gets progressively worse.

"It's like you don't even care that Katharine's dead!" I shout at her once we wrap and are back at the hotel.

"Everyone has different ways of showing grief!" Gianna snaps back. "And plus, it's not like we were best friends."

"It's not about that! A young person died who had their whole life ahead of them! It's a fucking tragedy!"

The night of the wrap party at the Jane Hotel is so much fun that between all the alcohol and weed, I can't remember it. All I have are the moments I managed to capture on my phone. Gianna and me posing with some members of the crew. Gianna and me drunk and wrestling on the couch. And then a single photo of me in a corner talking to a really gorgeous, tall, well-dressed Russian man who I would go on to marry less than two months after that night.

Gianna doesn't take the news about my new romance with Andrew very well.

"But you're *my* boyfriend!" she yells at me.

"I know, G, but I'm older than you, I need to settle down, and I always wanted to be with a Russian guy! I manifested this!"

I hate that it feels like I'm cheating on her. I resent her for being so irrational. Or am I in the wrong for expecting her to be okay with this sudden change? She's heartbroken, and so am I when I realize I can't have both of them. She wants me to choose.

I would be lying if I said there weren't times when Gianna and I were lying in bed together, smoking weed, watching reality TV, and laughing our asses off that I didn't look over at her and wonder if she was the one. And I knew she felt the same way. Our bond transcends anything either of us had ever felt before. It's more than friendship, and sometimes I feel as though I gaslit her into thinking it wasn't anything more as soon as I met Andrew.

She loathes Andrew. Her jealousy seeps through every pore of her being and poisons everything around her. She goes as far as to confide in a mutual friend of ours that she wants to have Andrew killed. Who knows if she's serious, but I wouldn't put it past her. Somehow this just makes me love her more.

Andrew is wary of Gianna too. He's figured out that we like to get high together and he worries about me when I'm with her. One night, he comes over to find us nodding out and slurring our words. He drags both of us to a Narcotics Anonymous meeting. Even though he knows nothing about the program, he's desperate for me to stop using.

He's never been with a drug addict before and the whole experience is too traumatizing for him. But he isn't going to give up on me. A friend of his gives him an old prescription of Suboxone strips to help me stop and I actually take them and eventually I stop getting high altogether. I tell Gianna about the miracle drug and beg her to start taking it too, but she refuses. She doesn't want my help.

Over the next few months, I see Gianna less and less. I try texting and calling, but it becomes clear from her silence that she's drifting further and further away from me. These winter months are the coldest and loneliest of my life. I spend most of my day cooped up at home in front of the TV, waiting for Andrew to be done with work. I still live with Viki and Liana, but I see them less and less now that they both have boyfriends.

I miss Gianna, my twin soul, but I don't give up on our friendship. It takes her some time to warm up to me again but she finally does. We enroll in a film class at SVA and meet up once a week. It's a far cry from what our friendship used to look like, but I'm just happy that we are healing. It feels as though we were in a relationship and are finally getting over the trauma of the breakup. Even with the boundaries set between us, we always maintain our crazy telepathic connection. I know what she's thinking and feeling at any given moment and it drives me kind of crazy. Even though we don't speak on the phone every day, we still text daily and she sends me memes and funny videos.

"Everyone is obsessed with you," she tells me like the proud mom I never had.

When the press tour for *Uncut Gems* kicks off that summer, Gianna is no longer my plus-one. In her place come my manager, my publicist, and my now-husband. I know this bothers her, as she was with me the entire time while filming, but she doesn't mention it. She's in acceptance. She's resilient. She keeps up with my hashtag on Twitter and sends me updates of people saying my performance is Oscar-worthy. On the night of the New York premiere, she sits alone in the general audience section cheering and clapping with her phone glued to her hand, filming every scene I'm in. Over time she even miraculously warms up to Andrew. Except when she tells him that he's the K-Fed to my Britney. Which I secretly think is hilarious even though Andrew does not at all.

I'm in L.A. staying with my friend Cole and her husband, Chris. I'm about to leave their house and head to a photo shoot for *Wonderland* magazine when I get the call from a friend Gianna and I had made on the *Uncut Gems* set. When I see her name flash on my phone, I immediately know something is up. I ignore the sinking feeling and hesitantly answer the phone.

"Gianna overdosed," she tells me. "She didn't make it."

I feel the air get sucked out from the atmosphere and the walls begin rapidly closing in around me. My knees give out and I collapse to the floor. This must be a mistake. Is this a joke? Is this a dream? Am I asleep? Can I rewind and delete this event from my inventory? This can't be happening. How could this be happening? I just fucking FaceTimed with her last night. I keep replaying our last conversation over and over. She was fine! She was happy! She said we were going to go to this Dior event at the Guggenheim together and it was going to be so much fun. We had plans!

When she called, I was in the car with someone and didn't want to be rude, so I told her I would call her back as soon as I got home. She had a splotchy black face mask all over her face and I thought she looked ridiculous, so I took some sneaky screenshots of her. I had no idea at the time that those would be the last photos I would ever have of her. Why didn't I call her back as soon as I got home? Instead, when I got home, I plugged my phone into the charger and went to the backyard to smoke a cigarette.

When I went inside to call her back, I had a slew of texts from her. They read:

> i wanna say i am so proud of u all the time every day and watching all of this happen for u makes me so happy blah blah blah

> but i also know how hard ur working and its really motivating me!!

> seeing your light shine so bright after all these years of crazy ass work u put in makes me want to work hard for my dreams too, and i re-read this beautiful letter you wrote me a couple years ago and it like reinvigorated my soul

> you are so special and you help me so much all the time i just wanted u to know ♥

I immediately tried calling her back to no answer. And then a weird thought crept in my head: What if she's dead? I quickly told myself, There's no way. I just talked to her and she was fine. But still. She always answers the phone. Always. So I texted her back telling her how much I love her and thanked her for always sticking by my side, and then I went to sleep.

That night I had the worst nightmare of my life. I dreamed of a scary drug-dealing stalker who was coming after me. When I woke up in the morning, I felt so unsettled. I texted Gianna about my dream, again receiving no answer.

Little did I know that at that exact moment, her lifeless body was lying on the cold tile floor, alone and undiscovered. I still can't bear to picture it. Her small and delicate frame, her silky auburn hair that shined a deep red in the sun, her smooth tan skin, her elegant fingers, her perfect little feet, her face. Her beautiful fucking face. I can't get the image out of my head.

By the time I hang up the phone, my Uber has arrived. I don't want to go, but I know if I stay here I'll lose my mind. I climb into the car and call Liana, sobbing. The ride is long and miserable. I feel like I'm going to throw up. I lie down on the seat and shut my eyes to stop the world around me from spinning. When I arrive at the shoot, I feel like a zombie on autopilot floating around the set. The stylists point to the racks of clothes and I feel nothing. I excuse myself and cry on the toilet for a moment before I take a deep breath and put the mask back on. My friends come to the set and stay with me the entire time, but the mood is somber. I try my best to be sexy, even with my puffy eyes and swollen face. I'm relieved once it's over.

I call an old client from the dungeon who's a respected detective at the NYPD and ask him to pull up Gianna's file and tell me everything. He calls me back and says, "It's not good, J." He saw the pictures of the scene. He says he would send them to me but advised me that if I saw them then that's how I would remember her for the rest of my life and that I should remember how she was when she was alive. I know he's right, so I force him to describe them to me in great detail. I just want to be there. I so badly want to put myself at the scene so she wouldn't have had to be so alone. She hated being alone more than anyone I know.

I obsessively wonder if she saw my texts before she passed. I pray that she did and that she knew how much I loved her. If only I had just called her back sooner, maybe she would still be here with me. I wish I could go back in time but I can't, and now I have to live the rest of my life wondering.

After Gianna's death, I retreat. I shut down. I stop answering the phone, even for Liana and Viki and Harmony. The only person I talk to is Chris, Cole's husband. He's older than us and knows what I'm going through. I talk to him as if he has all the answers. "Please please tell me I'm gonna be okay," I plead with him through hiccups, gasps, and snot-nosed sobs.

I sit in the darkness of Andrew's small studio apartment, rereading my text conversations with Gianna, scrolling through old photos, watching the videos on my phone of us play-fighting. In one clip I chased her down my hallway and blocked the doorway so she wouldn't go home. I wish I could teleport back to that moment and live there for the rest of my life.

All the special moments we spent together replay on a loop in my mind, like the year we spent Christmas together, just her and me, when Viki and Liana were in Berlin. It was the best Christmas I'd ever had, just the two of us in her cozy bed, buried under her big comforter, surrounded by her stuffed animals as the winter snow piled up outside.

Or the moment we met at that A.A. meeting. I was in one of my moods that day, and at the end of the meeting, we all had to hold hands in a circle and chant the Serenity Prayer. I usually hate that part because of my hyperhidrosis and how clammy my hands get, but Gianna's hands were clammy too. I apologized for it and she squeezed my hand tighter and laughed it off. She told me not to worry, she had the same condition. I had never met anyone else with it before and it felt like I finally found someone who understood me on a visceral level that most simply cannot.

I irrationally start thinking that maybe I should go back to A.A. and try to find another Gianna. But reality quickly dawns on me: There will never be another Gianna. She's a once-in-a-lifetime kind of person. There has never been anybody like her and there never will be anybody like her and that's a fact I need to accept.

So instead I set out in search of psychics and mediums to help me communicate with her. I just need closure. I just need to hang out with her again. Some of these people are total scammers. Then I find a medium out on Long Island. I book my appointment under a fake name and phone number, to ensure he won't be able to know any of my information. When I walk into the room, before I can say anything at all, he closes his eyes and says, "She was in so much pain. I'm surprised she even made it this far." The words hit me like a punch in the gut. He tells me she had been badly abused by her biological family, she wasn't going to make it in this world, and there was nothing I could have done to stop this from happening. And then he tells me, "She loved you the most. She might have even been in love with you." I know this is true, and my face is wet with a steady stream of silent tears.

As I'm getting ready to leave, he stops me. "Before I forget, she said she wants you to get a tattoo of her name on your ass." *Uncut Gems* won't be in theaters for another month. There's no way this man could know about the scene in the movie where I get Howard's name tattooed on my butt cheek. But Gianna knew! I start jumping up and down like a lunatic, screaming, "She's here! She's really fucking here! She's in the room!"

I tell him to tell her how much I love her and how devastated I am. I tell him about the text messages and my regret for not calling her back sooner. He reassures me that she knows how much I love her and encourages me to live my life and not be boring, because she will be living through me. I crack a smile. That sounds like her, and that's all I need to hear. As long as she'll still be with me, I'll be okay. But I'll certainly never be the same.

At her funeral, I throw myself onto her casket, desperately grasping for any remaining connection to her. I hold her lifeless hand in mine, running my fingers through her once vibrant hair. I lean over and whisper "I love you" in her ear and plant a kiss on her cold gray lips. At that moment, I feel like I would do anything to be with her, even if it means crawling into the casket with her.

As a way to keep her close, I request to bury her in my diamond cross necklace, the same one I wore in *Uncut Gems*. When I find out she will be cremated, I insist on keeping the ashes. I know Gianna would want to be with me, and her family graciously agrees.

The pain of her death takes a huge toll on my marriage. I push Andrew away completely, lashing out at him and blaming him for her death. I can't shake the feeling that if I hadn't fallen in love with him, I probably would have been with her that night and maybe even been able to save her. But Andrew reminds me that if I hadn't fallen in love with him, I might not be here either. He's not wrong. Despite the hurt and confusion I feel, I know that I can't let her death be in vain. I decide that I will never touch an opiate again for as long as I live. I've broken this promise many times before, but this time it feels different. I'm not fucking around anymore.

I catch a little glimmer of hope when I land a holiday campaign for Bloomingdale's. But the morning I arrive at the department store, a sinking feeling sets in when they ask me for ID. I worry they'll see that I'm permanently banned from the store. I'm relieved when they let me in without issue. As I stand in the bustling department store, waiting to get all dolled up, I take a moment to reflect on how far I've come. From being a dirty teenager stealing to get by, to running through this very store to avoid a creepy private investigator, to landing this campaign. This is a cosmic gift and it feels as if the universe is finally balancing the scales.

After the theatrical release of the movie, I start spending more time in L.A. and eventually get my own little apartment. Harmony graciously helps me move in, carrying the big boxes up the stairs for me. Unpacking everything reminds me how we went through all of her mom's stuff after she died and how the two of us have always been there for each other in our darkest times.

We have sleepovers where we spend hours going through my DMs on Instagram. She gasps at the A-list comedians, ballplayers, and rappers all lining up to take me out. I shrug and laugh. I don't care. I'd rather be with her watching *Gypsy Sisters* on TLC. Plus, I'm still heartbroken over the demise of my marriage. I feel like a failure. Like it's all my fault that Andrew filed for divorce.

When the pandemic strikes and everything shuts down, I realize pretty quickly that I'm going to have to put my acting pursuits on pause for the foreseeable future. The gaping hole in my soul where Gianna used to be and my grief over the apparent end of my marriage is only exacerbated by this professional hiatus, and I start feeling lonely during the long, never-ending days in lockdown. I know this isn't what Gianna would have wanted for me. She would have wanted me to be happy.

I decide to give Andrew a call and see how he's doing. By the end of the phone call, I have a one-way ticket back to New York. He picks me up at the airport with flowers and all my favorite candies. It's been a few months since we last saw each other but it's as if no time has passed at all. We slide right back into our pattern of immense love and extreme rage paired with crushing silence and the lingering pain of his absence.

As the weeks go by, holed up in his moldy little studio in Alphabet City, things start to fizzle again. It becomes clear that we really don't like each other as much as we thought we did. The love that we once shared seems to have dissipated and all that is left is a sense of resentment and frustration.

A PARTING GIFT

My hands tremble as I grip the pregnancy test, my whole future etched in the two menacing red lines glaring up at me. I call Andrew into the bathroom, expecting him to be excited. The look on his face is anything but. I feel the sting of silent rage burning inside me. He did this to me! This is all his fault! Without giving it much more thought, he leaves for work and I remain on the toilet seat, alone again in the claustrophobic bathroom in his studio apartment.

Why isn't he happy? He's been telling me since we first met that he wanted to have a baby with me. I can't make sense of it. I feel so betrayed, but mostly I am scared. I am an actress at the beginning of my career and it is no secret how pregnant women in Hollywood are treated. I have even heard pregnancy being referred to as a "career killer." But times are changing, right? Who really knows, and who am I to bet on that? I am just the new girl, after all, lucky to even be in the conversation.

Andrew and I get into these terrible explosive fights on a weekly basis where he disappears and leaves me alone for a few days. It is agonizing not to know where he is. This is not the kind of home I want to raise a child in. I know I'm destined to be a single mother if I go on with him, but I have to make a choice: to stay in this damaged toxic relationship or have an abortion and leave. I have had abortions in the past and have always been able to rationalize them in a way that I am never left traumatized. I'll be able to survive this.

Out of curiosity, I use an app on my phone to calculate the baby's due date based on my last period. What happens next changes everything for me. The due date is February 6: Gianna's birthday. It's like a lightning bolt strikes through the screen. It's like what Mistress Sadée used to say about being zapped by cell phones. I didn't believe her then but I believe her now. I remain frozen, eyes glued to the screen. I can't fucking believe it. Of all the days in the year! What are the chances?! I know this is more than a coincidence. It's as if Gianna has come down from the heavens and put this baby inside me herself. I realize this isn't a burden, this is her last gift to me. Because if there is something only Gianna and I could know, it's that it would take a whole baby to begin to fill the prolific void she left inside me. A baby would be the only way I could ever begin to feel better.

I instantly feel a deep sense of security that I'll be able to do this with or without Andrew. I will always have Gianna with me, even if only in memory and spirit. But that is enough for me to make the decision to proceed with this pregnancy.

Andrew is passive-aggressive and I can tell he isn't thrilled with me, but strangely, it doesn't affect me at all. I feel as though this baby and I are wrapped in a cast-iron shield. I tap in to an inner calmness I didn't know was there. As the strength surges through my body, I feel invincible.

I remember a conversation Gianna and I had on her big California king-size bed at the Carlyle.

"If I ever have a daughter, I want to name her Seven," I said.

"Oooh, I love that," she replied.

It's decided. I will have a daughter and her name will be Seven!

A few weeks later, I get a visit from Gianna in a dream. This one is different from the usual recurring dream I have of her, in which I am frantically trying to go back in time and warn her of her death so she can stop it from happening. In this dream, I plead with her, "Please be reborn as my baby!" But she just laughs and says, "Ugh, I don't want to come back as a boy!"

When I wake up, I have a sinking feeling. There will be no "Seven." I am having a boy.

At my twelve-week routine checkup, I'm sure I see a hint of male anatomy on the ultrasound. The doctor assures me it's much too early to make a determination. Still, I can't shake the feeling that my child will be a boy. And in the end, I'm proved right.

Even from beyond the veil, Gianna is with me, guiding me through this mess.

I'm faced with a series of challenges during my first trimester. Aside from being in a global pandemic with no end in sight and the physical and hormonal changes in my body, I also have to stop taking my mood stabilizers, a medication I have relied on for years. I give up my habit of chain-smoking Newports and, even more difficult, I let go of the Suboxone. Because everyone is in lockdown, I don't have the presence of my friends to help me through. I don't tell anyone about my pregnancy until I am well into my second trimester. It feels too delicate to share with the world yet, and I know how my friends feel about Andrew. I decide to keep it a secret.

The previous times I'd been pregnant, I would immediately summon all my friends into the bathroom and it would turn into this big convoluted ordeal regarding what I was going to do, knowing all along, deep down, that I would terminate. But this time it's different. I have Gianna's blessing. And now I have Molly too, the dog I fostered to alleviate the pain of isolation. Molly forces me out of the house and to the dog park, where I can connect with friends from the neighborhood. My sweet Molly, who brings me out of my shell and saves my life, we make the decision to adopt her.

• • •

It's been a while since I last spoke to Liana, and it feels strange not to be able to share the news with her. We've shared everything since we were kids, but now I'm on my own. She was starting to change and it terrified me. Once exuding unshakable confidence, she began constantly complaining about her appearance and shied away from the revealing garments she once loved. I suspected this was due to her boyfriend's influence, and it set something off in me. Seeing myself reflected in her doubt triggered me, and as she slipped away from me, I decided to cut the cord myself.

After Gianna passed away, I took my anger out on everyone, including Liana. I projected the issues and pain in my relationship onto hers. I worried that her boyfriend was judgmental and controlling without taking into account that Andrew was the jealous and controlling one. It's almost as if her relationship were a mirror for mine and I didn't like what I saw.

One day, I ask to come over to her place and she says no, citing the pandemic and her boyfriend's germophobia. I want to understand where she's coming from, but I housed her for a decade and made sure she had a roof over her head and a job to go to, and she won't let me come over because he said no? The Liana I knew would never let anyone tell her no. But more importantly, the Liana I knew would never let a man come in between her friendships.

Instead of arguing these points, I just stop talking to her. At first I think it will be for just a few days. But soon the days turn to weeks and the weeks turn to months. It makes me sad, but I just don't have it in me to reach out. She broke my trust, and I'd rather push her away and protect myself than potentially get hurt again. I can't handle much more after losing Gianna.

I go to all the doctors' appointments alone. After a few visits, the nurses politely ask me where my husband is. I shrug and tell them, "He couldn't find parking." The truth is, he doesn't ask to come, and I don't invite him. He stresses me out and makes everything about himself. The less we hang out, the better the chances are of us not fighting. Luckily, he works every day and comes home late at night, so I don't have to spend too much time with him.

Aside from the doctors and nurses and Andrew, the only other people I see during these months are when I join the protests after the murder of George Floyd. As a white woman, I feel a sense of duty to join the fight and stand in solidarity with the protesters. I ride my bike up and down the city, warning the front lines of approaching police and hoping my unborn son in my belly can hear our chants against injustice.

During my second trimester, Andrew receives a letter in the mail confirming the dissolution of our marriage. He hands it to me, and I can't help but giggle at our predicament.

"I wanna remarry you," he tells me.

I shoot him a concerned look. "We'll see."

Sometimes he's perfect. He randomly brings me big, beautiful bouquets of flowers. He gives me designer bags and jewelry. He brings home my favorite sweets. And sometimes he's the complete opposite. He hurls insults at me casually if he's upset. He'll disappear and lie to me. I beg him to understand the impact of his words and actions on both me and our unborn child, but he doesn't care. Despite my hope that our relationship would improve, I'm disappointed to find that this is not the case. His lack of consideration for my feelings and the future of our family terrifies me, and I find myself longing to escape from the tumultuous dynamic. I can't afford to move right now, so all I can do is pray that by some miracle I'll secure a role in a movie that will allow me to distance myself from this toxic situation. I get on my hands and knees in the tiny bathroom and beg God for a job far away from him.

And to my complete amazement, a role comes.

· · ·

I'm offered a role in a film by Steven Soderbergh alongside a dream cast with generous pay. The role does not call for a pregnant woman, but I simply can't turn down this opportunity. The twenty thousand dollars in my savings account is not going to be enough to raise a child. At six months pregnant, I make the decision to keep my condition a secret and accept the offer.

Filming *No Sudden Move* in Detroit for a month is a vastly different experience from my time on *Uncut Gems*. It's not nearly as fun without Gianna around the set. I don't have her to help me learn my lines and calm my anxieties. Forbidden from having visitors due to COVID restrictions, I feel isolated. The presence of my unborn child growing in my belly brings me some comfort. As I feel him kick within me, I'm reminded I'm not entirely alone. I work hard to clear a visit from Andrew with the production's insurance company, but his irresponsible behavior results in its cancellation. His lack of consideration for my health and that of our baby only adds to my frustration. How could he ruin the only opportunity for us to see each other? All because he wanted to go get drunk at a party. How could he be so careless? I start to worry about what he's going to be like once the baby comes. I can't shake the feeling of impending doom.

I make every effort to maintain a composed and cheerful demeanor in public. I suck in my belly and wear two pairs of Spanx under the costumes, which luckily fit me without needing any alterations. I am overjoyed to be working again and doing what I love and getting the opportunity to be part of a film of this caliber. The thought of my son one day watching the movie and seeing me share a romantic moment with Benicio Del Toro, all while he was growing within me, fills me with pride. However, the more successful I become, the more Andrew pushes me away. His ego just can't handle it, no matter how many times I've proved my loyalty to him.

As I enter my third trimester of pregnancy, we make the transition to a new apartment with high ceilings and an extra room for our son, Valentino. While Andrew is frequently absent, I take on the majority of the physical labor, moving furniture and assembling pieces for the baby's room. Despite my love for Andrew, his tendency to rely on me for tasks he is unwilling to do and his general incompetence can be stressful and overwhelming. I have my doubts about our relationship but I don't focus on them, as I want to keep my cortisol levels as low as possible.

During a routine checkup on January 16, three weeks before the due date, my doctor delivers the news no mother wants to hear: My blood pressure is approaching the danger zone and they want to induce labor today. I begin to panic. I don't have diapers or a crib. I don't even have a car seat or a stroller! I tell the doctor I feel fine and beg for a few hours to gather my things—and, more importantly, to have my maternity photos taken.

Once I get home, my best friends rush over with makeup and clothes, and within an hour I have my maternity photos and am on my way to the hospital to give birth. Due to COVID restrictions, only Andrew is allowed to visit me, but I keep Gianna's ashes in the floral pink urn by my bedside for the duration of my delivery. As I endure the intense pain, I grip her urn tightly and feel her presence with me, and I know that she is so proud of me.

Valentino has come a few weeks early, but he's absolutely perfect. He is the most beautiful little boy I have ever laid my eyes on. When I see him using every bit of strength to inch his body close to mine, I am filled with a love so visceral, it could shatter the earth. I am his. And he is mine. It's the kind of love that claws its way out of your gut, rips you apart, and puts you back together again. He is worth all the blood and pain, all the tears, and all the sleepless nights.

I wonder sometimes, if Gianna hadn't died, if he would be here. I think he would be, and so would she. I can picture her sassing me and bossing me around, reprimanding me when I'm being lazy, and telling me what to do because she *always* knew best. I can hear her voice so clearly yelling, "He's my son too, ya know?!" I just know she would have moved in with me and never left my side. I can't help but feel like I was so close to achieving my ultimate dream scenario. It feels like I played the lottery and got every number right except the very last one, instantly crushing any faith I had in life.

At night, I whisper in Valentino's ear and tell him all about his guardian angel, his aunt Gianna, and how much he would have loved her. Then I remind us that she's still here, inside both of us. She never left.

I feel closer to Gianna in her death than I do with Andrew in our home. There's no intimacy between us anymore. We don't talk unless it's about the baby and we haven't had sex since way before the birth. He leaves in the morning and comes home at night, after Valentino has already gone to sleep. He doesn't help me with feedings or diaper changes or cleaning or anything around the house. In fact, he somehow creates more work for me. His voice starts to irk me when he comes home and excitedly tells me he's taking up skateboarding and made a new best friend. I start to resent him. How could he have time to do all these things? Why does he get to go on with his life unbothered while mine has been flipped upside down? I'm starting to see how unfair this dynamic is.

One day, he comes home in the middle of the day as I'm lying in bed with our son, and I pick up a faint buzzing sound coming from the bathroom. I slip out of bed so as not to wake Valentino and tiptoe toward the bathroom, where I peek inside and find Andrew shaving his pubic hair. I feel a bolt of rage shoot through me then immediately diffuse itself. I'm too tired. I don't want to argue and I don't want to know. I run back into the bedroom and pretend to be asleep.

I get a text from Liana congratulating me on the birth. Even though I'm still mad at her, I invite her over to meet him. I may have my resentments but I wouldn't want Valentino to not get to know his auntie over a stupid grudge.

Her hands tremble as I place him in her arms. I see her eyes filling up with tears through her thick lenses.

"I can't believe you made this baby," she says in disbelief.

"I know, like, how am I somebody's mother right now?!"

We both start laughing and I feel my anger dissipate. I find it hard to believe that I didn't share my pregnancy journey with her, but I know it's for the best. We spent so many years glued to each other for fear of being on our own, and maybe we needed that distance to establish our own identities, separate from each other. We've come so far from the raggedy greased-up teenagers we used to be, from that first time I saw her on the 8th Street stoop in those pink patent-leather platform boots. It's truly a miracle that we are even still alive.

I'm having trouble lactating. I'll pump for hours for just a few droplets of milk. I make appointments with lactation specialists but nothing works. I feel like a defective cow. I wonder what's wrong with my body that it can't do what nature intended it to do. I can sense Valentino's frustration as he sucks away on my breast through the night, crying from hunger. I feel bad for him and I wish I could give him the milk he deserves. I have to resort to feeding him formula that gives him gas pains, causing him to stay awake crying after every feeding. The interruptions in my sleep pattern cause me to develop chronic sleep paralysis. It feels like I'm stuck in the confines of my own head, paralyzed and terrified, thrashing around to wake myself out of this hell.

My body is still recovering from his birth. During the delivery, I tore the skin between my vagina and my butthole in half and the stitches got infected. The antibiotics they prescribed to fight the infection caused me to get a temporary yet horrifying case of rheumatoid arthritis. All my joints are inflamed. I can barely bend my knees or my fingers, and I have to console a crying baby with a smile on my face every thirty minutes by myself. I frequently fall asleep sitting up, sometimes falling off the bed and hitting my head on the wall. Andrew sees this and does little to help.

"Hire someone!" he says.

I shake my head. "I don't have the energy to look for someone, and he needs to be raised by *both* his parents!"

As we emerge from the pandemic, so does Andrew's drinking, which luckily had been dormant due to all the bars being closed for so long. But now that things are starting to open up again, his old habits have resurfaced.

One night, he comes home wasted with his face swollen and clothes soaked in blood after getting jumped in front of Gold Bar. I rush to his aid and notice a gash on his head an inch wide. I plead with him to go to the emergency room. His speech is slurred as he pushes me aside and shouts at me to "shut the fuck up." I remain calm and talk to him like a zookeeper taming a wild hyena, but he continues to call me derogatory slurs. He starts knocking shit over and all I can think is: Thank God Valentino is at my dad's house for the night because he certainly would have woken up by now.

"You have to leave, Andrew," I tell him, this time with my camera phone aimed at him, carefully recording him for my own safety.

He storms out and I start packing up all his things into black garbage bags.

All the while I feel nothing. I'm on autopilot. I'm a mother protecting her nest, and this is the culmination of many other events that have led me to believe that he is not the man for me. I remember the time he called me "a fucking cunt" while holding Valentino in his arms or the time he called me "a fucking idiot" with Valentino when I opened his car door and lightly tapped the metal pole on the sidewalk. He is never going to stop being abusive, and the worst part is he doesn't even recognize his actions as abuse.

I remain stoic as I toss the last of his shit in the garbage bags, but inside I'm afraid. I hope this event sparks him to change, because I don't want to be a single mom. But then it dawns on me that I've been single in this relationship for years. I already am a single mom. He does nothing for us. I've always been on his team but he's never been on mine, and I can't keep wasting my time begging him to be someone he's not. He's shown me who he is and this is the time to do something about it.

The next day, we speak on the phone and I calmly tell him, "You need to take some time away from us and work on yourself. You have to get sober and be a real dad for Valentino." He doesn't seem apologetic and barely agrees to my terms. Later that night, I'm heartbroken when I discover he's been out all night again. He doesn't respect us, he is never going to change, and I have to get on with my life.

Now I'm alone with a dog and a baby, and the few chores he took care of, like walking the dog at night or taking out the trash, are delegated to me along with everything else. It's too much for me and I feel myself deteriorating. After a few weeks, I call Andrew and beg him to come back. I plead with him to go to therapy and work on his anger. I implore him to get his shit together. But he doesn't budge. He just keeps repeating, "No, you kicked me out!"

"I didn't have a choice!" He doesn't listen. "Okay, well, if you're not going to help me, then I'll just have to find a new dad for Valentino."

"Good luck. Who would want to date a single mom with a baby?"

I hang up on him before I say something I'll regret later.

I feel pathetic having begged him. I stop reaching out to him entirely. My silence triggers him and he calls me at all hours asking to see Valentino. He shows up hours late smelling of cigarettes with stale vodka on his breath and stays for less than an hour. I hate having him in the apartment.

"You can't only see Valentino here!" I desperately plead with him. "You need to get your own place! This isn't working for me!"

For the next few months, I do my best to keep a smile on my face for my son. My dad steps in to pick up Andrew's shifts, taking Valentino on the weekends so I can get some work done. Surprisingly, since becoming a mom, I have a lot more sympathy for my dad. I give him the grace to allow him to show up, and he's obsessed with being a grandpa. "This is the best thing to happen to me in the past twenty years," my dad says, beaming.

As much as I appreciate the help, I hate that I'm turning into my mom, a single parent being helped by her father. I remind myself that I'm different. My mom stayed in her miserable marriage. I did not. I had the will to change. I won't pass down the generational trauma to my kid.

I tell myself that this is temporary and I'm going to dig myself out of this mess.

One night, Andrew calls me asking for his passport. Apparently it was left behind in a drawer when I hastily packed up his things.

"No," I tell him. "I'm not giving it to you. You just went on vacation for ten days! You are not going again! You are taking care of your son!"

Later that same night, I'm eating at a restaurant, seated at a table outside with my friends for the first time in months, when he pulls up in his car and starts honking his horn and screaming, "She stole my fucking passport!"

The blood rushes to my face with the hot sting of embarrassment. I try pleading with him, begging him to not go, but he won't hear it. He doesn't see how him living his life as if he has no child is damaging to Valentino. It's obvious my son's emotional well-being is in jeopardy.

"Okay, I'll give you your passport!"

He follows me to my apartment and I make him wait outside. I run upstairs and rummage around until I find it, then I very carefully rip out the front page and stuff it in my pocket. I open the window and chuck the little booklet at him.

"Good luck getting a new one," I say with a devious grin before slamming the window shut. If I can't go on vacation, neither can he.

I start to hear whispers about Andrew's many girlfriends and convince myself to open my heart again. Since I never go out, meeting someone organically is out of the question, so I join a few dating apps. I quickly meet a man who checks all the boxes: smart, tall, handsome, rich, and successful. One night, after a movie date, he decides to walk me home. We're down the block from my apartment when I spot Andrew pacing outside on his phone. I quickly grab my date by the arm and spin him around, but it's too late, Andrew already spotted us.

He charges toward us with clenched fists like a raging bull. I step in front of my date, scared he might get punched in the face, and plead with Andrew to go away. "We're not together anymore! You're acting like a lunatic!" He ignores me and begins yelling at my date: "You know she's a drug addict!" My date remains calm, not giving him the reaction he's looking for. "She's mentally ill!" he continues.

I can't help but find his pathetic attempt at belittling me hilarious. It takes everything in me to not start laughing at him.

"We aren't together anymore!" I yell at him. "Get over it and fuck off!"

Surprisingly, my date still wants to see me after this, but for some reason I don't want to. It's ruined. He saw my life for all its horror, and even though he accepted it, I no longer feel sexy. I wanted to put Andrew behind me and build a new future, but the past seeped through to my present like mold and tainted everything.

For a few months after Andrew moves out, we engage in a dizzying dance of push and pull. Sometimes when he visits we end up having sex, which I always immediately regret. As soon as it is over, I insist that he leave and I scrub myself clean in the shower, desperate to rid myself of his scent. I change the sheets, trying to erase any trace of him and our encounter.

On one of his visits, a diamond-studded watch he gave me as "insurance" for Valentino goes missing. "I was going to sell the watch and put the money toward Valentino's future!" I yell into the phone. He denies stealing it and I threaten to file a police report. I change the locks, and in turn, he blocks my number for months.

12

SUDDEN STARFALL

t all starts when a friend tells me she saw Andrew at a restaurant in the East Village on a cold December night. She says he was wasted and when she asked about Valentino, he picked a fight with her. "That bitch won't let me see my son" are the exact words she quotes him saying. This sets off an earthquake in the depths of my core. How can he say I'm keeping him from Valentino when he's the one who's blocked my number for months? I have no way of contacting him and he doesn't check in either. Instead, he goes out drinking every night to strip clubs and dive bars and sweaty parties full of kids.

I make up my mind that I'm going to avenge myself. I've protected his discretions against me because I was humiliated by how he treated me. But now it feels like I have nothing left to lose. He's embarrassed me and Valentino enough for a lifetime. Revenge becomes my driving force. Exposing him for who he really is is all I can think of.

In a blind rage, I pull out my phone and open the Instagram app. I type a call to action: "Have you seen this deadbeat dad?" with a photo of Andrew wearing a shirt that so fittingly says "I'll trade this baby for a beer." I chuckle under my breath as I type out all my grievances. After debating with myself briefly, I decide to press send, opening the floodgates for my five hundred thousand followers on Instagram.

A part of me hopes that Andrew will see it and finally call me to see Valentino, but he doesn't. So I leave the post up for a full twenty-four hours. And when people start reaching out to me, divulging even more information about him, I come for him. I come for his mom, who I begged for help, which she ignored. I come for their family friend who hid a four-year-long affair with him behind the family's back. I don't hold back, and it feels so fucking good. Until Page Six writes about it and—just as with my decision to publish my first art book and preempt the malicious exposure of my past—the story spirals into something bigger than I intended it to.

"I need a miracle," I tell Viki around Christmas. "I'm not doing well." A few days later, I get a text from an old friend asking if he can pass my number along to a famous artist who's been asking about me. I don't think much of it at first. I've hooked up with celebrities before and I already know they're only after one thing. I'm so exhausted looking after Valentino by myself, I don't have the energy to embark on a new adventure. The days of spontaneously jumping in the car with Harmony and road-tripping to unknown destinations feel far behind me. And I'm still heartbroken over Andrew. But then I think back to the medium in Long Island who told me Gianna would be living through me. "She says she doesn't want you to sit around and be boring," he had said in her exact tone. Gianna was such a huge fan of this artist. She quoted him often and even ran up on him at a party to get a photo with him once. She would want me to do this. I give my friend permission to pass my number along and shift my attention back to trying to clean up the mess I've made of my life.

I discover that Andrew was paying my rent all along, unbeknownst to me, and although it doesn't excuse his absence, it does make me feel as though he didn't entirely abandon us. I start feeling really guilty for losing control and bashing him for the whole world to see and laugh at us. I can't help feeling like I'm going to be facing some karmic retribution for my impulsive, reckless actions.

I issue a public apology, acknowledging our relationship struggles in the hope that people will move on and just forget. However, I can't seem to. My mind keeps thinking about Andrew and the harm I caused him. I push the pesky thoughts aside and tell myself he deserved it after everything he put me through.

A text from the artist arrives shortly after, followed by dozens of phone calls. We talk for hours. Well, he talks for hours and I mostly listen, occasionally chiming in. When he does listen to me, he loves my ideas and thinks I'm really smart. Coming from him, this feels like a huge compliment. I'm giddy during this time. It's like he breathed a new life into me.

He invites me to Miami for New Year's, which I politely decline. I tell him I already have plans with my family. I can tell he doesn't like this answer. He insists I come. I tell him I'll only come if the people I had plans with can come as well. He agrees and charters a jet for my friends and me to fly to Miami the very next day. I leave Valentino at my dad's house, thinking I'll just be gone for the night.

We land at ten o'clock at night and rush to the hotel, weaving through New Year's traffic, worried about having enough time to change and make it to the club before midnight. Once we check in to the room, we all erupt into complete mayhem. My friends pop a bottle of champagne as I dig through the bags of designer clothes the artist had sent to the room. I frantically try on the different outfits, which I notice are all just different versions of the same thing. I finally land on a black bodysuit, accentuating my curves, and black leather boots. I do my makeup as fast as I can and yell at everyone to, "Hurry the fuck up!"

We scurry down South Beach to the venue, past the long line of people, and march straight up to the bouncer.

"Hi, we're on the list," I tell him as he eyes us up and down.

He shakes his head dismissively. "We're at capacity,"

I call the artist and don't get an answer. I look around at the tan, blond girls with Brazilian butt lifts getting let in before us and I start to argue with the bouncer, waving my phone in his face with texts from the artist to prove it.

"It's 11:58! I'm gonna miss my New Year's kiss 'cause of you!"

Eventually, the artist sends someone out to get us, but it's too late. It's 12:03.

Once inside, I head straight to the bar for a much-needed drink. I have to quiet the voices in my head saying: "What if he doesn't like me when he meets me in person?" I take a deep breath and down my drink, my nerves on edge as I make my way through the throngs of people on the dance floor. My eyes search the crowd, seeking out the artist amid the groupies.

Suddenly, I spot him leaning against the railing of the mezzanine, his gaze fixed on me. Our eyes lock and a jolt of electricity runs through me. The crowd parts before me, clearing the path straight to him. I make my way up the stairs, my heart pounding with anticipation as I approach him. My moment is abruptly stunted by another argumentative bouncer who must have missed the memo. I point to the artist as he makes his way toward us. The bouncer opens the red velvet rope and begins to apologize to me.

Without saying a word, the artist extends his hand and pulls me close. Our bodies press against each other as we move to the beat of the music. I can feel the heat emanating from him. He holds me tight, his hands scanning the folds of my body. My lips pressed gently to his neck, I know that this is the beginning of something truly special.

After our passionate introduction, I take a seat next to him. The music is too loud to have a decent conversation but we try anyway, yelling over the music and into each other's ears. I feel the stares of curiosity from the girls next to us as they side-eye me up and down.

After a few minutes, he motions for me to get up and follow him. He leads me through the crowd of screaming fans and iPhone flashes toward the back of the club. He opens a little door and we emerge from the chaos to a quiet little parking lot. It's empty except for a few guys who are starstruck once they realize who I'm with. The artist starts peeing on the wall and I quickly jump in front of him. "You better not take any pictures!" I yell at the boys, who already have their phones in their hands.

Once he zips his pants back up, he puts his arms around me and pulls me in close, kissing me passionately. He doesn't care about the boys in the parking lot or the fact that at any moment someone could take a picture of us.

"You make me feel like my high school girlfriend," he says, with little explanation.

Later in the night, I round up my friends and follow the artist to a party at a famous rapper's house on Star Island. In all our years of coming to Miami, we'd heard about the Gatsby-like parties he throws. So even though we are trying to play it cool and contain our excitement, we are actually freaking out.

I ride in the car with the artist and a few of his friends as my friends follow in the car behind. Once we arrive at the mansion, I see my friends getting stopped by security. I'm trying to get their attention from the backseat when the artist's friend says with a chuckle, "Can we just leave them?" I shoot him the death stare. The artist notices my frustration and gets the attention of a security guard and tells him to get them in. I hop out of the car and run to my friends, who don't seem all too happy. "We've been treated like shit at every corner," they say but laugh it off.

As we enter the mansion, the music is thumping. The artist gets swarmed by some people who look like old friends. When he's done greeting them, he turns to me and whispers, "I have no idea who any of those people are." We follow the artist and his entourage straight to the bar. As we laugh and dance, I can feel the looks from curious party-goers. I ignore it and let loose, twerking and doing splits for my friends, who cheer me on. Suddenly, I feel a tap on my shoulder. His annoying friend from the car pulls me aside and whispers in my ear, "You're doing entirely way too much. You need to chill out."

His words echo in my mind, and I can feel my confidence slipping away. I try to shake off the feelings of insecurity and embarrassment, but they stick to me like darts. Why do I care what this parasitic loser thinks? Why do I let his words affect me?

As I look at all the other girls, I realize I'm not like them. They're beautiful, but they willingly fade into the background, waiting for their come-up. They're party decorations, ornaments to be admired. I'm not like that anymore. I already had my come-up, and I'm not going back to being objectified and used as fuel for the egos of insecure men.

I scan the sea of neon party dresses and BBLs, looking for the artist, but he's nowhere to be found. My phone is dead, so I grab my friends and they gladly follow me out of the party. When I get back to the hotel, I can't help but feel like I fucked up. I overreacted. I'm too dramatic. I text the artist and thank him for an amazing night and pass out.

The next morning, I wake up thinking I'll be going home but instead I find dozens of missed calls and texts from the artist. I call him back and he picks up on the first ring. "Come to my room," he says.

This time, I don't spiral about what I'm going to wear. I throw on a pair of sweatpants and sneakers and go down to meet him.

Once I get to his room, I'm relieved his friend isn't there. I find him on the terrace getting a massage. I sit at the foot of the massage table as he turns his head and glances over at me. "Your lipstick is nice. I like how it matches the color of your lips," he says casually. I feel myself blushing. We spend the day playing UNO and a game that involves highlighting positive words in the dictionary and coming to the realization that there aren't many.

He invites me to dinner that night. On principle, I decide to wear my own clothes and not the ones he bought for me. Once we arrive at Carbone, he asks for more candles and rearranges them, creating a half-moon around the perimeter of the table. He removes the extra glasses and silverware and moves our entire table three feet to the right so we can get a better view of the slab of concrete on the side of the building.

After an hour of tweaks and adjustments, he very bluntly asks me, "Would you want to be my girlfriend?" I instantly burst out laughing. He can't be serious. A photographer circles the table, snapping candid photos of us midsentence. He follows up with: "How would you feel about taking our relationship public?"

I shut the idea down. "I think we should wait a few weeks. It just feels really fast to take such a big step, no?"

He gazes at me intently with a blank stare, nodding along, but it doesn't feel like he's really listening.

"If you're worried about me embarrassing you, I wouldn't do that," he says. "You have a son, and my mom was a single mom."

That's odd, I think to myself. Would he offer me the same courtesy if I had a daughter? I keep my observations to myself and listen as he discusses his lofty plans for our future. He wants to appoint a team to work on my wardrobe. I immediately think of an episode of *Keeping Up with the Kardashians*, where he did the same thing for his estranged wife in their early stages of dating. This all feels so surreal. I can't believe this is my life. I show him my friend Tammy's Instagram and he loves her style, hiring her and Liana on the spot to be my stylists. I tell him I tried to hire them as my stylists in the past but was advised by my management that they were "too editorial." I feel validated that I was right in my instincts all along. Once he lets my team know they will be styling me, there are no more discussions about it. I hope someday I can be listened to like that.

We go back to his hotel room, where I feel relaxed and at ease. I undress and get into bed. I put on the movie *Zola*, which I've already seen three times, and he falls in love with it. Once he's asleep, I slip out of his room and go back to my friends, eager to tell them all about my budding romance and the dream jobs I just secured for them.

The next morning, I open my phone and see a text message from a reporter at Page Six who somehow got my number. My heart skips a beat and I immediately google my name to see some heavily Photoshopped images of me from the dinner at Carbone the night before. To make matters worse, they dug up the story about Andrew from a few weeks ago and it's blasted all over gossip sites with thousands of comments underneath. I feel like a fool.

I thought I'd be happy when I could finally flaunt a new relationship in Andrew's face, but instead I just feel bad for him. I push down the feelings of guilt and go into damage control. My friends reassure me it's going to be okay, that it's not my fault.

"Did he leak these photos?" I ask Tammy. "Would he really do that?"

I'm not sure and I don't want to accuse him, but as I examine them more closely, they do seem to be shot in close proximity. I decide not to make a big deal about it and to surrender to the experience. It comes with the territory and I should have known better.

After a few days, I decide to wrap it up and head back home to my son. I've never been gone this long and I'm starting to feel guilty. Just as I'm about to leave, the artist surprises me by saying he's coming too. Excitement and nerves flood through me as I head back to New York, mentally preparing for the next phase of this whirlwind journey.

From the airport, I go straight to my parents' house. Being reunited with my son after five days is emotional. I wish I could just spend the rest of the evening with him, but the artist is only flying in for the night and he got us tickets to see the acclaimed Broadway play *Slave Play*, written by my friend Jeremy O. Harris, who I introduced him to via text after we watched *Zola*, since Jeremy wrote the film.

When I arrive at the theater, I'm disappointed to see that the artist brought his annoying friend along. As the curtain rises and the show begins, the artist is completely entranced by the raw and powerful performances onstage. His friend, on the other hand, spends the whole time on his phone.

As the night continues, I suggest we head to Carbone's original New York location, where I receive a text from Tammy saying, "Come to the bathroom." To my surprise, I find her in there with a mountain of clothes and multiple outfit options. I'm happy to see her but it's a little strange he didn't just tell me he didn't like my original outfit. Without protest, I slip into the garments. The artist is left speechless as I step out of the bathroom, effortlessly transitioning into my new role as the ultimate fashion girlie. And with that, the night takes on a whole new level of excitement. His photographer snaps photos of me all night long at the artist's encouragement. A part of me kind of feels like a show monkey, but I've been performing my whole life, so what's the big deal?

After dinner, we make our way back to his luxurious hotel suite. The anticipation builds as he teases me with hints of a surprise waiting for me. He unlocks the door and invites me inside. As I step into the room, my eyes are met with racks upon racks of the most beautiful clothing, the highly coveted and unreleased Diesel collection by Glenn Martens.

Without the slightest confliction this time, I begin trying on the clothes, each outfit more breathtaking than the last. The artist watches me in amusement, his eyes dancing with delight as he suggests pieces for me to model. "Why do you have so many bruises on your legs?" he asks me curiously. I glance down at my spotted shins and shrug. "I have a toddler," I say with a shrug and a knowing glance. He seems confused but accepts my explanation anyway. As I strike poses and twirl in front of the camera, he leans in to kiss me, the flashbulbs illuminating the room with a dazzling light. I slip into a slinky top, admiring myself in the mirror. But as I move, I realize that it's not quite right.

"I can't wear this with a bra," I say, shaking my head as I take it off and hand it to Tammy.

"I'll get you a boob job, if you want."

The artist's words cut through the air, sharp and unexpected. I look at myself in the mirror, taking in my post-baby body. They're not so bad, I think to myself.

"I'm good," I say, kindly refusing his casual offer. "I'm not getting a boob job."

But his words stick to me like a piece of lint on my clothes, and I can't shake off the uncomfortable feeling.

•   •   •

The next day, the artist goes back to L.A., and I try to go back to the comfort of whatever is left of my old life. The paparazzi have figured out where I live. I can't walk down the street without people yelling things at me. I focus on Valentino while taking calls from the artist.

"I sent the photos to Mel," the artist says, referring to *Interview* magazine editor in chief Mel Ottenberg and the pictures we took in the hotel room where we were making out and I was straddling him for most of them. "He wants you to write something on how we met. Is that cool?"

I try to steady my voice as I reply, "Yeah, I can do that."

"Show me whatever you write first."

I quickly type out a detailed paragraph recounting step by step how we met, sending it over to him with a sense of trepidation. He texts back almost immediately that this version isn't going to work. I'm confused because it's the truth.

A few minutes go by and he sends me a completely new version that sounds nothing like me and is completely fabricated. I immediately shut it down, telling him that it sounds dumb and that I'm not going to send it. He confesses that it was his annoying friend who wrote it. My mind floods with suspicion. I feel like he's using me in some weird, twisted game. It makes me feel dirty.

I stop responding via text and a few minutes later he calls me on a three-way with one of his assistants. I listen quietly as the master gaslighter insists that the fabricated version sounds great. I stand my ground and we make some edits over the phone, landing somewhere in the middle. But the seed of doubt has been planted in my mind, and I can't shake the feeling. I push the thoughts out of my head and remind myself how lucky I am to be in this position. I convince myself that over time, if he just stops to listen to me, he might fall for me and maybe I can help him overcome his demons.

When the feature drops on Interview.com, the site crashes from how many clicks our photos receive. I can tell the artist is elated by the amount of attention our relationship has been getting, but I feel vulnerable and exposed. I'm often so immersed in thought that I forget to eat. I'm spread so thin between my son and the demands of the artist that I don't have time to enjoy any of it.

Liana and Tammy come over to my apartment, armed with boxes and tape, and start packing up all my clothes. They don't ask my input, they ask *his*. I watch, powerless, as my old life shrinks to fit inside the cardboard boxes. When they have their back turned, I pull things out and hide them under my bed for safekeeping. The new clothes he got me won't fit inside my small place, so in the evenings, after I put Valentino to sleep, my friend comes over so I can go to the fittings in the old Nei-man Marcus building where the artist rented us an entire floor to play in.

I argue with the tailors because they never get my measurements right. I don't realize that it's because I'm shedding weight so rapidly.

Around this time, an NDA gets passed around my group of my friends. "I think you have to sign it too," Tammy says to me. Without thinking, I say, "No way." He can take over my life, but he's not taking my voice.

I spend the next week in New York with Valentino before I'm back on a plane to Los Angeles for a small commercial job. Once I arrive, I'm alerted by the production team that due to some ties with the artist's estranged wife, they can no longer work with me. I find it odd but they agree to pay me the full amount, so I let it go.

Now that I'm no longer committed, the artist moves his schedule around and we spend the next five days with each other. He accompanies me to a dinner I previously planned with Madonna. He introduces me to everyone as his new girlfriend. He even throws an intimate gathering in my honor and invites his friends and family. Dave Chappelle and Naomi Campbell are in attendance, as well as all my friends. Our crews mesh together seamlessly and the evening is filled with laughter and amazing music.

"I'm gonna get you a million-dollar deal," he tells me confidently. The next day, he puts me in touch with an Italian denim company and they start negotiating on my behalf.

I can't believe this is my life, but I can definitely get used to it.

The morning I'm due to fly back to New York, we wake up late. As I rush to get ready, he offers to accompany me to the airport. We hop in my rented Dodge Charger and speed down the highway, blasting his music from my favorite album. We're both belting the lyrics with the windows down as onlookers stare in disbelief. It's a surreal moment for me too.

A week later, we meet in Miami, preparing for a trip to Paris for couture week. Liana and Tammy join us to help with styling, and Viki is already there for work.

The first night in Paris is magical. We attend an intimate party at designer Rick Owens's concrete palace. The artist takes the aux cord and debuts his highly anticipated unreleased album. As the beat pulsates through the room, the crowd goes wild surrounding us. I sing along and dance until I'm dripping with sweat, unaware of the flashes of cameras going off. I'm just having the time of my life with my best friends. Throughout the night, the artist and I can't keep our eyes off each other, drawn to one another like magnets. I feel our connection becoming stronger.

When we arrive at the Schiaparelli show, paparazzi chase us down. People cry and snap pictures and scream his name as the crowd swarms our vehicle. The artist remains unfazed by it all. This is normal for him. He seems checked out a lot of the time, like he's lost in his little bubble of thought.

When we return to the hotel, tensions rise as he suddenly expresses that he doesn't think Tammy and Liana should be riding in the same car as us. I'm caught a little off guard, since he's developed a relationship with Tammy on his own.

"You hired them," I remind him. "It's just easier this way." But it's as if something in him has switched off. He begins quickly listing other things that have been bothering him. He says he doesn't like that I got my makeup done in his hotel room and he noticed Viki wearing a pair of boots he got for me. He suggests setting boundaries with my friends and I politely inform him that if I do that, then so does he. I let him know yet again how much I dislike certain members of his entourage who have proved to be opportunistic and duplicitous in the short time I've known them.

Our argument continues all the way to the home of one of the most prolific artists of our time. We spend hours in various corners of the massive warehouse mansion covered in breathtaking priceless pieces of art. Our voices echo as we talk in circles. Michèle Lamy—Owens's muse, collaborator, and wife—politely interrupts, urging us both to drop it and enjoy the rest of the evening. We pause our conversation and rejoin the party. However, the vibe has been knocked off its axis.

Back in New York, the artist goes silent.

"He's taking a monthlong phone break," his assistant informs me.

"Will he be coming for my birthday?" I ask her.

"Yes," she replies. Even though I find it odd, I can't say I'm not relieved to have a reprieve. I can focus on my son, uninterrupted by the never-ending phone calls and infinite texts. But it isn't long before I start to miss him. It feels jarring to go from so much to nothing at all in such a short span of time. I scan his annoying friends' social media for clues to his whereabouts. I carefully watch his assistant's Instagram and begin to notice a new girl popping up in her photos. She's beautiful in the same manufactured way they all are.

My ultimate dream comes true when I get asked to star in a Supreme ad shot by the inimitable Harmony Korine. I want to tell the artist, but his phone is still off. Harmony's always been one of my idols. I remember crowding around the big box television with Ella and her sister to watch the movie *Kids*. I lost my mind when I recognized the public pool in John Jay Park where I used to swim as a kid. The movie was like a mirror of my life at the time. Especially since it was shot in Yorkville.

On the day of the shoot, the artist finally emerges from his silent retreat and begins to text me. I tell him I'm on set and he asks to see what

I'm wearing. I hesitate and send him a photo of my flight-attendant outfit, knowing he won't be pleased. As I predicted, he hates it. He starts commenting on it, and I can feel my anxiety rising. "Maybe if you didn't fall off the face of the earth, I could have consulted with you!" I snap back, feeling a bit dizzy and faint.

As Harmony shoots away, I pop a piece of bubble gum in my mouth and bite down on it. To my absolute horror, I feel a piece of my back molar crack off into my mouth. I pretend nothing happened and carry on with the shoot, swallowing the tooth.

I can't go on like this. I'm falling apart.

When my birthday rolls around, I plan a big dinner party at my local French bistro, Lucien. The night starts off shaky when I'm instructed to go meet the artist at a hotel all the way on the other side of town, in the opposite direction of the party.

"Why can't he just come here?!" I yell to the air.

I'm met with paparazzi as soon as I step out my front door and into a waiting car. They end up tailing me. I call his assistant to inform her and she tells me to lose them. Calling on the skills I developed evading Rohan's private detectives, I hop out at a stoplight and run down into the subway and take two trains to get to the artist's hotel in the middle of nowhere. I did not intend to spend my birthday lugging a heavy bag across town, and when I arrive at the hotel I'm drenched in sweat and visibly annoyed.

I chug a glass of champagne as I anxiously await his arrival. Tammy and Liana frantically organize clothes on the racks they hauled over from the East Village, throwing different options at me.

"These are all approved by him," Liana says, pointing to a pile of clothes on the bed.

I quickly slip into the simplest outfit in the bunch: a latex bandeau and latex pantaboots that Liana had made for me.

"Okay, this is it," I say, looking in the mirror, feeling uneasy.

Tammy has been acting differently. She's more distant and secretive about her conversations with the artist. I feel like she's not telling me something. She's not herself lately. Her head is getting bigger by the day and I'm starting to feel like just another peg on the ladder. I can't help but wonder if she's doing all this just to get closer to the artist.

As he makes his grand entrance, my heart races with anticipation, but my excitement quickly fades when I spot his annoying friend looming behind him. I try my best to mask my true feelings, throwing my arms around him and kissing him as if nothing is amiss.

Five large Hermès boxes are brought into the room, and he informs us that for my birthday he has gifted us all with lavish Birkin bags. My friends are ecstatic, but I can't shake off the feeling that this is more of a farewell gesture than a birthday present.

He makes us re-create the moment several times for the camera. We do as we're told and awkwardly throw our arms up and scream for joy as he stands off in the background, looking on with pride. As we pose like puppets, I question his true intentions, feeling that this grand gesture is nothing more than a publicity stunt. I'm disconnected from the moment. I try to find gratitude for the lavish gifts, but the feeling of insincerity lingers.

As we make our way to the car, he seems different, distant and pre-occupied. The only time he engages is if the camera is on us, when he will grab me and kiss me passionately. Once we're alone in the car, I do most of the talking as he listens intently. As we drive through the cold city streets, I sense that our time together may be coming to an end.

The intimate dinner party quickly evolves into a massive rave in the empty storefront next door. My friend takes the aux cord and quickly sends everyone into a frenzy as the artist dances and sings along to re-mixes of his own music.

Just as I'm blowing out the candles, I look up and realize the artist is gone. I push past the crowd, dodging hugs from near strangers, and find him outside talking to his friend.

"He wants to go to another party," the friend informs me. "Come with us."

I look back at all my friends having the time of their lives in the storefront and decide to leave and go with them to the next spot. I climb in the SUV and regret immediately washes over me. The ride is awkward as we sit in silence. I keep thinking that I shouldn't have left my party. I'm visibly annoyed.

As soon as we arrive at the club, we're escorted to a private section and met with a group of guys sitting at a table, their eyes glued to their phones. A few wallflower girls, sprinkled along the sidelines, shoot looks at each other as I sit down. This is already the worst time ever. I feel like a fool for leaving my party. As tears begin to form in my eyes, I quickly wipe them away. The artist gets caught in a conversation for what feels like forever, leaving me alone with my racing thoughts. I quietly wait for the perfect moment to make my move. Finally, I walk up to the artist, my heart pounding with anger, and tell him I'm leaving. He doesn't try to stop me.

The next day, I text him that I'm not having fun anymore in this relationship, to which he asks me not to leave him.

"If you loved me, you would support me," he says.

"Who's going to support me, though?" I reply.

He calls, and we speak on the phone one last time. He tells me he had a good conversation with his soon-to-be-ex-wife and discovered a lot of information about me.

"I didn't know you were a drug addict," he says, as if I duped him.

"I told you! Maybe if you listened more. And not to mention, so were you!" At this point I'm yelling. "I told you I didn't wanna go public." He remains silent for once. "You said you wouldn't embarrass me."

I refuse to let him hear me crying, so I hang up and tell my publicist to inform the press that we are over. Shortly after, my million-dollar Italian denim deal falls through as well. "It's contingent on you being his girlfriend," I'm informed.

I text Liana and Tammy and tell them that I hope they can continue working for him, since I would hate if they'd uprooted their whole lives for nothing. Their replies come back late, and then Liana informs me that the artist wants them to dress his new girlfriend. I feel the sharp sting from the stab in the back and I know there's no coming back from this.

Everywhere I go, I can't escape it. Anytime I open my Instagram, I'm flooded with trolls. The comments border on harassment. They call me a clown, they tell me I'm a loser, a phony, a wannabe, a copycat, a junkie, a ho. The press takes anything I say out of context and turns it into a silly clickbait headline. I feel so embarrassed. How could I have been so dumb?

I glance over at my son. I refuse to let him see me like this. I wipe the tears off my face and pull myself together. I'm someone's mother, and I'm a fucking star regardless of who the fuck I'm dating.

I get a text from Mel Ottenberg asking if I'd be willing to open the LaQuan Smith runway show. I had been asked to walk in shows in the past but I always turned them down, under the advice that it's not typical for actresses to model unless it's for a major European fashion house. I decide that I'm going to do what the fuck I want. I'm tired of doing what I'm told.

Right before I hit the stage, a wave of anxiety washes over me and I start feeling delusional for thinking I could do this. I've never walked a runway before. I don't deserve to be here. I ignore the gremlin voices in my head, take a deep breath, and turn the corner, where I'm met with blinding lights and the unmistakable sound of applause.

I'm confidently strutting down the runway in my iconic black gown when I hear Saucy Santana's distinct voice yelling, "Go Julia!" For a moment, I let go of the doubts planted by the thousands of online trolls telling me that I was nothing without the artist. This is all the validation I need. The media dubs my look "the revenge dress"—following in the great tradition of Princess Di's Christina Stambolian off-the-shoulder look—and it soon finds its way to the prestigious Metropolitan Museum of Art, cementing its place in fashion history.

• • •

The next day, my friend Cole calls me and tells me her husband, Chris, shot himself.

"I'm in the hospital with him now. He's on life support," she tells me.

I had been at their home when I received the news of Gianna's passing. At one point in time, Chris was the only person I would pick up the phone for. Once I had Valentino, I would always make sure to bring him by Cole and Chris's house whenever we were in LA. When we hang up, I start scrolling through my camera roll to find the photos of Chris with Valentino in their pool. It was his first time in a swimming pool and Chris held him gently against his big burly tattooed chest adorned in thick gold chains.

"He's dead." The message pops up on the screen, and I feel the lump swelling in my throat. I curl over in bed and cry myself to sleep.

The very next day, I get on a plane to Milan for Fashion Week, where I meet Donatella and sit front row at the Versace show, which I certainly never thought would happen. Yet I'm heartbroken over the artist and even more so over Chris's death. I feel like I'm simultaneously living in my wildest dream and trapped in my worst nightmare. Soon the nightmare gets worse.

I'm getting ready for the Diesel show when I check my phone and see an urgent message from someone claiming to be one of Harmony's friends who's been trying to get ahold of me. I remain frozen as I hold my breath and stare at the glaring words on the screen: "Hey, it's about Harmony, it's important." I've been down this road before and I already know what she's going to tell me.

I call her back and she confirms my suspicion: "She was dead for two weeks before we found her." I feel the air get sucked out of the room and the walls close in on my head. I hang up and try to swallow the grief but her death rips me open to my core. Her passing eclipses the noise from the blogs and the tabloids, and everything else going on in my life feels stupid and inconsequential.

I pull up our messages and see she never responded to the last meme I sent her. She was already dead. I can't get the image of her lifeless body out of my head. She told me her worst fear was dying at home alone and not being found. I feel guilty. I could have done more.

My brain is in a fog, and everything around me is moving in slow motion. I'm forced to sit through hair and makeup, trying my best not to cry as I make arrangements over the phone for Harmony to be cremated. I think about how when I found out about Katharine's OD, I was also in a makeup chair on the set of *Uncut Gems*. Gianna was there to comfort me then. And when Gianna OD'd, Chris was there to comfort me. And when Chris killed himself, I took comfort in my friendship with Harmony, in those stupid, silly memes we constantly traded that took my mind off things. Now Harmony is dead too. What did I do to deserve this?

I randomly receive a text from the artist once he realizes I never signed the NDA. I'm busy dealing with Harmony's passing, so I ignore it. He starts calling me and my team, asking for them to get it signed. I write him a lengthy text in which I reiterate that I'm not signing jack shit.

"I can't be friends with you if you don't sign it," he warns me.

"I'll live," I text back.

After the Diesel show, I fly to Los Angeles with Valentino and start dealing with Harmony's funeral proceedings. I discover that due to her not having any family, I'm her next of kin and she left me a large portion of her money, which she inherited from her grandmother. I can't wrap my head around the fact that she's really gone. I keep expecting her to walk through the door and for this to all be one of her awful pranks.

Sara is by my side the entire time. I introduced them a few years ago when they both moved to L.A., and it always gave me so much peace of mind to know that they were looking out for each other in my absence. Sara helps me deal with the coroner and the detectives and together we organize the perfect memorial for someone as unique as Harmony. We'll start at the LGBTQ Center for the service, then a boat ride where we will disperse some of her ashes in the ocean, and we'll end the night at Dave & Buster's, her favorite place in the world.

The service is beautiful, just as she would have wanted it. Harmony used to brag about the charity balls she attended at the LGBTQ Center, so I know she would approve of the venue. The aroma of flowers fills the air, and white balloons sway gently overhead. We pull favors from all our friends and family, Uncle Paulie's provides sandwiches, and our friends put together heartfelt slide shows and T-shirts in her honor.

As I stand at the podium ready to speak, my heart feels heavy and tears stream down my face. I struggle to find the words, feeling numb, then filled with the deepest despair, and then numb again, in denial, wishing this nightmare away.

"She wouldn't want us to feel bad for her, she would hate that," I say, "so we just have to remember her as the rock star that she is."

Tammy and Liana arrive at Harmony's funeral late and look like shit. Tammy sits hunched over manically texting the artist about Coachella the whole time, while Liana peers over her shoulder anxiously. I feel defensive of Harmony. How could they be so disrespectful of someone who was their friend? How could they be so disrespectful of *me*? I wish I could just mourn in peace. Thankfully, they leave early and don't show up to the boat portion. I push them out of my mind and focus on giving Harmony the service she deserves, but when it's over, I send them both a scathing text. It's enough for Liana to immediately quit working for the artist, but Tammy says nothing. And in her silence, she says everything I need to know. I block her number. I can't accept that my friend of ten years would choose him over me . . . for clout. It's just another loss to add to the avalanche of loss I'm already buried under. No big deal.

After the memorial, Sara and I reminisce over our crazy adventures together: Ubering to Tijuana or getting kicked out of a shared Palm Springs weekend house for no reason, after which we went to a motel and made dozens of ads on Craigslist sending strangers to the house. One was for a needle exchange program, one was a keg party, one was a

Jesus-loving knitting group, one was a free furniture ad. "Come right in and take what you want!" was the header. We laughed more that night than in our whole lives combined. Harmony later informed us that she found out that strangers showed up to the house all weekend and ruined their vacation, just as we'd intended.

The next day, Sara and I go to Harmony's apartment. We climb onto her balcony through the balcony of her meth-head neighbor, who we haven't ruled out as a suspect. I pick the lock with a butter knife and duck under the blinds. Once inside, I'm hit with the awful stench of rotting flesh.

We turn the lights on and I carefully examine the room, retracing her steps from the way she left things. I notice empty bottles of vodka strewn around and tons more in her freezer.

"She was definitely on a bender," Sara says, pointing to the mess.

We start packing her stuff into boxes to put in storage. I go through her photo albums and trinkets. I find the gun she bought at a pawnshop in Louisiana. The clip is empty and there's a single bullet in the chamber. I quickly shove it in my bag. I find doodles that I mindlessly drew years ago that she put away for safekeeping. It warms my heart to see how much of me is in her home. I see the *Uncut Gems* poster she had me sign during my press tour.

The smell gets thicker as we walk through her bedroom toward the bathroom she died in. Her fluids are still all over the floor. As I move the towels around her bathroom, dead maggots fall out onto the floor. I gasp when I see a piece of her scalp with her hair on it stuck to the toilet. I get on my hands and knees and start scrubbing, the foam turning a dark burgundy color as it gets all over my hands. I don't care. This is my family.

We find her ID and I tell Sara we are going to need it for when she has to impersonate Harmony at the cell phone store. "It's the only way we'll be able to get her phone records," I tell her. And it works. The customer service rep is too busy fanning out over me that he doesn't even notice it's clearly not the same person.

Once we get a new phone with her same number, we are able to access her iCloud, and from there, we see who the last person she called is. I'm praying it won't be the same dealer I introduced her to years ago but when I put his number in my phone and his name pops up, I feel defeated.

"This is my fault," I tell Sara.

She reassures me it's not. "You were sick too! You didn't know!"

The only way I can live with myself is if I avenge her death. He has to pay, or else I will for the rest of my life.

We call the detective assigned to the case and tell him all about the dealer and how we know he's the one responsible, but he doesn't care. I tune him out when he starts telling me how hard it is to prosecute these kinds of cases and the DA most likely won't pick up the case. I guess I'll just have to get justice myself.

I start filming a movie called *The Trainer*, and unlike my previous experiences with acting, once I'm on set there are no jitters. Acting is my only escape. I used to get nervous and anxious and hyperfixate, but now I lose myself in the role and forget about everything else. It's the only way for me to release all the rage I have boiling under the surface and it provides a temporary reprieve from the grief and pain that gnaw at my soul. It's a way for me to channel my emotions and find some sense of catharsis. I know I can't run from my problems forever, but it's a way to cope in the moment, even though it's not a permanent solution. The moment the producers notify me that I'm wrapped for the day, I'm right back inside the boiling pot of rage.

One morning as I drive to work, I receive a distressing phone call from a lawyer representing Andrew, informing me that he is taking me to court for custody of Valentino. Despite the lawyer's reassurance that Andrew only wishes to establish a set schedule that works for both of us, my inner mama bear unleashes as I hurl insults at his lawyer.

I hang up the phone and call Andrew, my voice shaking with rage as I demand to know why he would do this to me now, knowing what I'm already going through. "You just want to punish me!" I scream at the top of my lungs.

Andrew remains unmoved, insisting we communicate through our lawyers before hanging up.

When I arrive on set, I pull into the lot and take a moment to compose myself. I throw my sunglasses on and make my way to my trailer with a smile on my face. At lunchtime, I begin the process of finding a lawyer to represent me.

After work that day, I drive through the drug dealer's neighborhood and look for him. I hit every street I used to meet him on years ago. I know he's got to be close. I keep Harmony's loaded gun in my glove compartment and fantasize about putting the single bullet left in the chamber right in his forehead. I curse the day I ever met him. I curse myself for ever giving her his number.

I continue my search every day, first in the evenings after work, then before my call time as well, and eventually even on my few days off. After weeks of aimlessly driving around, I finally spot him one morning standing over his car in a driveway on a residential street in West Hollywood. My heart races as I recline my seat and watch him closely through my rearview mirror, occasionally glancing at the glove compartment. The anger and the hatred I have for him build inside me as I watch him go about his life completely oblivious to the fact that he ruined mine.

I can't believe he's out here living his life like nothing happened, unaffected by the avalanche of destruction his actions caused. Harmony is gone, and in my mind it's his fault. He gets in his car and exits the driveway and I slowly pull out behind him, taking photos of his car and license plate for evidence. I follow him for a few hours, watching people hop in and out at a safe distance. A part of me wants to intercept his customers and tell them not to buy drugs from him and that it's poison, but he knows me and I can't blow my cover.

After a few hours, my babysitter informs me she can't stay any later, so I'm forced to abort the mission and go home early. But now that I know where he lives, I'm going to come back. At night.

I go back to his street and park at the top of his driveway night after night, but he's never there. Eventually, I get out of the car and walk toward the building. I notice a "For Rent" sign with a phone number on the lawn. I contact management, pretending to be interested in renting, and I make an appointment to go look at the only vacant unit, which offers me zero clues as to which apartment is his, since his name isn't on anything. This is proving to be much harder than I initially anticipated.

People ask me what it's like to be this famous. Truth is, I'm not a celebrity and I don't claim that title. I'm an artist in the role of a lifetime, playing *Me*. And nothing about my life has changed. I don't go clubbing. I never go to parties. Getting dolled up and being snapped by my paparazzo friend is my only thrill. We meet up on random street corners at all hours and it's like my own personal red carpet. One day, he calls and informs me that some powerful people asked him to stop shooting me, but he assures me that he told them to "fuck off." I'm touched by his loyalty, but I begin to wonder if I'm being blacklisted. Just last week, a role I secured a year ago was suddenly given to someone else. I brushed it off as bad luck, but now I'm not so sure.

I begin to feel discouraged. Why does everything feel like an uphill battle? It's hard not to compare myself to others in this industry, especially those who were born into the life. They just have it so easy. The worst feeling is seeing a fashion show entirely inspired by me and not receiving an invitation. Being purposely excluded from the conversation when I single-handedly started every trend of 2022 is annoying. But my fans quiet the gremlin voices in my head.

In every interview, I'm asked the same questions over and over. All they want is their next viral sound bite. And none of them ask me how I'm doing after so much loss. They don't care about Harmony or Gianna or Chris or how hard it is to be a single mom. They take my words out of context and twist them around to make me seem dumb. Sometimes I just want to disappear, but I can't. I have nothing to fall back on, no family wealth, no rich baby daddy. I have to keep going and prove that I'm more than what they make me out to be. It just means I have to go even harder.

I struggle to keep my life from falling apart as the pounds continue to melt off my body like butter. My period has become irregular, and I find myself eating vats of sheet cake and boxes of glazed doughnuts, but nothing sticks. I know I should be worried about my health, but with a murder to solve, a child to raise, and a movie to make, it's not a priority at the moment.

As I shed weight and lose my famous curves, something unexpected happens. Men no longer find me attractive, and strangely, it's liberating. I can finally walk around without getting honked at or cat-called. It's as if I've been living as a slave to the male gaze all my life, and I'm enjoying this newfound freedom. Being sexy had been my identity for so long, and I was consumed by it. I'm unlearning all the brainwashing and learning to love myself for more than just the way I look.

But the memories of this male attention still haunt me. I remember being followed off a train by a man with a boner when I was in the fifth grade, the masseur who took advantage of my vulnerable position, the Peeping Tom filming me on the toilet from under the stall, the driving instructor massaging his penis through his pants as I struggled to keep my eyes on the road, my "friend" who took photos of my vagina while I was sleeping and charged people five dollars to see them. I don't want men to like me anymore. I'm over it. I'm reclaiming my body and rejecting the notion that I exist only to be visually pleasing.

The movie wraps and my time in L.A. comes to an end just as Harmony's toxicology report comes back. We are shocked to discover she had multiple unidentified substances in her bloodstream and none of them were fentanyl. It seems she had a reaction to a multitude of things being taken together. Even though the dealer definitely sold her a pill that killed her, this changes everything and only leaves us with more questions.

The thought of leaving California fills me with dread. This place holds so many memories of Harmony, and I feel close to her here. The thought of leaving it all behind is painful. I try to hold on to the memories we made here, the laughter and the love that we shared. I drive by the kickball field and remember the time she insisted I come to her game. She was so proud of herself for joining a league. She wanted to see the look of pride on my face too. Every time I see a sign for UCLA, I remember when she forced me to come sit through a three-hour class with her so she wouldn't have to be alone. Every car wash reminds me of our rental-car escapades. The early-morning fog reminds me of driving through Culver City at sunrise to get us home from a wild night out. Every hike, every trail, any nail salon, any massage parlor reminds me of her. Malibu at night, roller-skating until the sidewalk ends, frozen yogurt on Sunset, walking to the gas station in the middle of the night. I don't want to leave this shrine to her that I've created in my head. I want to continue to wander through the graveyard of the landmarks of our past. I want to close my eyes and breathe in the air in hopes that there are traces of her still in it. The thought of returning home to my small apartment in New York, with all of its responsibilities and obligations, feels overwhelming. I am not ready to say goodbye. But I have to. As much as I resent Andrew, Valentino needs his dad.

Upon our return to New York, Andrew and I finally settle our custody agreement and he evolves into a dedicated father, taking Valentino for overnight stays multiple times a week and accompanying him on outings and adventures. He becomes reliable and dependable, consistently picking up and dropping him off and snapping into action when I'm working or attending events. His efforts to be an active and supportive parent make a significant difference in our family dynamic. I feel less alone, the weight on my back is significantly lighter, and I don't feel like I'm drowning anymore. Sometimes we even all hang out together, and I'm always in awe of how good he is with our son.

I may have chosen the wrong partner for me, but I definitely chose the right father for our son. And that's all that matters to me.

The walls of the city are plastered with the ad campaign I did for Supreme shot by Harmony Korine. I wake up early, determined to snag one of the posters before they get buried under fresh layers of ads. As I care-fully peel a poster off the scaffolding, a group of girls drives by, honking their horn and screaming my name out the window, waving their own ripped-off poster in the air.

After months away, I've returned to the city showing me more love than I ever anticipated. I can't walk a block without people stopping me to express their gratitude for the hope I give them. They say they love my authenticity and describe me as "real." They tell me I'm "a sex symbol for women," which is the highest form of compliment one could ever hope to receive.

Reflecting on my past, I now can admit that I was holding on to so much anger and pain toward this city that it was stopping me from being present. The bitter taste that lingered in my mouth was preventing me from savoring the full flavor and essence of what makes this city so magical. While I can't erase my history with this place, I can choose how I show up for the future.

I'm ready for a new start. I'm ready to release the resentment I've been harboring and focus on right now. And at this very moment, I am filled with gratitude for the people in my life and the opportunities that this city has blessed me with. I wouldn't be where I am today without the countless mistakes I made to get here. It's okay to live with regret. It's not okay to let it consume you.

Sometimes you have to say fuck it and throw your life down the drain just to see where you'll come out on the other side. The most pro-found beauty emerges from the ashes of destruction. And by that, I mean that sometimes you have to burn your life to the ground in order to experience the life that is truly meant for you. It is in letting go that we are forced to carve our own destiny. We must be willing to relinquish all we once held dear if we are holding on with fear. If you believe in the power within yourself, anything is possible. Because the truth is, anyone who is *someone* first started out as a delusional dreamer.

As I cross the street clutching my poster, a group of girls inside a restaurant recognize me and begin jumping up and down, holding their own poster up to the glass. I smile and wave as an unfamiliar feeling envelops me: joy. Everywhere I turn, I see girls dressed like me. It's a far cry from the days when I was bullied and called "weirdo," "freaka-zoid," "white trash," "prostitute," or my favorite, "weird white girl with the fat ass."

I was ridiculed for being different and for doing whatever I had to do to survive.

But now everyone is wearing latex.